FORLORN HOPE

*The Battle of White Bird Canyon
and the Beginning of the Nez Perce War*

by

JOHN D. McDERMOTT

IDAHO STATE HISTORICAL SOCIETY
Boise   1978

Library of Congress Cataloging in Publication Data

McDermott, John Dishon.
    Forlorn hope.

    Bibliography: p.
    Includes index.
    1. Nez Percé Indians — Wars, 1877. I. Title.
E83.877.M27   1978   973.8'3   78-2706
ISBN 0-931406-00-5
ISBN 0-931406-01-3 pbk.

Cover design by Judy Klein

Maps by Harry Scott and William G. Dougall

Printed and bound in the United States of America by
The Caxton Printers, Ltd.
Caldwell, Idaho 83605

To Joan

Contents

ILLUSTRATIONS

Foreword

Less than a year after General George A. Custer's ill-advised charge into a hostile Sioux camp on the Little Bighorn on June 24, 1876, the United States Army attacked White Bird's small Nez Perce camp in the lower canyons of the Salmon River. With support from a small group of volunteers from Mount Idaho, Capt. David Perry led 109 whites into battle against a substantially smaller Indian force. Even though White Bird's Lower Salmon band had been augmented by Joseph's Nez Perce followers from the Wallowa area to the west, Perry did not anticipate the kind of trouble that he headed into. His strength in numbers failed to save him from a fiasco that commenced a four-month campaign across Idaho and Montana. Although they had gone to considerable effort to avoid warfare with white ranchers and settlers, some of the Nez Perce — a minority who were driven from their homeland after Perry's unfortunate battle — gained a reputation for military success that contrasted remarkably with the peaceful tradition that they would have preferred to retain. Their spectacular opening triumph at White Bird contributed greatly to their confidence as warriors and brought national attention to a remote North Idaho battleground.

After Nez Perce National Historical Park was established in 1965, John D. McDermott undertook a thorough study of this episode for the National Park Service. With a grant from the American Revolution Bicentennial Administration and special assistance from Marcus J. Ware and Romaine Galey Hon, this revision of his account is being published by the Idaho State Historical Society in cooperation with the Nez Perce Park Cooperative Association and the Pacific Northwest National Park Association. All of this support is gratefully acknowledged.

MERLE W. WELLS
Idaho State Historical Society

vii

Acknowledgments

I owe a deep debt of gratitude to William A. Olson of Boise, Idaho, whose suggestions and assistance were of inestimable value. Twenty-five years ago, Bill became interested in the Battle of White Bird Canyon while vacationing in the area. As the years passed, his interest deepened and his knowledge grew. It was my pleasure to visit the scenes of the Salmon River killings and to spend several days walking White Bird Battlefield with him. Bill and I fought the battle many times, and, like the United States Army, our victory was one of knowledge rather than of arms.

I wish especially to thank Sara D. Jackson, then of the National Archives; Merle W. Wells, of the Idaho State Historical Society; and Earle Connette and Elain White, then of the Washington State University Archives, for their assistance in locating many of the materials used in preparing this volume. I also wish to thank Richard McWhorter of Prosser, Washington, who made the McWhorter Collection at Washington State University available for study.

Historians, present and past, of the National Park Service who read chapters of the manuscript or assisted in gathering information were Robert M. Utley, Frank B. Sarles, Don Rickey, Jr., Edwin C. Bearss, Erwin N. Thompson, Aubrey Haines, and John A. Hussey. I particularly wish to thank Robert L. Burns, former superintendent of Nez Perce National Historical Park, who participated in the field study and took many of the photographs used to illustrate this volume. Student trainee Michael Kannensohn of the University of South Florida assisted in gathering biographical data on enlisted men.

Others who provided information and assistance were Sam Watters and Richard Halfmoon, whose ancestors were on the winning side in the White Bird fight; the Rev. E. Paul Hovey, now of Portland; Marcus J. Ware, of Lewiston; C. H. Ketcham, of Grangeville; Mary K. Dempsey, formerly of the Montana Historical Society; Anna M. Ibbotson, formerly of the Washington State Historical

Society; and Glenn R. Downing, formerly of the Idaho State University Museum.

J.D.M.

Introduction

On May 15, 1965, President Lyndon B. Johnson signed a bill authorizing the establishment of Nez Perce National Historical Park in north central Idaho. The purpose of the act was to facilitate the preservation and interpretation of certain sites in Nez Perce Country, an area which the law defined as running as far north as the town of Pierce and Lolo Pass, as far south as Riggins, and as far east and west as the boundaries of the state. The act specifically named sites that related to early Nez Perce culture, the Lewis and Clark expedition, the fur trade, missionary activities, gold mining, logging, and the Nez Perce Indian War of 1877, but it did not restrict consideration of other properties. The only condition was that each site had to have exceptional value in illustrating the role of the Nez Perce Country in the history of the United States.

One of the twenty-two sites selected by then Secretary of the Interior Stewart L. Udall was White Bird Battlefield, the scene of the initial engagement between the United States Army and the nontreaty Nez Perce on June 17, 1877. Almost unchanged after 100 years, the site lies about one mile northeast of the small community of Whitebird and about twenty miles southwest of the town of Grangeville. U.S. 95 runs along a hillside above the battlefield and provides easy access.

To provide the general information needed to guide development and interpretation of White Bird Battlefield, the then Director of the National Park Service, George B. Hartzog, Jr., requested his historical research staff to study the engagement. It was decided that the study would concentrate on the acts that precipitated the conflict and on the Battle of White Bird Canyon and its consequences. The first part of the volume deals with the period June 13 through June 27, from the day that the first settler on the Salmon River died at the hands of three revengeful Nez Perce to the burial of the military dead on White Bird Battlefield by troops under the command of Brig. Gen. O. O. Howard. Later chapters treat the court of inquiry prompted by the defeat and attempt to pinpoint the reasons for the Nez Perce victory.

Research began with an examination of the standard books on the Nez Perce and the Nez Perce Indian War. Two things became immediately apparent. First, very little space in the volumes had been devoted to the Battle of White Bird Canyon. Most authors covered it in a page or two, apparently not because of lack of interest but because of the lack of material. Although Cyrus Townsend Brady, one of the early chroniclers, had mentioned that a court of inquiry had been held, no one had attempted to locate or consult the transcript of it. Second, there was little or no agreement among authorities concerning the sequence of events that occurred between June 13 and June 17. Information on the number of settlers killed, their names, their places of residence, in fact practically everything about them, varied considerably. Even the more recent volumes were as contradictory as some of the older works.

As the study progressed, a third fact became clear. In addition to the transcript of the court of inquiry, there were many other important documents in the National Archives relating to the first encounter and to the Nez Perce Indian War in general that had escaped the view of historians working in the field. This lack of use may have been partly because many military papers had already been printed as Congressional documents, and the file kept by the Adjutant General relating to the conflict had been microfilmed by the National Archives and made available to scholars at low cost. The easy availability of this material apparently gave historians a false sense of security and a belief that National Archives sources had been exhausted. A search for other manuscript materials in other repositories also proved fruitful, and contemporary newspapers yielded much information. An early local history, apparently overlooked, proved especially useful.

With the publication of books by Merrill Beal, Alvin Josephy, and Mark Brown, it has become fashionable to suggest that the Nez Perce Indian War has been thoroughly researched and the subject laid to rest. Certainly all three volumes contribute greatly to our knowledge of the conflict. Yet there is much that needs to be done, not only to expand and illuminate certain episodes, but to correct and re-evaluate accepted "facts" and interpretations. If this study succeeds in reopening the question, it will have served an additional purpose.

It was not possible in the time allotted for the project to discuss in detail the background of the Nez Perce Indian War and to trace the interaction of the two races that led to its inception. There are several books that handle the subject well listed in the bibliography. Let me especially recommend those by Alvin Josephy, Merrill Beal, Francis Haines, Helen Addison Howard, and Mark Brown. The two volumes by Lucullus McWhorter are essential in understanding the Indian viewpoint.

For those who do not have the volumes readily available, a few words of background are in order. Contacts with the Nez Perce followed traditional patterns. The first whites to meet them were the explorers Meriwether Lewis and William Clark in the fall of 1805. Mountain men, both British and American, were the next to visit them, and a profitable trade was established. The first missionary to settle in the heart of Nez Perce Country was Henry Harmon Spalding, in 1836.

The Christian influence exerted by Spalding and others tended to divide the Nez Perce into factions. One group began to adopt the white man's culture and to take his advice. The other tried to remain apart from the intruders and follow the old ways. Finally, in the early 1860's, they separated into two distinct groups. The catalyst was gold.

The discovery of gold in Idaho in 1860 brought thousands of white adventurers pouring into Nez Perce Country, and as settlements grew the demand for Indian land increased. In 1863 the more acculturated Nez Perce signed a treaty that reduced the holdings of the tribe by almost seven million acres. The Wallowa, Imnaha, and Grande Ronde river valleys of Oregon were opened to white settlement. In Idaho, the Snake and Salmon river valleys, part of Camas Prairie, and lands along the upper Clearwater were also ceded. The other group of Nez Perce, however, refused to sign the document or recognize it as binding upon them and continued to occupy their traditional homes outside the boundaries of the new reservation. Because of their refusal to accept the treaty, they became known as the non-treaty Nez Perce.

Principal among the non-treaty Nez Perce were the Wallowas in the Wallowa and Imnaha valleys of northeastern Oregon, the Lamtamas along the Salmon and its tributaries, the Pikunans on the highlands between the Salmon and the Snake, the Palouse in the big-bend country north of the Snake, and the Alpowai on the Middle Fork of the Clearwater. One of the most adamant in his refusal to accept the treaty was Old Chief Joseph of the Wallowas. Tearing a copy of the treaty to shreds and destroying his New Testament, he returned to his homeland in disgust. On his deathbed, his instructions to his eldest son were clear: "My son, never forget my dying words. This country holds your father's body. Never sell the bones of your father and your mother."

Young Joseph was not put to the test immediately because the Wallowa Valley proved barren of gold. Nevertheless stockmen coveted the land, and Gov. Lafayette F. Grover of Oregon clamored for action. Indian Bureau representatives who inspected the land in 1872 found that it was not particularly suited for cultivation and recommended that the upper reaches of the valley, the lake, and the bordering mountains be reserved as a permanent hunting grounds for the Nez Perce tribe. Consequently, President Ulysses S. Grant issued an executive order on June 16, 1873, setting aside 1,425 square miles of land for the purpose. However, the boundaries established by the executive order did not correspond to those claimed by Joseph or those recommended by the investigating committee, and all parties voiced dissatisfaction. Two years later the Indian Office had the order rescinded, and settlers renewed their efforts to wrest the valley from the Wallowas. Hostility reached the combustion point in 1876. Only the timely arrival of 1st Lt. Albert Gallatin Forse and a company of regulars from Fort Walla Walla prevented a clash between white ranchers and Joseph's band in September.

In response to the new evidence of unrest, Secretary of the Interior Zachary Chandler appointed a five-man commission to study the problem. The commission consisted of David H. Jerome of Michigan; A. C. Barstow of Rhode Island; William Stickney of Washington, D.C.; Brig. Gen. Oliver Otis Howard, Commander of the Department of the Columbia; and Maj. Henry Clay Wood, a member of Howard's staff who had previously studied the controversy. After meeting with the chiefs at Lapwai Agency in November, the commission recommended that the non-treaty bands be required to occupy unallotted lands inside the boundaries of the reservation, by force if necessary.

On January 6, 1877, Commissioner of Indian Affairs J. Q. Smith gave Lapwai Indian Agent John B. Monteith authority to implement the recommendations of the commission. Pursuant to instructions, Monteith sent Indian ambassadors to the camps of the non-treaty Nez Perce to inform them that the government wished them permanently encamped on the reservation by April 1. With Joseph's brother, Ollokot, acting as emissary, the non-treaty Nez Perce were able to postpone the date of removal and received permission to speak with Howard at Lapwai on May 3.

The Lapwai council convened on schedule. Although Howard

permitted the Indians to recount their grievances, he considered the issue closed. When Toohoolhoolzote, a medicine man, defied the general by questioning his authority and the right of the United States to take Indian land, Howard had the old chief ushered to the guardhouse. Realizing the futility of further resistance, the chiefs agreed to terms.

On May 8 Howard began a tour of the reservation with the principal chiefs, and each of them selected a settlement site before the journey's end. On May 14, Howard addressed the Indians for the last time and informed them that they had thirty days in which to make the move. It was a solemn moment. The Nez Perce had expected more time, and many protested, but Howard was firm. On May 15, the non-treaty Indians sadly left for their homes to gather their belongings. In a short time they were on the road to the reservation, and by June 2 they had gathered at Tepahlewam (Split Rocks), an ancient rendezvous site at the head of Rocky Canyon near Tolo Lake, about six miles west of Grangeville and about eight miles south of the southern border of the reservation. It is here that our story begins.

What They Said

In 1862 he started to Warren with a posse of men and on the head of the Owyhee river they rescued a man and wife from the Indians by killing the Indians.

BIOGRAPHICAL SKETCH OF LARRY OTT

On the Salmon River a few miles above the mouth of White Bird Creek is the grave of a white man killed by Nez Perce at the outbreak of hostilities. The history of the case as told by a half-blood of good repute is that before the war a young married Indian couple were met in their forest camp by this same white man, who, having the ascendency in arms, tied up the husband and subjected the woman to unwarranted indignities. For this was his life forfeited.

OLD-TIMER'S STATEMENT

The blood that cried for vengence of his murdered kin and clan.

JOSEPH, THE NEZ PERCE (Poem)

The Indians, White Bird's Band, were raised around here and had lived and trafficked with the whites, who were nearly all storekeepers, for a good many years. Many causes of dissension had grown up amongst them, and in nearly every case the whites were to blame. They were in fact crowding the Indians, taking forcible possession of every little plot of ground that would grow anything along the river and the creeks following into it, and covering the hills with their stock. I could not for anything be the apologist for the Indians, but could not shut my eyes to what I saw and also my ears to what I heard, and in my opinion the white people were to blame for the trouble.

FIRST SERGEANT MICHAEL McCARTHY

It is the old story of aggression by the whites on lands which the savages believed to be by right their hunting grounds; of unavailing efforts by the Government to induce roving bands to live upon a reservation; of threats to employ force; and of a sudden revengeful outbreak on the part of the Indians, attended by horrible massacres of settlers and their families.

THE TIMES (London), July 3, 1877

It was bad men on both sides who made the trouble.

CAPTAIN JOEL G. TRIMBLE

1

The First Raid

On June 13 the Nez Perce remained in camp near Tolo Lake. Although they had to stand within the boundaries of the new reservation within twenty-four hours or feel the wrath of General Howard, there was no sense of urgency among the warriors. They had agreed to move; they intended to do it in their own fashion and with dignity. The young men were sullen but under control. To pay tribute to their camping place and bid it a final farewell, the chiefs decided to stage a war parade. Perhaps they were also aware of the therapeutic value of a warlike demonstration in purging pent-up feelings of resentment and hatred.

One of the positions of honor in the parade was behind the horse column. In conditions of war the chiefs selected some of their best men to bring up the rear in order to prevent the enemy from launching a surprise attack. In the ceremony two warriors mounted on a single pony were the honor guard. This day Shore Crossing and Red Moccasin Tops were awarded the place of courage.

Shore Crossing was the son of Eagle Robe, a chief who had been killed in March of 1874 by a rancher named Larry Ott in a property dispute.[1] According to the Nez Perce he was slow to anger but a

1. Larry Ott was born on February 19, 1836, in Blair County, Pennsylvania. He settled permanently in Idaho in 1864, and in 1872 he began farming and ranching on the south side of the Salmon River at Horseshoe Bend. In the beginning he fenced only a small parcel of land, but in the spring of 1874 he decided to extend his fence line to enclose a small piece of property that had been formerly used as a campground by the Nez Perce. The Indians objected, but Ott ignored them and began plowing. In a fit of anger, Eagle Robe threw a rock at Ott and knocked him to the ground. Ott retaliated by pulling his revolver and shooting the chief, who died a few days later. A grand jury looked into the matter but discharged the case, because the Indian witnesses refused to be sworn on the grounds that it was unnecessary. Agent Monteith believed that Ott had not been justified but was powerless to act. The failure to convict Ott was but one example of the general lack of law enforcement in cases involving the Nez Perce and another addition to a long list of Indian grievances. "Lawrence Ott," *An Illustrated History of North Idaho* ([Spokane?]: Western Historical Publishing Company, 1903), p. 513; Mark H. Brown, The *Flight of the Nez Perce* (New

formidable enemy when fully aroused. Indeed, few rivaled him in strength or valor. Red Moccasin Tops was the son of Yellow Bull and the grandson of Tomahas, one of the Cayuse murderers of Marcus Whitman. The men were first cousins, or brothers in Nez Perce parlance. Shore Crossing held the reins, and Red Moccasin Tops mounted behind him. In passing through the village, the horse they were riding stepped on a piece of canvas covered with drying *kouse* roots and scattered them in every direction. The owner of the property, Yellow Grizzly, flew into a rage. "See what you do!" he cried. "Playing brave, why not go kill the white man who killed your father?" A moment passed before Shore Crossing replied. "You will be sorry for your words," he said, and urged the horse forward.[2]

After the parade, Shore Crossing retired to his lodge and sought comfort in liquor recently obtained from an unprincipled trader. On his deathbed Eagle Robe had asked his son not to seek revenge, but the words of Yellow Grizzly were insulting to a proud warrior. Liquor helped to make things clear, and Shore Crossing soon reached a decision. His father would be avenged.[3]

Red Moccasin Tops agreed to join in the vendetta. The warriors

---

York: G. P. Putnam's Sons, 1967), p. 64; O. O. Howard, "The True Story of the Wallowa Campaign," *The North American Review* (1879), 129:56.

2. I have followed Lucullus McWhorter in the details of the incident that prompted Shore Crossing to begin the bloodbath on Salmon River. One of the Indians whom McWhorter relied upon in writing his history was Two Moons, who rode at the end of the horse column and undoubtedly witnessed the episode. Unfortunately, McWhorter does not specify the exact source of his information; and in an account of Two Moons reproduced later in the book, the warrior does not go into the details surrounding the departure of the avengers. He does indicate, however, that the main cause of the outbreak was liquor rather than insult. Because of the lack of definite evidence for the McWhorter version, it must be accepted with some reservation, and other plausible accounts must be related. Yellow Bull claimed that Shore Crossing became intoxicated one evening and rode through the camp firing his rifle and boasting of his bravery. An old man was not impressed and challenged him to prove his courage by killing the murderer of his father. In 1878 Duncan MacDonald wrote that the insult came from the relative of a girl whom Shore Crossing had compromised. See Lucullus V. McWhorter and Two Moons in *Hear Me My Chiefs* (Caldwell, Idaho: Caxton Printers, 1952), pp. 188–190, 201; Account of Yellow Bull in Edward S. Curtis, *The North American Indian*, 20 vols. (Seattle: E. S. Curtis, 1911), 8:164; and Duncan MacDonald, "Goaded to the War-Path," *The New North-West* (Deer Lodge, Montana), June 21, 1878, p. 2.

3. Although McWhorter accepts the statement of Camille Williams (War Singer) that Shore Crossing was a teetotaler, Two Moons, Yellow Bull, and Joseph among others state that the warrior had been drinking heavily. See Two Moons in *Hear Me*, p. 201; Yellow Bull in Curtis, *North American Indian*, 8:164; and "Chief Joseph Was a Great Indian," *The Indian School Journal* (1904), 5:39.

needed a third man to hold their horses when they went into action. Swan Necklace, the seventeen-year-old nephew of Shore Crossing, was their choice.[4] The boy was alone when his uncle found him. Receiving instructions to follow, the would-be warrior obeyed. He mounted behind Shore Crossing, and without explanation the riders moved out of camp in the direction of Salmon River.[5]

The Indians took an old trail that wound up the north side of White Bird Hill and then descended into the little valley watered by White Bird Creek. From there they could follow the stream to its confluence with the Salmon. Six miles upriver on the west bank of the Salmon stood the home of Larry Ott. When the men reached the homestead of J. J. Manuel of White Bird Creek, they paused to sharpen their knives on the rancher's grindstone. Manuel found them friendly and felt no alarm.[6]

About three miles above the mouth of White Bird Creek, the warriors stopped at a store owned by Harry Mason and attempted to trade a horse for a rifle, but the trader declined. Mason was a bit apprehensive and kept a hand on a revolver under the counter as he dickered with the Indians. He had administered a whipping to two Nez Perce in the spring; and although a council of arbitration ruled in his favor, Mason was still uneasy in the presence of young warriors who might hold a grudge. After pricing some other items, the Nez Perce departed.[7]

Crossing the Salmon, the warriors drew near the Ott ranch early in the afternoon. It was then that Swan Necklace fully understood

4. At the time of the outbreak the boy was known as Red Sun-rayed Grizzly, but after the war he "put away" the name and took that of his father, Swan Necklace. Yellow Wolf found it more comfortable to refer to the Indian by his later name and historians have followed suit. Lucullus V. McWhorter, *Yellow Wolf: His Own Story* (Caldwell, Idaho: Caxton Printers, 1948), p. 44n.

5. A letter from L. P. Brown to the Commanding Officer of Fort Lapwai on June 14 definitely establishes that the parade took place on June 13. McWhorter states that Shore Crossing spent the night brooding over the insult before deciding to take action and that the war party left the camp early the next morning. Subsequent testimony, however, will show that the avengers departed before noon on June 13 and stopped at a number of places on White Bird Creek and Salmon River before darkness came. Most historians follow McWhorter's lead and perpetuate the error. See Brown to Col. David Perry, June 14, in O. O. Howard, *Nez Perce Joseph* (Boston: Lee and Shepard, 1881), pp. 90–91; McWhorter and Camille Williams in McWhorter, *Hear Me*, pp. 190–191.

6. Byron Defenbach, *Idaho: The Place and Its People*, 3 vols. (Chicago: American Historical Society, 1933), 1:415.

7. Harry Mason was born in 1830, apparently in England. When about eighteen years old, he signed on a whaling vessel and sailed around Cape Horn to San Fran-

the purpose of the trip.[8] But Larry Ott was nowhere to be found.[9] After a thorough search of the area failed to disclose their prey, the warriors decided to visit another white man whom they hated. He was Richard Devine, a retired sailor who lived near the mouth of Carver Creek many miles upriver. The Nez Perce had accused him of the murder of a crippled Indian, and to the avengers he appeared a worthy substitute for Ott.

The Indians recrossed the Salmon to pick up the main trail on its east bank. Four miles farther upstream they stopped to buy food from Charles P. Cone, a friend of the Nez Perce who owned a ranch near the mouth of Slate Creek.[10] The warriors also tried to purchase ammunition, but Cone refused them. He thought it strange that the young men were traveling up the river so late in the day, especially since two of them rode the same horse. He also noted the poor quality of their mounts. The Indians usually selected their best animals when taking a long trip.[11]

Covering another six miles, the warriors came to the Henry El-

cisco. The dream of quick riches kept him in California for more than a decade. In 1861 he formed a partnership with his friend Henry Elfers and headed for Warrens (then Washington Territory, later Idaho Territory), to try his luck in the new goldfields. The following year Mason and Elfers settled on John Day Creek and began raising stock. Mason later sold his share in the ranch to Elfers and moved to Mason Prairie, where he kept a stage station. In 1872 he returned to Salmon River and bought a ranch and store about three miles upriver from the mouth of White Bird Creek. Helen J. Walsh, "Personal Experiences of the Nez Perce War," University of Washington Library, Seattle, pp. 1–6; Howard, *Nez Perce Joseph*, p. 102; Helen Addison Howard, *Saga of Chief Joseph* (Caldwell, Idaho: Caxton Printers, 1965), p. 155; Chester Anders Fee, *Chief Joseph: The Biography of a Great Indian* (New York: Wilson–Erickson, 1936), p. 82; Francis Haines, *The Nez Perces: Tribesmen of the Columbia Plateau* (Norman: University of Oklahoma Press, 1955), p. 219.

8. Camille Williams to McWhorter, *c.* May, 1942, item 103, packet 164, McWhorter Collection, Washington State University Library Archives, Pullman; McWhorter, *Hear Me*, p. 191.

9. Ott had made a trip to Florence, where he had fallen ill. He later returned to the region and served as a scout for Capt. Trimble. "Lawrence Ott," *North Idaho*, p. 513; E. R. Sherwin, *et al.*, to Governor Brayman, Slate Creek, June 30, 1877, in Eugene B. Chaffee, editor, "Nez Perce War Letters to Governor Mason Brayman," *Fifteenth Biennial Report of the Board of Trustees of the State Historical Society for the Years 1935–1936* (Boise: The Society, 1936), pp. 55–56.

10. Cone was one of the few settlers in the canyon who actually purchased his land from the Nez Perce. In 1863 he paid Chief Whistle Knocker $1200 for the land, and he continued to maintain good relations with the Indians throughout the rest of his life. "Charles P. Cone," *North Idaho*, p. 550.

11. H. W. Cone, "White Bird Battle," manuscript in the files of the Idaho State Historical Society, Boise, p. 2.

fers ranch, which stood on the bank of John Day Creek not far from its confluence with the Salmon.[12] Elfers and two others were busy milking cows when the party appeared. Not being able to see clearly in the twilight, Catherine Elfers headed toward the house to inspect her rental rooms. She thought that perhaps the travelers might wish to engage them, since it was almost dark. As she returned from her chore, she saw that the men were Indians. They said the purpose of their visit was to inquire after some horses that had strayed from their camp on Camas Prairie. Receiving a negative reply, they continued on their journey, finally reaching the cabin of Richard Devine late at night.[13]

The avengers left their horses in charge of Swan Necklace and entered the shack, where they found Devine awake. He was no match for the young warriors, and they killed him with a bullet from his own rifle. Following the murder, the party decided to retrace its steps and pay a return visit to Jurden Henry Elfers. The German had some fine horses, and his heart had not always opened to the Nez Perce.[14]

Early on the morning of June 14, Elfers started for his hayfield and pasture, located on an elevated plateau behind his homestead

12. Then forty-two years old, Jurden Henry Elfers was a native of Hannover, Germany. Entering Idaho in 1861, he settled on John Day Creek a year later and almost immediately began to prosper. At first in partnership with Harry Mason and John Wessell, Elfers became the sole owner of the spread in 1872. In addition to his ranch, Elfers derived income from a general store and hotel, did a thriving dairy business, and prospected for gold in partnership with Philip Cleary and M. Dasey. Elfers married his German wife October 16, 1871. By June 1877 three children had blessed the union, and the Elferses expected another child in six months. "Henry Elfers," *North Idaho*, p. 451.

13. Little is known of the early life of Richard Devine, except that he was an Englishman by birth and a sailor by profession. Forsaking the sea in later life, he decided to try his hand at ranching and built a cabin on the bank of the Salmon River near its juncture with Carver Creek. He shortly won an unenviable reputation among the Nez Perce for cruelty and brutality. Devine was fifty-two years old in 1877. J. W. Poe, "Beginning of Nez Perce Hostilities," *Lewiston Teller*, April 13, 1878, p. 2; Robert G. Bailey, *River of No Return* (Lewiston, Idaho: Bailey Publishing Co., 1943), p. 184; McWhorter, *Yellow Wolf*, pp. 145–146n; Yellow Bull in Curtis, *North American Indian*, 8:165; Defenbach, *Idaho*, 1:416; Cone, "White Bird Battle," p. 2; Camille Williams to McWhorter, January 2, 1934, item 75, packet 164, McWhorter Collection; McWhorter, *Hear Me*, pp. 121, 192; Charlotte M. Kirkwood, *The Nez Perce Indian War Under Chiefs Joseph and Whitebird* (Grangeville, Idaho: Idaho County Free Press, 1928), pp. 40–41.

14. Henry Elfers apparently got along with his Indian neighbors better than did most settlers on the Salmon. He had not done any of them direct physical harm. One

about two hundred yards southwest. After driving the stock to pasture, he intended to try out a new mowing machine on his hay crop. Elfers sent his twenty-one-year-old nephew, "Harry" Burn Beckrodge, ahead with the calves.[15] Robert Bland, a hired man, followed with the cows, and Elfers brought up the rear with the horses. Perhaps half an hour elapsed between the time Beckrodge left the corral and when Elfers reached the pasture.[16]

When Shore Crossing, Red Moccasin Tops, and Swan Necklace reached the Elfers ranch, they secreted themselves near the path leading to the pasture. To attract the attention of anyone who might pass by, they staked their horses in a little patch of oats that bordered the trail. As each man approached the hiding place, he was picked from the saddle by a bullet from Devine's rifle. While the avengers ambushed the unsuspecting rancher and his helpers, Catherine Elfers churned butter in the milkhouse on the bank of John Day Creek. The sound of rushing water drowned the noise of death as she went about her work. Later she returned to the house.[17]

After rounding up the finest of Elfers' horses, the three Nez Perce began a hunt for arms and ammunition. They entered the ranch house and found a rifle belonging to a man in Warrens, which an expressman had left at the ranch a few days before, and a handful of cartridges. Taking the loot, the young men departed and con-

---

tribal historian, however, referred to him as an "uncomprising enemy," and McWhorter claimed that he was prone to set his dogs on defenseless Indians. The evidence seems to indicate that the Nez Perce respected Elfers whether they liked him or not. They agreed to permit him to sit as a member on the council of arbitration convened to determine the justice of the whipping Mason gave to two Nez Perce. The fact speaks well of him, because it must have been common knowledge that he and Mason had been in partnership only a few years before. The avengers may have been among those who resented the decision of the council and accorded Elfers more than his proportionate share of blame. "Henry Elfers," *North Idaho*, p. 451; Statements of Catherine [Elfers] Cleary, April 16, 1888, and September 23, 1890, and statement of Philip Cleary, September 23, 1890, Claim of Catherine Cleary, no. 2723 (hereafter cited as Cleary 2723), Records of the United States Court of Claims, Record Group 123, National Archives (hereafter cited as Court of Claims Records); McWhorter and Camille Williams in *Hear Me*, pp. 192, 212; Cone, "White Bird Battle," p. 2; Bailey, *River of No Return*, p. 184.

15. Although Beckrodge's real name was Burn, he was universally known as Harry after a brother of his who had lived with the Elferses and had died before Burn joined them. See *North Idaho*, p. 52.

16. Kirkwood, *Indian War*, p. 41; Catherine Cleary, September 23, 1890, Cleary 2723.

17. "Elfers," *North Idaho*, p. 451; Catherine Cleary, September 23, 1890, Cleary 2723.

tinued northward down the trail leading to Slate Creek. Catherine saw the Indians leave but did not suspect that anything was wrong.[18]

At least three men saw the smoke from Devine's rifle. Not all of them, however, interpreted it in the same way. A packer, John T. Johnson, seeing the smoke from the mountain prairie far above the hayfield, reasoned that some boys were after coyotes and continued his journey. Victor, a Frenchman working a claim on the bank of Salmon River, also saw it but became suspicious and left his claim to gather his colleagues and investigate. When a third man, named Whitfield, who had been hunting in the vicinity, saw the smoke he rushed to the site and discovered the bodies of the three men lying on the trail only a few yards apart.[19]

Without telling Mrs. Elfers what had happened, Whitfield hurried two miles up John Day Creek to notify Norman Gould of the tragedy. Gould operated the Elfers' lumber mill and was a good friend of the family. Whitfield found Gould at home with George Greer, another Salmon River settler. He quickly told his story, and the three men started back to the ranch to break the news to Catherine. In the meantime Victor and his companions reached the pasture, where they too discovered the bodies. They reported their findings to Mrs. Elfers, but she refused to believe them. Not until Gould arrived and had the bodies brought to the house did she begin to accept the fact of her husband's death.[20] The men decided to take Mrs. Elfers and her children and seek safety among the Cones and Woods on Slate Creek.[21]

II

When the Indians neared Slate Creek, they left the main trail and climbed upward to a path that followed the contour of the mountaintop in order to avoid passing through the tiny settlement. Two miles below the mouth of the tributary, they returned to the

18. Fee, *Chief Joseph*, p. 118; Yellow Bull in Curtis, *North American Indian*, 8:165; Statement of Norman Gould, September 12, 1890, Cleary 2723; *North Idaho*, pp. 52–53.

19. "John T. Johnson" and "Elfers," *North Idaho*, pp. 541, 549.

20. Gould, September 12, 1890, Cleary 2723; Kirkwood, *Indian War*, pp. 41–42; "Norman Gould" and "Elfers," *North Idaho*, pp. 478, 541.

21. On June 16, Philip Cleary and several others returned to the Elfers ranch and buried the bodies. They laid Elfers near a large weeping willow tree that grew by his bedroom window. After the war Mrs. Elfers had the bodies removed to a graveyard on a hill on the opposite side of John Day Creek. After spending six weeks at Slate Creek, Mrs. Elfers returned to the ranch and engaged Cleary to manage it for her. Kirkwood, *Indian War*, p. 42; Marriage Certificate, Cleary 2723.

lower trail bordering the Salmon and almost immediately encountered Charles Cone. Before continuing their journey, they warned him that the Nez Perce were on the warpath and that it was dangerous to be out alone. The rancher took the Indians at their word and spread the alarm to settlers in the immediate vicinity.[22]

About one mile above the mouth of White Bird Creek, the warriors met Samuel Benedict, who was out looking for his cows. Red Moccasin Tops had been wounded by Benedict in a foray almost two years before, and the Nez Perce was anxious to even the score.[23] The Indian opened fire, wounding Benedict, who fell to the ground. The white man escaped further injury by playing dead, and the Indians left him to return to the camp on Camas Prairie.

When Shore Crossing and Red Moccasin Tops reached Round Willow, they halted momentarily and sent Swan Necklace ahead with the news of their killing. Carrying a rifle and riding a roan horse taken from Henry Elfers, the boy paraded into camp and delivered the message to his people. Big Morning, the brother of Yellow Bull, relieved Swan Necklace of his plunder and rode among the lodges crying: "This is the horse and this is the gun they have brought back! You must all remember that we have to fight now!"[24] Amidst the movement and the shouting, Shore Crossing and Red Moccasin Tops made their triumphal entrance.[25]

Volunteers for a second raid were not hard to find among the young men, and in a short time at least seventeen warriors joined

22. Cone, "White Bird Battle," pp. 2–3; *North Idaho*, p. 53.

23. According to J. W. Poe, who apparently investigated the matter thoroughly in 1878, some Nez Perce attempted to force their way into Benedict's store to obtain liquor late on the night of August 29, 1875. Grabbing his rifle, Benedict opened fire and succeeded in driving them off. According to Poe, he killed one Indian in the process and wounded one or two others. However, Isabella Benedict claimed that her husband had wounded two Indians but killed none, and that the dead Indian found near their store the following morning had been killed with his own pistol. On the other hand, Nez Perce historians declare that the shooting occurred in broad daylight and that Red Moccasin Tops was the only casualty. According to them, he took some buckshot in the back of his head but quickly recovered. Sometime before or after the incident, the Nez Perce state, Benedict apparently murdered an Indian named Chipmunk for stealing liquor from under his nose. Affidavit of Isabella [Benedict] Robie, November 9, 1889, Claim of Isabella Robie, no. 10557 (hereafter cited as Robie 10557), Records of the Assistant Attorney General for Claims Cases, Record Group 205, National Archives; Poe, "Beginning," p. 2; McWhorter, *Hear Me*, p. 210; Isabella Benedict to Alonzo Leland, April 17, 1878, *Lewiston Teller*, April 26, 1878, p. 1.

24. Yellow Bull in Curtis, *North American Indian*, 8:165.

25. Camille Williams in McWhorter, *Hear Me*, pp. 194–195. Round Willow was also known as Thorn Creek. It was located about three quarters of a mile from the summit of White Bird Hill.

the ranks of the avengers.[26] Among them were Bare Feet, Red Elk, Strong Eagle, Stick-in-the-Mud, and Geese Three Times Lighting on the Water, the only Wallowa who chose to go. Leadership naturally fell to Yellow Bull, a buffalo hunter and warrior of some repute who had been with Looking Glass in the Crow–Sioux battle on Pryor's Fork a few years before.[27] The war party quickly prepared themselves for battle and galloped out of camp.[28]

Joseph and Ollokot were absent when Swan Necklace brought the news of the raid. They were busy herding cattle across the Salmon and butchering beef in preparation for a feast.[29] The remaining chiefs went into council after Yellow Bull and the marauders had left. Some apparently argued that war was inevitable and that they should move rapidly to prepare for it. But Old Rainbow and others urged caution and restraint. Before the meeting ended, most of the participants had agreed to chart a course of neutrality. They would wait to see how the whites reacted. Perhaps there was still a chance for peace. In any event the chiefs determined to leave Tolo Lake. It was now a bad place.[30]

26. Poe gave the number of recruits as seventeen or more, and O. O. Howard followed suit. See Poe, "Beginnings," p. 2, and Howard, *Nez Perce Joseph*, p. 103. Eyewitnesses reported that the total party numbered between eighteen and twenty-five. See George Popham, "From the Scene of Hostilities," *Lewiston Teller*, June 30, 1877, p. 4; Helen Walsh, "Incidents of an Indian Murder," *Lewiston Teller*, September 9, 1877, p. 2; Robie, November 9, 1889, Robie 10557.

27. Camille Williams in McWhorter, *Hear Me*, pp. 194–195; Yellow Bull in Curtis, *North American Indian*, 8:165.

28. Two Moons and Yellow Wolf stated that Swan Necklace rode into camp after dark on June 14 and the second war party departed the following morning. See McWhorter, *Hear Me*, p. 201, and *Yellow Wolf*, pp. 45–56. However, contemporary accounts of the second foray prove that the Nez Perce returned in force to Salmon River on the afternoon of June 14. See Popham, "Hostilities"; Isabella Benedict to Mrs. Orchard and Mrs. Dougherty, June 19, 1877, *Idaho World* (Idaho City), July 13, 1877, p. 1.

29. Thirty-seven years old, Joseph was very striking in appearance. Of him Lieutenant Forse wrote: "I thought he was the finest Indian I had ever seen not only physically but intelligently. He was about six feet in height, powerfully built, and strength of character written on every feature." His role was that of a diplomat and statesman; he was a civic rather than a military leader. His younger brother Ollokot was a warrior of renown and served as Joseph's confidant and advisor. See Albert Forse, "Chief Joseph as a Commander," *Winners of the West* (November, 1936), 13:1; McWhorter, *Hear Me*, pp. 178–181; Alvin M. Josephy, Jr., *The Patriot Chiefs: A Chronicle of Indian Leadership* (New York: Viking Press, 1961), pp. 314–315, 329–330.

30. Two Moons in McWhorter, *Hear Me*, pp. 201–202; McWhorter, *Yellow Wolf*, p. 45; C. E. S. Wood, "Chief Joseph, The Nez Perce," *Century Magazine* (1884), 28:136–137.

III

In the morning, Two Moons stepped from the darkness of his
tepee to see Joseph and Ollokot approaching camp leading twelve
horses packed with fresh meat. He mounted and rode to greet the
brothers and tell the disquieting news. The intelligence must have
been painful to Joseph: the search for peace had occupied him almost constantly since the death of his father, and he felt that unless
he acted swiftly and forcefully it would elude him forever. When
Joseph and Ollokot reached the camp, they found most of the
lodges already down. Riding about the tepee circle, they pled with
their people to remain. "Let us stay here till the army comes," they
said. "We will make some kind of peace with them."[31] But none took
their counsel, and the exodus continued. Soon the lodges of the Wallowas stood alone. The rest of the Nez Perce headed for a camping
place called Drive-Inn (Sah-pah-tsas), named for a large cavern near
the Red Rock area.

Joseph and Ollokot spent the rest of the day and night on Camas
Prairie. A relative tried to persuade Joseph to return to Fort Lapwai
and explain that the Wallowas had no part in the killing, but the
chief replied: "I can hardly go back. The white people will blame
me, telling me that my young men have killed the white men."[32]
Experience had taught him that frontiersmen often had difficulty in
distinguishing one Indian from another. After dark, the Indians reported, white raiders fired several shots into the camp, but none in
the party was injured. The next morning Joseph and Ollokot decided to join their tribesmen on Cottonwood Creek.[33]

31. Two Moons was in his early forties. His father was a notable Salish warrior; his
mother was a Nez Perce. McWhorter, *Hear Me*, p. 30; Account of Wetatonmi [wife of
Ollokot] in McWhorter, *Hear Me*, pp. 195–196.

32. Account of Three Eagles in Curtis, *North American Indian*, 8:24–25n.

33. Wetatonmi and Two Moons in McWhorter, *Hear Me*, pp. 196, 202; McWhorter, *Yellow Wolf*, p. 45; Yellow Bull in Curtis, *North American Indian*, 8:165.

What They Said

Mr. Baker wanted to come to the prairie and inform the people, but Manuel did not deem it safe for any of them to leave.

GEORGE POPHAM

That there was also in the house, furniture consisting of 12 cane-bottom chairs, rugs (made from rags), one homemade lounge, six ordinary cheap paintings, one parlor stove, and one kitchen stove with fixtures. There was also in the house clothing for my husband, four children, and myself — clothing enough to last my children for three years. My husband was a good provider and kept us well-provided with clothes. There was also one gold watch and chain bought in San Francisco in the spring of 1863, one black enameled breast pin, two sets of gold sleeve buttons, one set of earrings, two gold crosses, which were all used from two to 14 years.

CLAIM OF ISABELLA BENEDICT ROBIE

When all was still, I cautiously crept to the house under the cover of the night. August lay just as I had seen him fall. They had taken his gun and left his body unmolested. Satisfying themselves with the supper I had prepared, they had hurried on to other scenes of bloodshed and pillage. I could find no clue to my husband's whereabouts. I searched everywhere, and called his name, but could find no trace — only some blood stains on the window, as though he might have escaped through it.

ISABELLA BENEDICT

He turned and looked at them, lowering his gun without a word. I shall never forget that look. There was prophecy in it. He knew that he was giving up his last chance.

HELEN WALSH OF HARRY MASON

It would make your heart ache to see little children walk here and sleep here for 36 hours [and] never cry except when you name Indians.

LETTER FROM SLATE CREEK

If you never see me again in this world remember that my love was strong to the end, and that I will wait for you in the next.

HELEN WALSH

2

The Second Raid

It was mid-afternoon on June 14 when the war party led by Yellow Bull made its first stop, at the ranch of John J. Manuel on White Bird Creek.[1] The homesteader and his family were aware of the possibility of an attack and had just started for the ranch of a neighbor when the Indians appeared.

James Baker, a seventy-four-year-old bachelor who lived one mile southwest on White Bird Creek, had brought the news of the wounding of Samuel Benedict a few hours before.[2] Accompanied by Conrad Fruth, one of his employees, he reached the Manuel spread about noon. Baker intended to continue on to Camas Prairie to warn the settlers there, but Manuel convinced him that he would be safer if he stayed at home, so the old man returned to his ranch. An hour later he returned, this time with Patrick Brice, an Irish prospector who lived near Warrens.[3]

Manuel, his father-in-law George Popham, and the other two men discussed the matter at length. The rancher was determined to remain where he was, but Baker and Brice decided to leave and try

1. A native Virginian, Manuel migrated to Idaho during the gold rush. In 1873 he bought a ranch from Arthur Chapman on White Bird Creek, one mile east of the present town of White Bird. Manuel owned about 300 head of cattle in partnership with Benjamin F. Morris. In the late 1860's he married Jennet Popham. Her father, George Popham, was a frequent visitor and had been at the Manuel ranch since the fall of 1876. Statement of J. J. Manuel, February 6, 1878; statement of Benjamin F. Morris, August 16, 1890; and statement of George Woodward, August 16, 1890, in Claim of Benjamin F. Morris, no. 2718 (hereafter cited as Morris 2718), Court of Claims Records. See also the account of Maggie Manuel Bowman in "William Bowman," *North Idaho*, pp. 529–530; Popham, "Hostilities."

2. Baker was one of fifty-seven settlers who had petitioned Howard on May 7 to move the non-treaty bands to the reservation. His ranch stood near the center of the present town of Whitebird. Cone, "White Bird Battle," p. 4; Brown, *Flight of the Nez Perce*, p. 61.

3. Patrick Brice was born in Londonderry, Ireland, in 1837. At the age of fourteen he emigrated to the United States. After spending some time in Oregon, he moved to Idaho to search for gold. Statement of Patrick Brice, November 23, 1897, Claim of Patrick Brice, no. 7427 (hereafter cited as Brice 7427), Court of Claims Records.

to reach Mount Idaho. On the White Bird Divide near Thorn Spring they saw a band of Indians approaching and quickly returned to the Manuel ranch. The men decided at once to take Jennet Manuel and the children and flee with them to the Baker place, because it was much easier to defend. In an emergency its stone cellar might afford them needed protection. Popham and Brice volunteered to stay behind and lock the doors, while the rest of the party started down White Bird Creek. Manuel put his six-year-old daughter Maggie on his horse, and their eleven-month-old son rode with his mother. Baker took the lead.[4]

After they had traveled a short distance, they found themselves face to face with the marauding party. Baker was the first to fall. Although mortally wounded by a number of arrows, he was able to raise himself long enough to gasp, "Goodbye, Jack, they've got me."[5] Manuel was the second victim. When a bullet struck him in the hip, he slid from his horse. Driving an arrow into the back of his neck, the Indians left him for dead.

Picking up the weapons dropped by Baker and Manuel, the warriors took the woman and her children back to the ranch. During the shooting Mrs. Manuel lost control of her horse, took a bad fall, and injured her knee. The baby also was injured in the fall. As the result of the barrage directed at her father, Maggie suffered two arrow wounds, one in the upper arm and the second in the back of the neck, but neither appeared to be serious.

Surrounding the ranch house, the war party gave Brice and Popham an ultimatum. The Nez Perce told them that if they would surrender their weapons, they would not be harmed. Believing it useless to resist, Popham and Brice handed over a Henry rifle and a shotgun and, true to their word, the Indians took them and left. Mrs. Manuel remained in the house to care for herself and the children, while the men took to the brush. Some of the Nez Perce kept watch in the vicinity and, fearing that the Indians might change their minds and finish the job they had begun, the men returned hidden but stayed close to the house in case they should be needed.[6]

4. Patrick Brice, "The Nez Perce Outbreak," *Idaho World* (Idaho City), September 14, 1877, p. 2; Popham, "Hostilities"; Maggie Bowman in *North Idaho*, p. 529. The third Manuel child, Julia, was in school at Mount Idaho.

5. Maggie Bowman in *North Idaho*, p. 530.

6. Manuel, February 6, 1878, Morris 2718; Statement of John J. Manuel, February 13, 1878, and statement of George Popham, August 13, 1890, Claim of John J. Manuel, no. 3496 (hereafter cited as Manuel 3496), Court of Claims Records; Brice, "Nez Perce Outbreak"; Popham, "Hostilities"; Maggie Bowman in *North Idaho*, pp. 529–530.

II

Earlier that morning, Isabella Benedict saw her husband approach the house, sitting his horse with difficulty.[7] She ran to help
him and found that he had been shot through both legs and was
bleeding profusely. Slipping off his horse, Benedict lay down in the
shade of a large tree that stood in the yard and told his wife to send
their older daughter to fetch "Hurdy Gurdy" Brown, his closest
neighbor, who kept a store about three-fifths of a mile down the
Salmon River.[8]

When Brown arrived, Benedict related his story and warned his
friend that the Indians would return to finish their work. He told
Brown that he should be ready to defend his life and property as
well, because the assault marked the beginning of an uprising.
Brown chose to discount this because he knew of the bad blood between Benedict and some of the Indians. Convinced that the attack
was an isolated incident and nothing more than a judgment rendered in payment for an old debt, he prescribed a cold-water treatment for Benedict's wounds and returned to his cabin.[9]

Not long after Brown left, five Frenchmen arrived. They worked
a mining claim on the opposite bank of the Salmon River and had
come by boat. Unaware of what had been happening, they had not
carried rifles. After hearing Benedict's story, the miners decided to
return to camp for their guns, leaving August Bacon with the family.
Isabella gave the Frenchman a fine breechloader to use in the event
that Indians arrived before the party returned.[10]

7. Samuel Benedict was a Canadian by birth who migrated to Idaho in 1862 during the gold rush and in 1868 settled near the mouth of White Bird Creek. On February 7, 1863, he married fifteen-year-old Isabella Kelly, a fiery redhead of Irish
ancestry. The Benedicts had four children, two of whom were attending school in
Mount Idaho at the time of the outbreak. In addition to farming and raising horses,
cattle, hogs, and chickens, Benedict ran a general store and wayside inn and did
blacksmithing. In 1874 he obtained a franchise from the county to operate a ferry
across the Salmon River. "Edward W. Robie" and "William G. Brown" in *North Idaho*,
pp. 464–465, 543. See also Benedict to Leland, April 17, 1878; Robie, November 9,
1889, and statement of Charles F. Cone, Robie 10557; M. Alfreda Elsensohn, *Pioneer
Days in Idaho County*, edited by Eugene F. Hoy (Caldwell, Idaho: Caxton Printers,
1951), 2:71; Bailey, *River of No Return*, p. 205; Poe, "Beginnings"; McWhorter, *Hear
Me*, pp. 210–211.

8. Benedict to Orchard and Dougherty, June 19, 1877; Robie, November 9, 1889,
Robie 10557.

9. Account of Isabella Robie in Kirkwood, *Indian War*, p. 50.

10. Affidavit of John Doumecq, Abstract of Evidence, May 10, 1898, Robie 10557;
"John Doumecq," *North Idaho*, p. 525.

After the men left, Isabella went into the garden to gather lettuce and onions for supper. As she returned to the house, she saw a band of Nez Perce approaching. She broke the news to her husband, who lay on a bed in a small room that opened off the parlor. Telling her to flee with the children, Benedict prepared to meet his foe. Bacon moved to the front door with rifle in hand.[11]

Isabella and her children left by the rear door and ran toward the back gate. She saw that she was being observed by Indians on a hillside above her and, realizing the danger of her position, returned to the safety of the house. When she entered the room where her husband had been, she found it empty. Firing began. Bacon, who still stood in the doorway, suddenly lurched backward and slumped to the floor. Then Indians began to push through the door, but one warrior took pity on the woman and her children and told them to go to the Manuel place. Isabella guided the children from the house and hurriedly followed them to the bank of White Bird Creek and the protective cover of some willows.[12]

After watching his wife and daughters leave the house, Benedict had apparently crawled through the open window in his bedroom and limped toward a footbridge spanning White Bird Creek. There his enemies found him. Struck by a volley from Nez Perce rifles, Benedict fell into the water.[13]

Crouched among the willows, Isabella and the children remained hidden while the Indians pillaged the house and store. Feasting on the supper prepared for the Benedicts, they gathered their loot, including a keg of whiskey, and left. When they had gone, Isabella slipped back to the house. She found no traces of her husband except blood stains on the window sill in the bedroom. She covered Bacon's body with a quilt, collected a few trinkets and the little money that was left, and began to work her way along the creek toward the Manuel ranch.[14]

After leaving the Benedict ranch, the war party headed up the trail to the store operated by H. C. Brown. Luckily for Brown, he

11. Isabella Robie in Kirkwood, *Indian War*, p. 50.

12. Benedict to Orchard and Dougherty, June 19, 1877; Kirkwood, *Indian War*, p. 50.

13. Camille Williams to McWhorter, *c*. May, 1942, McWhorter Collection; Brice, "Nez Perce Outbreak"; McWhorter, *Hear Me*, p. 212. On June 20 Louis Boucher returned to the Benedict ranch and found it destroyed by fire. He saw the body of Benedict "laying in the creek" but made no effort to retrieve it. When others later searched for the corpse, it could not be found. Affidavit of Louis Boucher, August 1, 1890, Robie 10557.

14. Isabella Robie in Kirkwood, *Indian War*, pp. 50–51.

learned of the presence of the Indians before they were upon him. As he sat reading on the porch, he heard someone calling to him from the opposite bank of the Salmon. "The Indians are coming," the voice told him, and remembering Benedict's warning he moved quickly. Shouting to his sister and her husband to head for the boat, he grabbed his hunting bag and rifle and climbed to the top of a high rock to survey the path leading from the Benedict ranch. The Indians, he observed, were only a short distance away. He made his way swiftly down from the vantage point and back to the boat, where he found his brother-in-law, Albert Benson, fumbling with the rope holding the skiff to its mooring. Brown cut the line with his hunting knife as Benson scrambled aboard to take a seat by his wife. Brown shoved the boat into the current and leaped in, while Benson began pulling on the oars. They were not far from the bank when the Indians opened fire. One bullet cut a furrow in Brown's shoulder and a second hit Benson in the arm, but the boat soon glided out of range. On reaching the far bank the party disembarked, safe for the moment.[15]

III

About 2 p.m. on the afternoon of June 14, William Osborn rushed into the Mason store to tell his brother-in-law that the Nez Perce had murdered two Frenchmen on John Day Creek.[16] William George, French Frank, and old Shoemaker had just finished lunch and were sitting around the table talking.[17] Harry Mason lay on a cot in one corner of the store. He had injured his eye with a whip while driving cattle and was sensitive to strong light. Mason seemed to accept the news calmly, because the killings appeared to be an isolated incident. But after Osborn left, he began to clean and load his

15. *Ibid.*, 46; McWhorter, *Hear Me*, pp. 212–213.

16. Mason and William Osborn married sisters, Anna and Elizabeth Klein. Osborn located one-half mile upriver and operated a placer mine on the bank of the Salmon. About forty-eight years old, he was born in Massachusetts and reached Idaho as early as 1864. Elizabeth Osborn was born in Hesse-Darmstadt, Germany, in 1842 and married Osborn on October 29, 1867. After his wife died in 1876, Mason asked his sister and her husband, Helen and Edward Walsh, to live with him. Walsh was a Civil War amputee with one arm and was apparently having difficulty making a living, so the couple accepted. Helen reached the Mason ranch with her two children early in the fall of 1876; Edward planned to follow a year later. See Walsh, "Personal Experiences," pp. 1–4.

17. H. W. Cone identifies French Frank as François Chodoze. Apparently all of the men were in the employ of Mason at the time. H. W. Cone in Bailey, *River of No Return*, p. 187.

weapons. If there really were Indians on the warpath, he wanted to be ready for them. As a further precaution, he sent William George below to warn the families living between the Mason ranch and White Bird Creek.[18]

Before going very far, George met a man named Koon, who told him of the wounding of Samuel Benedict that morning. George then decided to return to the store and inform Mason, taking Koon with him. This time, Mason sent George directly to the Baker place to tell the old rancher to gather his neighbors and seek refuge at the Mason store. Mason believed his buildings were more defensible because they stood in the open, and there was a good place to hide the women and children on the mountain in back of the house. When George returned sometime later, he brought word that the settlers on White Bird Creek had decided to make their stand at the Baker cabin and carried an invitation for Mason to join them.

About 6 o'clock in the afternoon, Mason; his sister Helen Walsh and her two children; Osborn, his wife Elizabeth, and four children; and William George set out for the rendezvous point. Mrs. Walsh rode one of the horses and held her daughter Masie on her lap. A second horse carried the older Osborn children and little Edward Walsh. The rest of the party started out on foot.

Passing the Benedict ranch on the opposite bank of White Bird Creek, Mason and his followers forded the stream and approached the Baker cabin. Suddenly the night air rang with war whoops, and the travelers saw Indians advancing toward them through the twilight. The warriors called for the men to come forward to parley, but Mason refused and firing began.

Baker's garden and orchard were surrounded by a fence. Protected as it was from rummaging cattle, the grass grew high inside the fence and afforded the besieged party a refuge from sight if not from bullets. The Nez Perce maintained their position but did not advance. They kept up a haphazard fire as the last rays of light disappeared from the narrow gulch.

When complete darkness fell, Mason, Osborn, and their charges waded across White Bird Creek and found shelter in the thicket bordering the stream. Soon after, the Nez Perce left, and the fugitives decided to make their way back to the Mason ranch.

William George did not follow Mason when the firing began but started for Camas Prairie to find help. He lost his way in the dark-

18. The following treatment of the Mason Affair is based primarily on three accounts written by Helen Walsh. See "Personal Experiences," pp. 5–29; "Incident"; and her reminiscence in Kirkwood, *Indian War*, pp. 43–45.

ness and returned to find the party on the trail leading back to Salmon River. George had been wounded by a stray bullet; the tip of
his little finger had been shot away, a minor but painful injury.[19]
Mason gave George instructions on how to find his way to Mount
Idaho without following the established trail, and he soon departed.

By the time the weary group reached the ranch, the sun shone
brightly in the east. French Frank and Shoemaker were in the process of preparing breakfast in the midst of chaos. During the night,
the Nez Perce had paid Mason a visit and ransacked his buildings.
Frank and Shoemaker had heard them coming and escaped by hiding in the brush.

Mason's plan was to gather food at the ranch and cross the Salmon River to hide during the day. After dark they would return to
the east bank and attempt to reach Mount Idaho before daylight.
They found some bread, cake, and cold meat in the basement and
each took a handful. The rest went into sacks carried by the men.
While Shoemaker stayed behind to let out the calves, the rest of the
party started for the boat landing near the Osborn cabin, which
stood on the bank of the Salmon one-half mile upriver.

Just as they reached the bank of the river, the war party appeared. Hurrying to the cabin, the refugees barricaded themselves
inside. Mason went to the room in the rear and poked his Winchester through a crevice in the logs. He had a clear shot at the Indians
and was about to pull the trigger when Osborn called for him to
stop. The miner knew some of the Nez Perce and believed that there
was still a chance to avert bloodshed. Osborn's wife also begged him
not to shoot, so Mason relented.

There was no chance to parley, however. A volley from the Indians came crashing through the only window in the cabin. The
three men rushed to the opening and raised themselves to return
the fire, but before they could steady their weapons, a second volley
sent them sprawling. Osborn regained his footing long enough to
shout, "You devils you!" before he toppled backward.

The Frenchman moved only once after he fell. Mason was not
dead, but a bullet had shattered his right arm and he bled freely.
The Indians continued to send volley after volley through the window, and to escape the barrage the women and children took refuge
under one bed and Mason rolled under the other. Sensing that their
victims were helpless, the warriors stormed into the cabin. Helen

19. C. A. Sears, "Letter from Mount Idaho," *Idaho Tri-Weekly Statesman* (Boise),
July 3, 1877, p. 2; *North Idaho*, p. 53.

Walsh handed her revolver to Mason, but he was too weak to hold it. "If I could only shoot," he moaned.

The intruders soon discovered the hiding place of the survivors. They were able to dislodge the women and children by jumping up and down on the bed. One Indian dragged Mason out by his shattered arm and began pulling him across the floor toward the door. "Oh shoot me!" he cried in pain. Pulling a revolver, the warrior obliged. The raiders raped the women before releasing them.[20] "You go now," one of the warriors told them. "You go Lewiston. You go Slate Creek. You go where you like." It was about 6:30 when the war party rode away, leaving the women to stare at their dead.

They decided to go to Slate Creek because it was the closest settlement, but before they departed Elizabeth Osborn insisted on changing her dress. Her husband was dead and she would wear black. Soon in her mourning clothes, she trudged after Helen Walsh and the children, who took the lead. A few miles upriver they reached the Titman ranch. Taking milk from the deserted house, the women gave it to the children but declined to drink themselves. "As for ourselves," Helen Walsh wrote, "we did not seem to realize that we should ever want any thing."

While they were resting, Shoemaker walked in. His chores in letting out the calves had detained him so that he arrived after the cabin had been attacked. He had taken to the river when the shooting started and had stood in water up to his neck until the war party left. After conferring with the women, Shoemaker decided to push ahead to Slate Creek to get help. Putting little Annie Osborn on his back, he moved quickly down the trail. Not too long afterward a rescue party led by William Wilson reached the women and brought them all to safety.[21]

IV

Mrs. Walsh and Mrs. Osborn found many settlers gathered at Slate Creek. Among them were Mrs. Elfers and her children, the Hiram Titmans, the E. R. Sherwins, and the Van Sickles, whom they knew as friends and neighbors. Soon there were about forty women and children and thirty men huddled together in a stockade built of

20. In her accounts of the affair, Helen Walsh indicated that she and Elizabeth had been treated kindly by the war party. Apparently she did not wish the fact of their misfortune known. A diarist who visited Slate Creek on June 26 reported that the women had been raped and would not show themselves because of their shame. Michael McCarthy, Diary, June 26, 1877, Journals and Papers of Michael McCarthy, Library of Congress (hereafter cited as McCarthy, Diary). See also *North Idaho*, p. 54.

21. "William J. Wilson," *North Idaho*, p. 571.

heavy timbers. The night before, an Indian woman named Tolo had carried the word of the outbreak to Florence, twenty-six miles distant, and a dozen or more miners had responded to the call.[22]

One of them, William Wilson, had had military experience, having served with the Second Missouri Light Artillery during the Civil War. He supervised the construction of defenses. The men dug a trench three feet deep around the buildings owned by Charles Cone. Placing eleven- to twelve-foot fir logs on end in the ditch, they formed the stockade. The defenders filled in cracks between the firs by placing other upright logs behind them. Inside, a stone cellar afforded a measure of security for the women and children. A bluff to the east overlooked the fortification and posed a tactical problem, but Wilson solved it quickly. He ordered his men to dig a rifle pit on its top and posted sentinels to maintain a steady watch. Whether the Nez Perce came along the trail hugging the bank of the Salmon or took the high road along the canyon rim made no difference: the settlers would be ready for them. As an added precaution, the men each night removed the planks from the bridge that spanned Slate Creek, cutting off the possibility of a sudden attack from the north under cover of darkness. The river ran high during that June, and its width and swiftness made crossing a hazardous undertaking. Feeling more secure, the settlers and the miners relaxed a bit — and waited and watched.[23]

V

Isabella Benedict and her daughters approached the Manuel ranch late in the evening on June 14. She passed the body of Baker on her way to the homestead and saw Manuel lying inside the fence. When she reached the house she found Jennet Manuel and her children inside, and shortly afterward Popham and Brice emerged from the thicket. Isabella learned that Jack Manuel was still alive, although he was badly wounded and might not survive the night. She tried to persuade Mrs. Manuel to accompany her to the safety of Mount Idaho, but Jennet refused, saying she would not leave her

22. Cone, "White Bird Battle," pp. 3–4; "Wilson," *North Idaho*, p. 571; Walsh, "Personal Experiences," pp. 29–31; Statement of Hiram Titman, 1888, Claim of Hiram Titman, no. 4945, Court of Claims Records; and Cleary, September 23, 1890, Cleary 2723; Kirkwood, *Indian War*, p. 42. Cone reported that twenty-five miners came to the rescue, but Wilson stated that there were twelve and Cleary placed the number between twelve and fifteen.

23. "Wilson," *North Idaho*, p. 571; "Charles P. Cone," *North Idaho*, p. 550; Cone, "White Bird Battle," p. 3; H. W. Cone in Bailey, *River of No Return*, pp. 184–185; Walsh, "Personal Experiences," p. 30; Elsensohn, *Idaho County*, 2:279–281.

husband. Because Isabella was afraid to make the trip alone, she had no choice but to stay at the ranch. While they were talking, six Indians rode near the house. Fearing for their lives, Isabella, her daughters, Popham, and Brice sought cover in the thicket.[24]

During the night Isabella and the girls became separated from the men, and when Brice called to them in the morning they mistook him for an Indian and refused to answer. Thoughout the daylight hours of June 15, Popham and Brice gave what help they could to Manuel, still lying in the grass, and to his wife and children in the house. Popham risked his life many times by exposing himself to the watchful eyes of Nez Perce sentries in order to care for his son-in-law. An Indian discovered Brice when he attempted to reach the house with water but allowed him to return to the thicket unharmed. As the day drew to a close Isabella reached a decision. Whatever the cost, she must reach Mount Idaho. After dark she took the children and started up the trail. She thought that if she could reach Camas Prairie before dawn broke, she might have a chance.[25]

24. Benedict to Orchard and Dougherty, June 19, 1877.
25. Brice, "Nez Perce Outbreak."

What They Said

I shall never forget my father when he came up to shake hands with me, tears running down his cheeks. He said, "Oh, my boy — is it possible? Only a few moments ago you and Ready were reported killed."

LUTHER P. WILMOT

My Kingdom in Heaven for a drop of water.

LEW DAY

Father was still alive and choked out that I should try to get away, but mother did not want me to go. Father said, "He'll be killed here anyway." Lynn Bowers took off her heavy skirt so that she could run faster, and we both sneaked away toward Grange Hall, through the high bunch grass.

HILL NORTON

With what guns Joe Moore could crawl out on the ground and secure, he had kept up a constant fire until his ammunition was exhausted. He then secured a shotgun and cut cartridges for bullets, used the powder, loaded the shotgun repeatedly, and kept the Indians at bay until morning. It was heroism of an unusual order. Scarely able to move from the loss of blood, he worked energetically to keep the hostiles off, always passing a reassuring word of comfort.

JENNIE NORTON

We finished getting the harness off the dead horses, and as we could not move the dead horses out of the road, we pulled the wagon around them by hand. This took a little time and the Indians, in a large group, were galloping toward us. Doug and I pulled the saddles off our horses and tied some of the harness and lasso ropes to them and the wagon. Doug and I mounted our horses, leaving our saddles on the ground, and away we went, as the Indians were getting nearer and were firing.

JOHN R. ADKISON

We spread out, searching the tall grass for Jyeloo. We found him. I saw his body myself, all covered with blood. He had many gunshot wounds on his body and legs — eleven in all. His head, crushed, was all over blood. Blood on the ground. I saw he had drawn his sheath knife. It was in the grass not far from him — must have been shot from his hand. We did not find the rifle.

YELLOW WOLF

3

The Norton Party

About 4 p.m. on the afternoon of June 14, Lew Wilmot and Pete Ready drove their wagons up to Cottonwood House, a combination store, hotel, saloon, and stage station eighteen miles west of Grangeville.[1] Returning from Lewiston with a load of merchandise for Vollmer and Scott, the proprietors of a general store in Mount Idaho, the freighters looked forward to a pleasant pause before beginning the last lap of their journey.[2]

The owner of the establishment, Benjamin B. Norton, was on the porch waiting to greet the men.[3] His wife, Jennie, his nine-year-old son, Hill, and his wife's nineteen-year-old-sister, Lynn Bowers, were

1. Luther P. Wilmot was born in 1839 in Freeport, Illinois. His father took the family west to Oregon and eventually settled near Fort Walla Walla, Washington. Luther married Louisa Haworth on October 4, 1863, and in 1866 they moved to Idaho. The couple had four children at the time of the outbreak and were expecting a fifth in a matter of days. Ready was born in Detroit in 1849. After spending some time in the goldfields in Colorado and Montana, he migrated to Idaho and settled on Camas Prairie in 1870. Norman B. Adkison, *Nez Perce Indian War and Original Stories* (Grangeville, Idaho: Idaho County Free Press, 1966), pp. 20–21; "Peter H. Ready," *North Idaho*, p. 564.

2. Luther P. Wilmot, "The Norton Massacre," in Adkison, *Original Stories*, p. 21; W. A. Goulder, "Northern Idaho," *Idaho Tri-Weekly Statesman*, March 4, 1876, p. 2; McWhorter, *Hear Me*, p. 221n; J. G. Rowton to McWhorter, item 4, packet 179, Mc-Whorter Collection.

3. Named for the lumber used in its construction, Cottonwood House was built in 1862 by a man named Allen. In 1874 it became the property of Norton, an experienced carpenter and former miner. Norton married Jennie Bowers in 1864, and their only child, Hill, was born in December, 1867. Lynn Bowers had been living with the Nortons for several years. She was a great help to her sister, who appeared to be saddled with enough chores to distract any woman. In addition to being a stage-station proprietor, postmaster, hotel keeper, bartender, and merchant, Benjamin Norton was also a livestock raiser and dairyman. He had a special love for horses and bred some of the finest animals in the country. Norton also had political ambitions but had been unsuccessful in his quest for elective office. Defeated for co-auditor in 1864 and probate judge in 1868, he appeared to have won election to the Territorial Legislature in 1866 but soon found himself disqualified for failure to measure up to the

there also, and from their demeanor it appeared that something was brewing. They had heard rumors of Indian unrest, Norton told them, and they were hoping to hear the latest news from the pair. Wilmot did his best to allay the fears of the family. He was confident that trouble was not imminent, because the Nez Perce still had their women and children with them. If they intended to hit the war trail, he said, they would first remove their families to a place of safety; at least that was the way it had been in the past. The argument apparently did not impress Mrs. Norton, because she pleaded with the men to spend the night. Wilmot had a reputation as a crack shot and would be an added asset in a tight situation, but he was anxious to return to his home and family and declined.[4]

As the teamsters were preparing to leave, a messenger from Mount Idaho arrived. He was Lew Day, an old acquaintance of Wilmot, who carried dispatches from L. P. Brown to the commanding officer of Fort Lapwai. He told the men that the Nez Perce were acting unfriendly and had been practicing war maneuvers and that he was to inform Capt. Perry of the situation. Settlers in the vicinity were streaming into Mount Idaho for protection. After obtaining a fresh horse, he was soon on his way again.[5]

Before he was out of sight, another wagon appeared. It contained John Chamberlin, his wife, and two daughters. They were on their way to Lewiston with a load of flour and intended to spend the night at Cottonwood House. They became alarmed at the news and also attempted to detain the freighters, but to no avail. Firm in their resolve to push ahead, Wilmot and Ready climbed aboard their wagons and bumped down the trail. When they reached Shebang Creek, a branch of the Cottonwood, they went into camp for the night.[6]

The Nortons and the Chamberlins soon decided to make their

---

requirements prescribed by law. Account of Jennie [Norton] Bunker in D. W. Greenburg, "Victim of the Nez Perce Tells Story of Indian Atrocities," *Winners of the West* (February 15, 1926), 3:8; Statement of Jennie Bunker, July 20, 1898, and statement of Lynn [Bowers] Schafter, July 20, 1895, Claim of Jennie Bunker, no. 9816 (hereafter cited as Bunker 9816), Court of Claims Records; D. W. Greenburg, "Old Luna Clock Rich in History," *Lewiston Morning Tribune*, May 3, 1936; *Twenty-Seventh Biennial Report of the Secretary of the State of Idaho, 1943–1944* (Boise: The Secretary, 1944), p. 71; Elsensohn, *Idaho County*, 1:297.

4. Wilmot, "Norton Massacre," p. 21.

5. July 20, 1898, Bunker 9816.

6. Statement of James Chamberlin [father of John], September 15, 1890, Claim of James Chamberlin, no. 8632 (hereafter cited as Chamberlin 8632), Court of Claims Records; Wilmot, "Norton Massacre," p. 22.

way to Grangeville, and the Nortons' hired man, Joe Moore, agreed to go with them. But before they had completed preparations to leave, Lew Day returned. Not more then twenty minutes had passed since he left the way-station. Day told them he had encountered three or four Nez Perce near the Old Board House on Craig's Mountain. They had pretended to be friendly and had ridden along with him for some distance; but when he told them he was getting cold and urged his horse ahead, they opened fire. One of the bullets hit Day in the back, but he managed to stay in the saddle and found shelter in nearby timber. He held his own in the exchange of shots that followed, and the warriors soon left, making it possible for him to return to Cottonwood House.[7]

Mrs. Norton dressed Day's wound as best she could while the men readied Chamberlin's wagon for the trip to town. They left Cottonwood House about 9 p.m. The night was starlit, and visibility was good. Norton, Day, and Moore rode horseback and Chamberlin drove the wagon containing the women and children.[8]

After traveling a few miles, they reached the camp of Wilmot and Ready. Again the settlers urged the men to come with them, but again the freighters declined. "This is the last time we will see you boys alive," one of the settlers called as the wagon moved down the road.

Wilmot and Ready rolled under their wagons and prepared to sleep. Perhaps an hour later they heard what sounded like gunfire, but it was very faint. At 3 o'clock the men awakened, fed the horses, and continued their journey. They had gone about three miles and were near Cottonwood Butte as the sun began to shine and warm them. It was then that they heard the first war cry.

Unhitching the horses from the wagons, the men mounted them and galloped up a stock trail branching off to the left of the main road. The Indians were about one quarter of a mile behind and coming fast, but Wilmot and Ready had all the lead they needed.

7. "Killing of Norton," *Lewiston Teller*, June 30, 1877, p. 2. The reporter who prepared the article based it in part on a statement obtained from Lew Day before he died.

8. Accounts conflict concerning the number of men on horseback and the number of men in the wagon. The *Teller* of June 30 reported that only Norton rode a saddle horse, but in a letter written on July 17, Mrs. Norton indicated that all the men except Chamberlin were mounted. In an interview in 1926, she specifically mentioned the horsemen and discussed the fate of each. See copy of Jennie Norton to her mother and sister, July 17, 1877, Mount Idaho, item 36, packet 188, McWhorter Collection, and Greenburg, "Victim."

After following the freighters for four miles, the warriors gave up the chase and returned to the wagons in search of plunder. Among the items left behind, they found twelve bottles of Martel brandy, one dozen baskets of champagne, and a barrel of whiskey.

Only when Wilmot and Ready reached Nathaniel Markham's ranch, about two miles north of Grangeville, did they feel safe from pursuit. They found the house empty and continued on their way to the settlement. As they neared the town, a crowd of men came to meet them.[9]

II

The freighters had been correct in thinking that they had heard gunfire about an hour after the Chamberlin wagon left their camp. About seven or eight miles from Cottonwood House, the party ran into a band of warriors. Whipping their horses into a run, they were successful in eluding their pursuers for a time: the chase continued for about four miles before an Indian bullet sent Lew Day tumbling from the saddle. Chamberlin stopped the wagon long enough to permit the badly wounded man to climb aboard, and they were off again. Norton was the next to be hit. A rifle ball smashed into his leg, and another disabled his horse. He made it to the wagon before the Nez Perce could intercept him, but one of the harness horses took a bullet and fell. Dragging a dead weight, the wagon skidded to a halt.

Norton, Chamberlin, and the women and children remained in the wagon. Day found cover behind a dead horse, and Moore joined him later. Apparently Moore lost his horse about the same time that the wagon stopped, and he was wounded when he reached the rest of the party. Two of his fingers had been shot away, and shortly after he assumed the defensive position near the wagon, he was hit again, this time in the hip.

Day received a number of other wounds before much time passed, and he began calling for water. When Norton attempted to bring him some, he was hit in the thigh. The bullet severed the femoral artery, and it was apparent that he would soon bleed to death. Gathering her courage in desperation, Jennie Norton begged her husband to permit her to go to the Indians and plead for their lives. He finally assented, because all other avenues of hope appeared to be closed. She was about to jump from the wagonbox when a bullet found her. It ripped through both legs and knocked

9. Wilmot, "Norton Massacre," pp. 23–25.

her from her perch, and in the subsequent fall to the ground she also dislocated an ankle.[10]

In the meantime Chamberlin decided to run for it and moved off through the grass with his wife and children. Losing his sense of direction, he guided his family toward Tolo Lake instead of toward Mount Idaho. Norton called his son to him after the Chamberlins left and told the boy to make his escape and bring help if possible. He told Lynn Bowers to go with Hill, and after the girl shed her heavy skirt so that she could run faster, they slipped into the night and headed toward Grangeville.[11]

Mrs. Norton crawled under the wagon and took shelter near one of the dead horses. Moore continued to keep the Indians at bay during the rest of the night. When morning came, warriors circled the wagon a few times and then left, apparently to secure more ammunition.

Mrs. Norton decided to attempt to reach the ranch of J. W. Crooks near Grangeville and began dragging herself through the grass. She had gone only a short distance when she heard a horse approaching. Thinking it was an Indian, she covered her head and prepared to die. The man dismounted, and she heard a pistol cock. Suddenly Moore cried: "Don't shoot, for God's sake; it is us." The rider was Frank Fenn, one of the volunteers from Mount Idaho.[12]

Fenn had discovered Hill Norton stumbling through the brush near Grange Hall and learned of the attack on the wagon.[13] After forming a relief party consisting of Charles Rice, George Hashagen, and the three Adkison brothers, he rode down the road in search of the beseiged party.[14] The first to reach the scene, he mistook Mrs. Norton for an Indian and was about to fire when Moore cried out.

The men placed the dead and wounded in the wagon and sent James Adkison hurrying back to Grangeville to bring more volunteers. John and Doug Adkison cut the harness from the dead horses

10. Bunker, July 20, 1898, Bunker 9816; Greenburg, "Victim"; Norton to mother and sister, July 17, 1877; "Killing of Norton"; Kirkwood, *Indian War*, pp. 52–55; Poe, "Beginning."

11. Hill Beachy Norton, "Hill Beachy Norton Speaks Out of the Past," in Adkison, *Original Stories*, p. 39; Statement of Hill Norton, *Lewiston Morning Tribune*, December 18, 1938, reproduced in part in Elsensohn, *Idaho County*, 1:299; Schafter, July 20, 1898, Bunker 9816; Norton to mother and sister, July 17, 1877.

12. Greenburg, "Victim."

13. Norton, "Norton Speaks," p. 39; Elsensohn, *Idaho County*, 1:298–299; account of Frank Fenn in *Lewiston Tribune*, April 17, 1927.

14. There may have been a seventh man in the party. Elias Darr claimed to have

and, chucking their saddles, hitched their mounts to the wagon. As they finished, the men saw a large band of Indians approaching rapidly. Fenn, Rice, and Hashagen formed a rear guard, while the Adkisons leaped on the backs of the wagon horses and urged them forward. The warriors began to close the distance; but before they were able to draw near enough to do any damage, they observed a group of white riders racing down Crooks' Lane to meet the wagon and abandoned the chase. James Adkison and the reinforcements escorted the wagon into town and saw to the care of the wounded.[15]

Not long afterward, another relief party left Grangeville to find the Chamberlins. A few hundred yards from where the wagon had been, they found the body of John Chamberlin. Both children were with him. Hattie, the older girl, was dead, but the other child was still alive. She was in bad condition, however, suffering from an ugly neck wound. She had also lost the tip of her tongue, probably severed in a fall, although some claimed that an Indian who had grown tired of her crying had cut it off. When Cash Day found the little girl, she was trying to hide behind the corpse of her father. Remembering back to the scene, J. G. Rowton wrote: "May such trials be forever gone."[16] Within a mile of the wagon, Rowton found Mrs. Chamberlin in hysterics. She had been shot in the breast with an arrow and raped repeatedly.[17]

III

On the morning of June 16, Five Winters, Going Fast, and Jyeloo left camp at White Bird Canyon and rode back to Camas Prairie. Coming to the ranch belonging to Ab Smith about three miles southwest of Grangeville, they entered the house and found it deserted. After helping themselves to everything that happened to catch their fancies, the Indians decided to rest a while. They had been drinking heavily and soon lapsed into sleep. When they awakened, Going Fast left the house to bring the horses.[18]

been present, but he is not mentioned by Adkison or any of the others who wrote about the affair. According to Darr, he fell behind in the retreat to Grangeville due to a poor horse and took shelter in some rocks. See his statement in McWhorter, *Hear Me*, pp. 219–221.

15. John R. Adkison, "The Norton Rescue," in Adkison, *Original Stories*, pp. 36–37.

16. Wilmot, "Norton Massacre," pp. 24–25; J. G. Rowton, "A Tribute to Mrs. Bunker," *Winners of the West* (March 30, 1926), 3:2; "Shocking Details," *Idaho Tri-Weekly Statesman*, July 21, 1877, p. 2.

17. Rowton, "Tribute," p. 2; Chamberlin, September 15, 1890, Chamberlin 8632; Sears, "Mount Idaho."

18. McWhorter, *Yellow Wolf*, pp. 47–48.

Twenty volunteers under George Shearer were scouting in the vicinity, and when J. G. Rowton noticed some movement at the Smith homestead, he went to investigate. He saw Going Fast and reported his find to the rest of the company, who quickly moved into action.[19] Seeing the body of horsemen riding hard toward the ranch, Going Fast called to his comrades. He and Five Winters hastily mounted and galloped away, but Jyeloo had a game leg and a bad back and had to move more slowly. He had some difficulty in catching the horse brought for him, and by the time he was ready to leave, the volunteers were only one quarter of a mile away. The horse turned out to be a poor runner, and the posse soon closed the gap.

When he came to a fence Jyeloo dismounted and set out on foot. Before he had traveled very far, he was hit several times in the back and slumped in the tall grass. Shearer galloped up to the Indian and emptied both barrels of his shotgun; then, dismounting, he broke the stock of his weapon over the head of the old warrior and crushed his skull. While the volunteers were busy with Jyeloo, the other Nez Perce made good their escape.[20]

IV

Going Fast and Five Winters made their way to the camp at Drive-Inn. After hearing their news, about thirty warriors hurriedly mounted and returned to the scene of the attack. They found Jyeloo. The misshapen head and eleven bullet wounds testified to the fury of his assailants. Half of the party returned to camp with the body, while the rest went to the Smith ranch.

As they were poking around the house, one of the Indians noticed a white man approaching. He was Charles Horton, a single man of about thirty-five who was on his way home. The warriors concealed themselves until Horton drew close and then gave chase. On the side of a steep hill about two miles from the house, they caught him. Five Times Looking Up rode along side the fleeing rancher and drew an arrow to his bow. Reacting quickly, Horton grabbed the arrow and nearly wrenched the warrior from his saddle. Going Alone fired, and the chase ended. Horton got up again, but a second bullet finished him.[21]

19. Account of Rowton in McWhorter, *Hear Me*, p. 222.

20. McWhorter, *Yellow Wolf*, pp. 48–49; accounts of Rowton, Elias Darr, and David B. Ouster in McWhorter, *Hear Me*, pp. 222–223, 224–225n.

21. McWhorter, *Yellow Wolf*, pp. 48–49; Rowton in McWhorter, *Hear Me*, p. 224; L. P. Brown, "From the Scene of Hostilities," *Lewiston Teller*, June 30, 1877, p. 1.

When they returned to camp the Nez Perce went into council. The Alpowai and Palouse bands under Looking Glass, Red Echo, and Naked Head had already gone back to their homes on the Clearwater, where they believed they would be safe from war. "We will move to Lahmotta," said the chiefs, and the remaining bands under Joseph, White Bird, and Toohoolhoolzote began the march to White Bird Canyon. It was about 8 o'clock when the caravan left Cottonwood Creek.[22]

22. McWhorter, *Yellow Wolf*, pp. 48–49; McWhorter, *Hear Me*, p. 224; Brown, "From the Scene." White Bird, Chief of the Lamtamas, was about seventy years old. In his youth, he had been a famous buffalo hunter and fighter. Toohoolhoolzote was the leader of the Pikunans. He was a gifted orator whose influence spread beyond his little band of followers. McWhorter, *Hear Me*, pp. 181–184.

What They Said

This lovely burg is nestled at the fringe of the precious metal bearing hills of Northern Idaho, about 65 miles east of Lewiston, with a fertile valley spreading out before it, where grain is raised in abundance and superb quality. Fruit such as apples and their kindred flourishes majestically. There is no church and no minister in that infant town, yet its citizens are good, true and moral for all that. A Grange Hall is now erected three miles this side of Mount Idaho, which, when completed, will be a magnificent and indeed useful structure. It will also do service in that event as a high school. A semi-weekly mail visits Mount Idaho, and Baird Bros. do a fine express business to that point per stage. L. P. Brown, an esteemed and highly respected citizen, keeps a good hotel, and whosoever calls feels like "Home Sweet Home." Warrens diggings are the nearest mines yet the whole country about is saturated with gold, silver and precious metal which time and labor alone will yet develop, when many perhaps will sleep beneath Mount Idaho.

LEWISTON TELLER, June 2, 1877

In the afternoon of June 14, 1877, two friendly Indians, Looking Glass and Yellow Bear rode up to my place and told me that Joseph's band were on the war path, were very near my place, and I should go at once; that they had already killed seven white men. I then started to go to my house. They then called me back and told me to go immediately. I then told my two hired men what I had heard, and told them to take my three stallions from the stable and go to town. I got on my horse and started to town ahead of the two men, and as I started I could see the Indians coming.

ARTHUR I. CHAPMAN

We were afraid that the Indians would ride through the town at night and shoot into the crowded houses and tents, so wagons and logs were tied across the lanes in Mt. Idaho at night. We felt they could sneak in through the trees any time and kill us in our beds. A sort of fort was built later. Trenches were dug, logs stacked up and Uncle Loyal who ran the mills gave many sacks of flour to make it safer.

HARRIET BROWN ADKISON

We returned to Mount Idaho and I got to see my wife and babies. But only for a few moments, for I remembered that I had on my wagon, one barrel of whiskey, one dozen Martel Brandies and one dozen baskets of Champagne, and I knew there would be a lot of drunk Indians around those wagons. I proposed to some of the boys that it would be a good time to "Get us some Indians."

LUTHER P. WILMOT

4

Developments At Mount Idaho

The little town of Mount Idaho lay about sixty-five miles southeast of Fort Lapwai. Nestled against the northern base of the mountains that skirted the Salmon River, it was the seat of government in Idaho County. It had its beginning early in 1862, when Mose Milner, better known as California Joe, erected a roadhouse on the site to provide sustenance and accommodations for travelers headed from Lewiston to the Florence mines. In July Milner sold his interest to Loyal P. Brown and James Odle.[1] Brown became the sole owner of the property in 1865, and it was he who laid out the town and promoted its development.[2]

By 1877 Mount Idaho was still a lively community, although the hustle and bustle of the early gold-rush days were gone forever. L. P. Brown continued to dominate life in the settlement. His hotel was the largest building in town, and his hospitality and cuisine left most travelers with pleasant memories. One satisfied customer wrote: "It is precisely like living at home with a good uncle. The food is choice, abundant and well cooked."[3] Brown also owned a grist mill that was capable of grinding thirty barrels of flour in a ten-hour period.

At the time of the outbreak, there were two general stores in Mount Idaho; a Mr. Rudolph operated one of them, and Vollmer and Scott managed the other. Rudolph apparently occupied space in

1. Elsensohn, *Idaho County*, 1:106–108; Bailey, *River of No Return*, pp. 336–337.

2. Loyal P. Brown was born in Stratford, New Hampshire, on September 26, 1829. He left Boston in 1849 to try his luck in California and spent a year mining for gold on the Middle Fork of the American River at Rector's Bar. In 1850 he moved to Trinity River and engaged in trading and packing. In 1852 he settled at Scottsburg on the Umpqua River and remained in southern Oregon until he decided to leave for Idaho in 1862. He was a member of the Territorial Council and in 1875 he was instrumental in arranging the boundaries of Idaho County so that Mount Idaho became the county seat. He married his wife Sarah on October 24, 1855. "L. P. Brown," *North Idaho*, p. 574; H. H. Bancroft, *History of Washington, Idaho and Montana* (San Francisco: The History Company, 1890), p. 553n.

3. W. A. Goulder, "Northern Idaho," *Idaho Tri-Weekly Statesman*, February 24, 1877, p. 2.

one end of Brown's Hotel. The village also had a drugstore kept by
C. A. Sears and a blacksmith shop run by F. Oliver. J. B. Montgom-
ery owned the only saloon in town and was the subject of discussion
among the members of an active temperance organization. According to one newspaper reporter, "the Champions of the Red Cross"
were so successful in their campaign against King Alcohol that his
power was already "very feeble" in that part of the country. Although the town had yet to build a church or acquire a minister it
did have a new jail, and a new courthouse was a source of pride.[4]

Three miles northwest of Mount Idaho stood Grangeville, then
in its infancy. After the local chapter of the Grange decided to con-
struct a meeting place and a mill, John W. Crooks offered to donate
the land in order to encourage settlement on Three Mile Creek,
where he was the principal property owner.[5] The farmers erected
Grange Hall and the mill in 1876. Both structures apparently
needed some finishing work, but both were operable when hostilities
began. A boarding house, a blacksmith shop, the residence of
Crooks, and one or two other family dwellings completed the scene.

Beyond the twin villages of Mount Idaho and Grangeville was
Camas Prairie, a relatively level plain rich in grass and acquiescent to
the plow. Its western boundary was Craig's Mountain. Other spurs
of the Blue Mountains bordered it on the north and east. Settlers
grew a variety of grains and raised livestock on the prairie, and the
slopes of the mountains were fertile ground for fruits of many
kinds. The main exports were flour, pork, and beef. They found a
ready market in the mining towns of Pierce, Elk City, Florence, and
Warrens.[6]

II

Rumors of trouble with the Nez Perce had been bruited about
for some time, and many of the settlers were understandably ner-
vous when the tribes went into camp near the mouth of Rocky Canyon. The treatment of the Indians by a number of whites in days

4. W. A. Goulder, "Northern Idaho," *Idaho Tri-Weekly Statesman*, March 4, 1876,
pp. 3–4; "Mount Idaho," *Lewiston Teller*, June 2, 1877, p. 1.

5. John W. Crooks was born in Indiana in 1820. He crossed the plains to Oregon
in 1852, and ten years later he settled on Camas Prairie. He secured the land that
became the site of Grangeville in 1865. He operated a stage line between Lewiston
and Grangeville for many years. See Defenbach, *Idaho*, 1:479n.

6. Goulder, "Northern Idaho," March 4, 1876, and February 24, 1877; Howard,
Nez Perce Joseph, p. 109; Herbert Joseph Spinden, *The Nez Perce Indians*, Memoirs of
the American Anthropological Association, Vol. 2, pt. 3 (Lancaster, Pa.: New Era
Print Co., 1908), p. 176; Defenbach, *Idaho*, 1:480.

past had not always been kind; in fact, it had often been brutal and murderous. The Nez Perce list of grievances was as shocking as it was long. Murder, rape, assault, fraud, and unlawful possession of property were but a few of the crimes committed against them.[7] The guilty became anxious, and the innocent were wary — provocation had been great, and reprisals often visited the clean and the unclean at the same time.

Apparently the first warnings of impending disaster reached Mount Idaho on June 13. John Adkison was one of those who received intelligence from an Indian friend that there might be trouble.[8] John Crooks visited the Indian camp in the afternoon and received warnings to return to his home as quickly as possible. He took the advice and left immediately. One warrior followed him most of the way to Grangeville, and at one point the Indian rode up to Crooks and flourished a revolver in his face. Crooks notified a number of settlers of the incident, and many of them chose to spend the night in town.[9] Early on the morning of June 14, Cyrus Overman, a rancher who lived near the head of Rocky Canyon, arrived in Mount Idaho with a number of his neighbors and reported that the Nez Perce were practicing war maneuvers. The day before, he had seen them stage a mock war parade, and some of the Indians had openly stated that they intended to fight if the soldiers came to put them on the reservation. Alarmed by the actions of the warriors, Overman thought it best to take refuge in the settlement and await developments at a safer distance.

Later in the morning, some of the Nez Perce entered the town in quest of powder and cartridges. One Indian offered storekeeper Wallace Scott $2.50 for a can of powder, a price so far in excess of its value that it reinforced fears that hostilities might begin at any moment. L. P. Brown believed that the situation was serious enough to be reported to the authorities, and he sent a messenger with a letter to the commanding officer of Fort Lapwai.[10]

About 4 o'clock that afternoon, Looking Glass and Yellow Bear

7. McWhorter listed twenty-eight Nez Perce who had been murdered by whites between 1861 and 1877. In the late 1870's, James Reuben is supposed to have submitted a list of thirty-two names. McWhorter, *Hear Me*, pp. 116–131. See also Haines, *Nez Perces*, pp. 180–184; Brown, *Flight of the Nez Perce*, pp. 44–67.

8. Harriet Brown Adkison, "Inside Mount Idaho Fort," in Adkison, *Original Stories*, p. 42.

9. *North Idaho*, p. 56.

10. Brown to Capt. David Perry, June 14, 1877, in Howard, *Nez Perce Joseph*, pp. 90–91.

rode up to the ranch of Arthur Chapman, who owned a spread on Cottonwood Creek seven miles from Mount Idaho.[11] They told the rancher that the Nez Perce were on the warpath and that seven white men had already been killed. The Indians advised him to leave at once because the rest of their tribesmen were nearby and they could not guarantee his safety. Leaving his hired men to follow with his prize stallions, which he would not abandon under any conditions, Chapman rode on ahead to spread the word.

When he reached Mount Idaho Chapman gave the alarm. The citizenry quickly formed into a volunteer company of irregulars and elected Chapman its captain. After placing mounted pickets at strategic points on the approaches to town, the new commander sent the rest of the volunteers to warn families living in the vicinity. Lew Day agreed to ride to Fort Lapwai to solicit the aid of the military and galloped down the road leading to Cottonwood House.[12]

As late afternoon grew into evening, settlers poured into Mount Idaho. The townsfolk busied themselves by casting bullets and making preparations for the defense of their lives and property. The men feared that the warriors might ride through the settlement at night and fire into the crowded shops and houses, so the volunteers blocked the street with wagons and logs. On a hill near the north end of town, they began the construction of a stockade. H. E. Croasdaile, a retired English naval officer, superintended the work. When finished, the stockade was circular in shape and perhaps 150 feet in diameter. Apparently the settlers made three of the walls by building rail fences parallel to each other and then filling in the intervening space with rocks and logs. Flour sacks piled on the ground made the fourth wall. The fortification reached about five feet in height, and a narrow passageway at the west end provided access to the interior. Tents both in and about the stockade housed the refugees, but it appears that all of the settlers sought refuge in Brown's Hotel and some of the other buildings during the first night.[13] During those watchful hours and in the days and nights to come, the villagers and

11. Looking Glass was the leader of the Alpowai band and was one of the most respected warriors among the non-treaty Indians. McWhorter, *Hear Me*, pp. 182–183.

12. Statement of Arthur Chapman, November 23, 1886, Claim of Arthur Chapman, no. 1102 (hereafter cited as Chapman 1102), Court of Claims Records; James P. Canby to AAG, Department of the Columbia, August 6, 1877, in Claim of Henry Croasdaile, no. 7439, Court of Claims Records.

13. Adkison, "Inside Mount Idaho Fort," p. 44; J. Loyal Adkison and Norman B. Adkison in *Lewiston Morning Tribune*, January 12, 1958, p. 1; Accounts of Harriet Adkison and Alice Overman in Elsensohn, *Idaho County*, 1:115, 2:527; *North Idaho*, p. 60.

their guests maintained their morale by singing such hymns as "On-ward Christian Soldiers" and "Nearer My God To Thee." John Row-ton and John Adkison achieved reputations as fine singers during the siege. One evening when the children were especially fearful, Rowton climbed to the top of a large pine tree growing inside the stockade and quieted them with his rendition of "I'll Remember You, Love, In My Prayers."[14]

At Grangeville, settlers chose Grange Hall for their defense. They obtained logs about sixteen feet in height to make a wall around the building and piled sacks of flour against the walls in the upper story to make it bullet-proof.[15]

Very early on the morning of June 15, Arthur Chapman left Mount Idaho to keep a rendezvous with Looking Glass and Yellow Bear. He reached a point near his ranch about 5 o'clock and found his friends and two other Indians waiting for him. The Nez Perce told Chapman the names of those who had been killed to date, among them Lew Day. Chapman persuaded the brother of Looking Glass, an Indian named Tucallasasena, to ride back with him to Mount Idaho.[16]

During Chapman's absence Hill Norton reached Grange Hall, and the news of the tragedy spread quickly throughout both settle-ments. The attack confirmed the worst suspicions of the settlers: the war had spread from the Salmon and White Bird Creek to Camas Prairie, and it threatened to engulf them at any moment. After L. P. Brown learned that Day had not been able to get through to Fort Lapwai, he wrote a second letter to Capt. Perry. A half-breed named West agreed to make the journey.[17]

Chapman returned to Mount Idaho shortly after the first relief column brought in the Norton party, and he talked Tucallasasena into carrying another dispatch from Brown to Perry. West left shortly after 7 o'clock, and the Indian followed an hour later.[18]

The rescue of Mrs. Chamberlin and her child and the arrival of Wilmot and Ready were occasions of sorrow and rejoicing. The rape of Mrs. Chamberlin and the brutal killing of her three-year-old daughter must have terrified the women and children who waited in the stockade. Few were exempt in the Indian war. It would have

14. Greenburg, "Victim"; Adkison, "Inside Mount Idaho Fort."

15. Elsensohn, *Idaho County*, 1:130–131.

16. Chapman, November 23, 1886, Chapman 1102.

17. Brown to Perry, 7 a.m., June 15, 1877, in Howard, *Nez Perce Joseph*, p. 95.

18. Chapman, November 23, 1886, Chapman 1102; Brown to Perry, 8 a.m., June 15, 1877, in Howard, *Nez Perce Joseph*, pp. 95–96.

been less of a shock to the Nez Perce women and children: they had learned this bitter lesson in years past and would learn it again in the months to come.

Mrs. Norton and Mrs. Chamberlin were taken to Brown's Hotel and put in an upstairs bedroom. Mrs. Norton was bleeding badly, and her friends feared that she would not survive. In the absence of Dr. Morris, who was away on a trip, his brother began treatment by running a silk handkerchief through the wounds in both of her legs. Gentle hands placed Lew Day and Joe Moore on litters in the dining room.[19] Brown opened his doors to all comers and fed them without charge. His wife, Sarah, helped to nurse the wounded and make her guests feel at home.[20]

It was not long after that John Swarts discovered Lynn Bowers hiding in the brush and brought her to town. The girl was unharmed but nearly crazy with fear.[21] Refugees continued to straggle into Mount Idaho, and by the second day the village contained about 250 people. Henry C. Johnson, a bachelor who owned a ranch about eight miles southwest of Grangeville, was one of the last to arrive.[22] The rest were given up for dead.

Later in the day, Lew Wilmot persuaded seven volunteers to accompany him in an attempt to recover the liquor he had left behind in his wagon. All feared the consequences should the war party find the alcohol. When the men reached the place where the Norton party had been attacked, they saw about sixty warriors galloping in their direction and quickly retreated to Grangeville.[23] The settlers spent the rest of the day strengthening their defenses and hoping for relief from Fort Lapwai. There were few rifles in town, and pickets passed their weapons to those who relieved them.[24]

On the morning of June 16, clouds hung on the horizon and the promise of rain helped to dampen spirits already dampened. The killing of Jyeloo created a stir and brought satisfaction to some, but

19. Greenburg, "Victim"; Adkison, *Original Stories*, p. 43.

20. Statement of L. P. Brown, September 27, 1890, and Claimant's Brief, 1897–1898, Claim of L. P. Brown, no. 2714, Court of Claims Records; Brice, "Nez Perce Outbreak."

21. Schafter, July 20, 1898, Bunker 9816; Kirkwood, *Indian War*, pp. 56–57.

22. Statement of Henry C. Johnson, August 18, 1890, and statement of I. A. Watson, August 23, 1890, Claim of Henry C. Johnson, no. 3501, Court of Claims Records.

23. Wilmot, "Norton Massacre," p. 25.

24. Adkison, "Inside Mount Idaho Fort," p. 44.

it was an empty victory. The settlers knew there were many warriors close at hand, and if they chose to attack the town, many would die — perhaps all of the defenders. Only soldiers could bring them the help they needed, and there had been no word from Fort Lapwai.

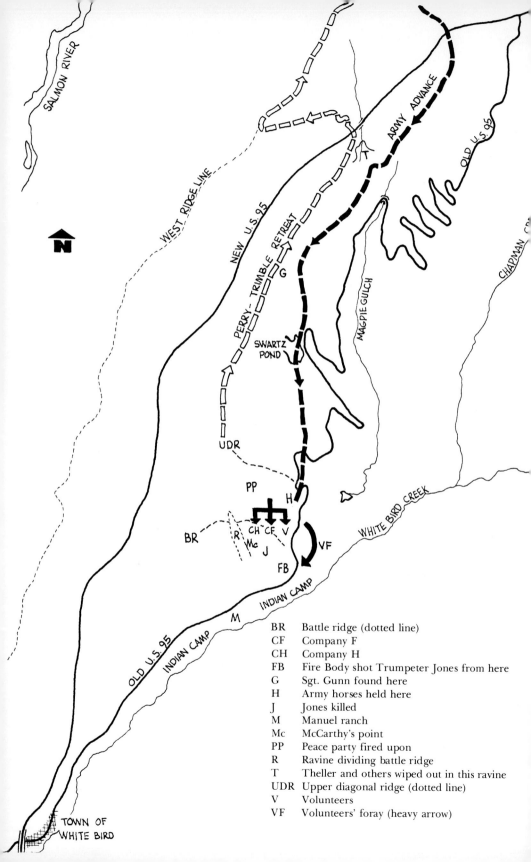

SALMON RIVER

WEST RIDGE LINE

N

NEW U.S. 95

PERRY - TRIMBLE RETREAT

ARMY ADVANCE

OLD U.S. 95

CHAPMAN CR.

T

G

MAGPIE GULCH

SWARTZ POND

UDR

PP

H

BR

R   CH CF V

Mc

J

VF

FB

WHITE BIRD CREEK

INDIAN CAMP

M

INDIAN CAMP

OLD U.S. 95

TOWN OF
WHITE BIRD

BR	Battle ridge (dotted line)
CF	Company F
CH	Company H
FB	Fire Body shot Trumpeter Jones from here
G	Sgt. Gunn found here
H	Army horses held here
J	Jones killed
M	Manuel ranch
Mc	McCarthy's point
PP	Peace party fired upon
R	Ravine dividing battle ridge
T	Theller and others wiped out in this ravine
UDR	Upper diagonal ridge (dotted line)
V	Volunteers
VF	Volunteers' foray (heavy arrow)

What They Said

Morning of June 14. Eventless, not a thing to break the monotony, except mosquitoes. A chorus of them sang me to sleep last evening but the music is "too touching."

MICHAEL McCARTHY

Like a thunderbolt from a clear sky, came the news of a hostile attack.

ASSISTANT SURGEON JOHN FITZGERALD

War, bloodshed and other horrible stories are in the mouths of everyone.

MICHAEL McCARTHY, June 15

I immediately had "boots and saddles" blown, and ordered the pack mules to be packed with five days rations I had on hand, which preparation was made in half an hour. In the meantime I hurried to the Post and reported for orders.

JOEL TRIMBLE

Then there was a pallor like of death itself, which seemed to seize the countenance of those knowing agents of the government. All business of Watkins's Court was quickly suspended, and there was a gathering to and fro, in hot haste, and orders given and dispatches sent for troops, and the fullest evidence given that no preparation had ever been made by Howard for any emergency whatever.

LEWISTON TELLER

The time of busy preparation had come. As before a battle, when men are often pale and thoughtful, and little is spoken by one to another, so now, officers and men were mostly silent, but in constant motion. Arms, ammunition, provision, means of transporting, everything was being put in readiness with skillful and steady nerves, without over haste, and without confusion.

O. O. HOWARD

5

Help From Fort Lapwai

General O. O. Howard docked at Lewiston at 8 o'clock on the morning of June 14.[1] With him were his aide-de-camp, Lt. Melville Wilkinson, and Indian Inspector Erwin C. Watkins.[2] Howard and his companions had left the Headquarters of the Military Department of the Columbia in Portland on May 30 to visit a number of trouble spots in the Northwest. The general had arranged the trip so that the trio would arrive in Lewiston one day before the Nez Perce were supposed to have completed their journey to the reservation. Watkins wanted to inspect the agency near Fort Lapwai, and as departmental commander Howard wanted to be close at hand in case of an emergency.

In the early 1860's Lewiston had been the home of miners, gamblers, desperadoes, and harlots, but by 1877 the village had

1. Howard was born on November 8, 1830, at Leeds, Maine. He graduated fourth in his class at West Point in 1854. Rising to the rank of major general of the Volunteers during the Civil War, he took over command of the Army of Tennessee in the summer of 1864 and led General Sherman's right wing on the March to the Sea. After the war he became head of the Freedmen's Bureau and served until its demise in 1872. President Grant used him as a special emissary to the Apaches, and he succeeded in persuading Cochise to come to terms. He became commander of the Department of the Columbia in 1874. He was known as a man of strong religious conviction. Howard lost his right arm in the Battle of Fair Oaks in 1862, and the Indians commonly referred to him as "Cut Arm." J. G. deR. Hamilton, "Oliver Otis Howard," in Dumas Malone, editor, *Dictionary of American Biography* (hereafter cited as DAB) (New York: Charles Scribner's Sons, 1943), 9:279–281; John A. Carpenter, "General Howard and the Nez Perce War of 1877," *Pacific Northwest Quarterly* (October, 1958), 49:129.

2. A native of New York, Wilkinson made captain during the Civil War before being mustered out on June 30, 1866. Later in that year he received a commission in the peacetime Army, and in 1871 he achieved the rank of first lieutenant in the Third Infantry. Also a native of New York, Watkins had a military background. He had served as a captain in the Volunteers before resigning his commission on April 5, 1865. Howard described the Indian inspector as "a large, full-built, wholesome man, backed up with genuine courage in any dangerous position." Francis B. Heitman, *Historical Register of the United States Army*, 2 vols. (Washington, D.C.: Government Printing Office, 1903), 1:1008, 1037; Howard, *Nez Perce Joseph*, p. 76.

settled into comparative quietness and respectability. Howard found its setting especially charming and later described it in his book:

> The hills behind this pretty town, and close to it, look like regularly constructed fortifications. The line of the table-land is just above the chimneys, and nearly horizontal; and the white fence of a burying place on the top, in the distance, adds to the idea of a constructed parapet.[3]

Lewiston stood near the confluence of the Clearwater and Snake rivers, and the town could boast of several well-to-do merchants, a mill, and a newspaper.

On hand to meet the party were Capt. David Perry, the commanding officer of Fort Lapwai; his wife; Capt. Joel Trimble, commander of Company H of the First Cavalry; Lt. Peter Bomus,[4] the post quartermaster; Charles Monteith, clerk at the agency and a brother of the agent; and a host of prominent townsfolk. After the formalities of greeting were over, Howard turned to the business at hand. "How is Chief Joseph?" he asked. Putting the general at ease, Capt. Perry replied: "All right, at last accounts. The Indians are, I think, coming on the reservation without trouble."[5] Others in the party confirmed the statement, and a few enlarged upon it. The situation appeared to be so well in hand that Howard decided to stay in Lewiston while Watkins made his inspection. Perry convinced his commander, however, that a rest at Fort Lapwai would be more enjoyable, and the general agreed to make the journey to the post twelve miles southeast of town. Mrs. Perry remained in Lewiston in order to board a steamer going down the river. She had made arrangements to visit friends at The Dalles.

The trip was a pleasant one. The quality of the road and the beauty of the landscape impressed the general, and they soon drove through the gate of Fort Lapwai to find relaxation in Perry's quarters. Later in the day, after Howard was comfortably settled, Perry decided to get in some target practice and left for the range, a short distance from the garrison.

About 6 o'clock that evening, the first courier from Mount Idaho came galloping into Fort Lapwai. In the absence of Perry, who was still at the range, Lt. Bomus received the message. The young lieutenant read the communication from L. P. Brown with interest.

3. Howard, *Nez Perce Joseph*, p. 87.

4. Peter Spoor Bomus graduated from the U.S. Military Academy on June 15, 1870, and became a second lieutenant in the First Cavalry. He made first lieutenant on June 5, 1876. Heitman, *Historical Register*, 1:229.

5. Howard, *Nez Perce Joseph*, p. 88.

After finishing the letter, he looked up to see that Capt. Perry had returned from his outing and was walking toward his quarters. Bomus quickly handed him the envelope.[6] Perry read:

MOUNT IDAHO, June 14, 1877

COLONEL PERRY: — DEAR SIR: Mr. Overman, who resides at or near the head of Rocky Canyon, eight miles from here, came in today and brought his friends. They are very much alarmed at the action of the Indians, who are gathered there. He says there are about sixty lodges, composed of the Salmon River Indians, Joseph and his band, with other non-treaties, and that they are insolent, and have but little to say to the whites, and that all their actions indicate trouble from them. Mr. Overman is regarded as a very truthful man, and confidence can be placed in all his statements. Some of the other neighbors have likewise moved over this way, where there are more people.

Yesterday they had a grand parade. About a hundred were mounted, and well armed, and went through the manoeuvres of a fight — were thus engaged for about two hours. They say, openly, that they are going to fight the soldiers when they come to put them on the reservation, and I understand that they expect them up on Friday next. A good many were in town to-day, and were trying to obtain powder and other ammunition. Mr. Scott told me to-day that they offered him two dollars and half for a can of powder. Up to this time, I think they have been buying all the arms, &c., that they could get, but do not believe they can make any purchases now. They have a strong position at the head of the canyon, among the rocks, and should they make any resistance could give the troops much trouble. I do not feel any alarm, but thought it well to inform you of what was going on among them. Early this morning one Indian came here, and wanted to know when General Howard was coming up. As the stage came up last night, they perhaps thought we might know when he would be up. They are evidently on the lookout for the soldiers. I believe it would be well for you to send up, as soon as you can, a sufficient force to handle them without gloves, should they be disposed to resist. Sharp and prompt action will bring them to understand that they must comply with the orders of the government. We trust such action will be taken by you, so as to remove them from the neighborhood, and quiet the feelings of the people.

I write this for you own information, and at the suggestion of many settlers who are living in exposed localities.

Very respectfully yours,
L. P. Brown[7]

Perry immediately took the letter to Howard. Perry trusted Brown's judgment that the situation was not yet critical, and Howard held the

---

6. Trimble to Maj. H. Clay Wood, January 29, 1878, letter no. 301, Letters Received, Department of the Columbia, Records of United States Commands, Record Group 98, National Archives (hereafter cited as Letters Received, DC).

7. Howard, *Nez Perce Joseph*, pp. 90–91.

same opinion. Before taking drastic action, Perry suggested, they should send a detachment to Mount Idaho to investigate the matter; Howard assented.[8] The detail consisted of Cpl. Joseph Lytte and Pvt. John Schorr of Company F of the First Cavalry and the post interpreter, a half-breed named Joe Rabusco.[9]

As dawn broke on Friday, June 15, the little detachment rode out of Fort Lapwai. After traveling only twelve miles, the mission came to an abrupt and exciting end. As Lytte and his companions neared Craig's Mountain, they saw horsemen approaching at great speed. They turned out to be Nat Webb and Putonahloo, friendly Nez Perce who were bringing news of the killings on the Salmon. Webb had been visiting in the camp near Tolo Lake when the avengers returned from their initial raid. He had immediately decided to ride to Fort Lapwai with the news, but he feared that a quick departure might arouse the suspicions of the non-treaty Nez Perce and lead to his capture and possibly his death, so he spent the night in the village and then left as soon as daylight appeared. As the young Indian drew near the detachment, he began to shout for the soldiers to stop. He told them that fighting had broken out and that it was useless to go any farther. Wheeling their mounts to the rear, Lytte, Schorr, and Rabusco joined the couriers of doom in their race to Fort Lapwai.[10]

8. Testimony of Captain David Perry, Transcript of a Court of Inquiry Concerning the Conduct of Captain David Perry During the Nez Perce Campaign of 1877, pp. 113–114, file no. QQ1738, Records of the Office of the Judge Advocate General, Record Group 153, National Archives (hereafter cited as CI). The text of that portion of the transcript concerning the Battle of White Bird Canyon appears in Appendix 1, below.

9. Joseph F. Lytte was born in Buffalo, New York. About thirty-three years of age, he was five feet seven inches tall. He was one of the more experienced soldiers in Company F, having completed an enlistment in the Fifth Artillery. John Schorr was born in Cincinnati, Ohio, on June 26, 1853. When he enlisted in the Army on April 13, 1875, he gave his previous occupation as carrier. He was five feet six inches tall, blue-eyed, and brown-haired. Registry of Enlistments in the United States Army, 1798–1914, Vol. 1875, Microcopy No. 233, Record Group 94, National Archives (hereafter cited as Registry of Enlistments, followed by year). See also John Schorr, "Participant in Whitebird Massacre Recalls Fatal March into Ambush," *The Idaho Statesman*, September 13, 1931, section 2, p. 2; Schorr obituary, clipping from unidentified Dayton, Ohio, newspaper, *c.* June, 1935, item 9, packet 179, McWhorter Collection.

10. Account of John Schorr in McWhorter, *Hear Me*, p. 223; John Schorr, "The White Bird Fight," *Winners of the West* (February 28, 1929), 6:7; Statement of Joe Rabusco, December 19, 1899, Claims of the Nez Perce Indians, Senate Executive Document 257, 56th Congress, 1st Session, p. 100 (hereafter cited as Nez Perce Claims); Account of Nat Webb in McWhorter, *Hear Me*, p. 231.

At exactly 11 o'clock, the messengers came in sight of the post. As they rushed through the cavalry camp a short distance from the fort, one of the riders relayed the news to Capt. Trimble, who happened to be about. "The Indians are killing the citizens at Mount Idaho," was the cry as the party swept by. Trimble immediately called for his trumpeter, and in a short time the notes of "Boots and Saddles" roused the camp into hurried movement. Trimble issued orders to load the pack mules with five days' rations and galloped to post headquarters for orders.[11]

Howard and Perry listened intently as Rabusco attempted to interpret the foreboding tale told by the Indian messengers. The half-breed had some difficulty in making the translation, and the officers were not quite sure just what had happened. Apparently three or four Indians had committed a murder on Slate Creek, and the killing had something to do with Larry Ott. Howard and Perry decided to take the Indians to the agency, located four miles north of the post, and have them repeat their story for Inspector Watkins and Agent John B. Monteith.[12] This time Perrin Whitman, the agency interpreter, did the translating but he was unable to clarify the account.[13] One thing was certain: all of the men feared that trouble was coming, unless they acted swiftly. It appeared that the killing was an isolated incident, but the hatred it had generated might explode into widespread violence at any moment.[14] To stem the rising tide of hostility, Monteith suggested that Jonah Hayes, the acting head chief of the treaty Nez Perce, ride to the camp at the mouth of Rocky Canyon and urge constraint and compliance. Joseph's brother-in-law, another agency Indian, volunteered to go with Jonah, and it was not long before the Indians left on their errand of peace.

Perhaps an hour had passed when the emissaries returned to Fort Lapwai accompanied by West and Tucallasasena, who carried

11. Trimble to Wood, January 29, 1878.

12. John B. Monteith was the son of a Presbyterian minister and had been appointed agent of the Lapwai Agency in February, 1871. Alvin M. Josephy, Jr., *The Nez Perce Indians and the Opening of the Northwest* (New Haven, Conn.: Yale University Press, 1965), p. 441.

13. Perrin Whitman was the nephew of Marcus Whitman. He went west in 1843 with his uncle and remained in the Northwest. He was about forty-seven years old and had a reputation as an able interpreter. Clifford M. Drury, *Marcus Whitman, M.D.* (Caldwell, Idaho: Caxton Printers, 1937), pp. 93, 324–325.

14. Perry to Lt. Col. James W. Forsyth, *c.* October 22, 1878, letter no. 1024, Letters Received, DC.

dispatches from Mount Idaho. Although West had left the hamlet an hour earlier then Tucallasasena, the Indian had overtaken him in the road, and they were together when they met the Indian ambassadors sent by Monteith.

A crowd gathered on Perry's front porch shortly after the messengers rode into the fort. All the officers were there, and the ladies of the post soon arrived. Included in the assemblage were a number of agency Indians who had been in the non-treaty village on June 13, but who had left after it had become obvious to them that some of the warriors were serious in their claims to resist any attempt to put them on the reservation. Howard felt the excitement of the moment and, aware of the need to maintain his poise, he made an effort to appear cool and self-possessed as he opened the packets and read, first to himself and then to his officers, the letters from Mount Idaho.

MOUNT IDAHO, 7 A. M., Friday, June 15, '77

COMMANDING OFFICER FORT LAPWAI
    Last night we started a messenger to you, who reached Cottonwood House, where he was wounded and driven back by the Indians. The people of Cottonwood undertook to come here during the night; were interrupted, all wounded or killed. Parties this morning found some of them on the prairie. The wounded will be here shortly, when we will get the full particulars. The whites are engaged about forty of them, in getting the wounded. One thing is certain: we are in the midst of an Indian war. Every family is here, and we will have taken all the precautions we can, but are poorly armed. We want arms and ammunition and help at once. Don't delay a moment. We have a report that some whites were killed yesterday on the Salmon River. No later word from them; fear that the people are all killed, as a party of Indians were seen going that way last night. Send to Lewiston, and hasten up. You cannot imagine people in a worse condition than they are here. Mr. West had volunteered to go to Lapwai; rely on his statements.

                                                    Yours truly,
                                                    L. P. Brown

MOUNT IDAHO, 8 A.M., June 15, 1877

COMMANDING OFFICER FORT LAPWAI.
    I have just sent a despatch by Mr. West, half-breed. Since that was written the wounded have come in, — Mr. Day mortally; Mrs. Norton with both legs broken; Moore shot through the hip; Norton killed and left in the road, six miles from here. Teams were attacked on the road and abandoned. The Indians have possession of the prairie, and threaten Mount Idaho. All the people here, and we will do the best we can. Lose no time in getting up with a force. Stop the stage and all "through travellers." Give us relief, and arms and ammunition. Chap-

man has got this Indian, hoping he may get through. I fear that the people on Salmon have all been killed, as a war party was seen going that way last night. We had a report last night that seven whites had been killed on Salmon. Notify the people of Lewiston. Hurry up; hurry! Rely on this Indian's statement; I have known him for a long time; he is with us.

L. P. Brown

P. S. — Send a despatch to town for the express not to start up, unless heavily escorted. Give the bearer a fresh horse, and send him back.

CHAPMAN

Howard then examined West, who spoke English, and the messenger gave a graphic account of the murders and outrages that had been committed. After making arrangements to forward the messages to Inspector Watkins and Agent Monteith, Howard wrote a note to Brown, informing him that help was on the way. He sent his aide-de-camp to Walla Walla, the closest telegraph station, to communicate his orders for troops and supplies to headquarters. Finally, he dispatched Quartermaster Bomus to Lewiston to procure pack animals to carry supplies for Perry and his command, who prepared to move to the scene of the outbreak.[15]

Howard's way was clear. Necessity forced him to send immediate relief to Mount Idaho; he had to stop the killings and insure the safety of those living in the vicinity. He had only two companies of cavalry available at Fort Lapwai for duty, but they would have to suffice. He hoped the small contingent might also serve another purpose — that of containment. He wanted to keep the Indians occupied while he marshalled troops to deliver a crushing blow. His orders would start two more companies of cavalry marching from Wallowa and a detachment of infantry steaming up the river from Walla Walla. Additional troops and supplies would be forthcoming from more distant posts under his command. It would take time to assemble the strength he needed, and time was precious, but above all Howard did not intend to "feed the enemy with driblets."[16] Much depended on Capt. Perry and his men.

When Bomus had not returned from Lewiston by the time retreat sounded, Perry felt that he could wait no longer and asked for permission to begin without the pack train. Howard granted the request.[17] The force consisted of Company F and Company H of the

15. Howard, *Nez Perce Joseph*, pp. 92–96; Howard to Assistant Adjutant General, Military Division of the Pacific, August 27, 1877, Letters Sent, DC.

16. Howard to H. Clay Wood, June 17, 1877 (telegram), Letters Sent, DC.

17. David Perry, "The Battle of White Bird Cañon," in Cyrus Townsend Brady, *Northwestern Fights and Fighters* (Garden City, N.Y.: Doubleday, Page & Co., 1913), p. 112.

First Cavalry. Perry commanded Company F, and he selected 1st Lt. Edward R. Theller of the Twenty-first Infantry for his junior officer because Howard wished to retain Bomus at Lapwai to continue his duties as post quartermaster. There were forty-nine enlisted men in Company F, and they carried cooked rations that would last them for three days. Capt. Trimble commanded Company H, and his first lieutenant was William R. Parnell, a very capable officer who had a great deal of combat experience. Fifty-four men were available for duty in Company H, and their pack animals carried rations good for five days. Each of the soldiers carried forty rounds of ammunition.[18] To complete the complement, Perry enlisted the aid of Joe Rabusco and a number of friendly Nez Perce, including Jonah Hayes, Abraham Brooks, Joe Albert, Robinson Minthon, Frank Husush, Henry Yumushakown, Amos Wapsheli, Itskea Levi, Matthew Sottoks, Yuwishakaikt, and Wishtashkat.[19]

When everything was in readiness, Perry turned to Howard:

Good-by, general!
Good-by, colonel. You must not get whipped.
There is no danger of that, sir.[20]

A few horses plunged and reared and bucked, but soon the men had them under control, and the column moved off into the darkness. Mrs. Theller was the only wife left at the post to bid her husband adieu. Mrs. Perry, on her way to The Dalles, would soon receive a message from her husband that would send her to Portland to stay with Mrs. Howard. The wives of Trimble and Parnell were both at Walla Walla. After troops left, the period of waiting began. To relieve himself from anxiety, Howard read, wrote, studied maps, counted days for the marches, and paced his room. But he did have confidence in his men. In a dispatch which he had given Wilkinson, he had written: "Think they will make short work of it."[21]

18. Muster Rolls of Company F and Company H of the First Cavalry, April 30 to June 30, 1877, Regular Army Muster Rolls, Records of the Office of the Adjutant General, Record Group 94, National Archives (hereafter cited as Muster Rolls).

19. Abraham Brooks testified that there were only ten scouts, including Rabusco, who left Fort Lapwai with Perry, but Amos Wapsheli added the name of Matthew Sottoks and Lucullus McWhorter presented strong evidence in favor of Robinson Minthon. At Cottonwood yet another Nez Perce, Abraham Watsinma, joined the party. Nez Perce Claims, pp. 81, 84, 96; McWhorter, *Yellow Wolf*, p. 65.

20. Howard, *Nez Perce Joseph*, p. 99.

21. *Ibid.*, pp. 98–100.

What They Said

Captain Perry has done much hard service in the Indian Campaigns in this country, is thoroughly conversant with it and the best mode of operating against these Indians.

LT. COL. GEORGE CROOK (1868)

He was a fine horseman and could ride farther and show less fatigue than any of his men.

MICHAEL McCARTHY OF CAPTAIN TRIMBLE

There is a loss of the bones forming the septum between the nasal cavities, and an opening of considerable size between mouth and nose from loss of portions of hard palate, requiring the constant wearing of a plate to make eating and speech possible.

MEDICAL REPORT ON WILLIAM PARNELL

Company Commander thinks Trumpeter Jones is now a good soldier and truthful man. His yielding to drink was temporary and he is now under going punishment for what he did while intoxicated. He asks remittance of a part of his sentence, namely the fine.

O. O. HOWARD

Rudyard Kipling had a similar character in mind when he created Private Mulvaney.

MICHAEL McCARTHY OF JAMES SHAY

6

Military Biography

Chance and circumstances combined to put the men who rode out of Fort Lapwai in the same place at the same time, but they varied greatly in background and experience. The commander of the expedition, David Perry, was the senior officer of Company F of the First Cavalry. He was born in Ridgefield, Connecticut, on June 11, 1841. Like so many other officers who served in the frontier Army, Perry had learned to soldier during the Civil War. He received a commission as a second lieutenant in the First Cavalry on March 24, 1862, and on July 1 of the same year he earned his first promotion. On November 12, 1864, he became a captain, the rank he held at the time he became the commanding officer of Fort Lapwai. At the Battle of Five Forks, fought sixteen miles southwest of Petersburg, Virginia, on April 1, 1865, Perry won his first brevet for gallant and meritorious service.[1]

After the war the First Cavalry moved to the Northwest to participate in campaigns against the Snake Indians. On December 26, 1866, Company F engaged a large band of warriors on the Owyhee River in Idaho and won a smashing victory, killing thirty of the enemy and losing only one man in the process. For his part in the action, Perry received a second brevet, that of lieutenant colonel. During the years that followed, he continued to serve on the far-flung frontier. His company was one of those that fought against the Modocs in their stronghold at Lava Beds, and on January 17, 1873, Perry received a wound in a battle with the Indians near Tule Lake.[2]

Perry was apparently a capable officer, if not a flamboyant one. In 1868 Lt. Col. George Crook of the Twenty-third Infantry paid

1. *Obituary of David Perry, Military Order of the Loyal Legion of United States, Circular No. 16, Series of 1908, Washington, D.C.,* File of David Perry, ACP, Records of the Office of the Adjutant General (hereafter cited as ACP); Heitman, *Historical Register,* 1:785.

2. George W. Webb, *Chronological List of Engagements Between the Regular Army of the United States and Various Tribes of Hostile Indians Which Occurred During the Years 1790 to 1898, Inclusive* (St. Joseph, Missouri: Wing Printing and Publishing Co., 1939), pp.

him a high compliment in a letter to departmental headquarters. "Captain Perry is an excellent officer," he wrote. "I assure you it is no easy matter to find an officer who is so conversant with his duty and who is so willing to do it and do it thoroughly." Crook particularly appreciated the captain's knowledge of Oregon and his ability as an Indian fighter.[3]

Perry stood a little over six feet in height and carried himself very erect. According to Howard, the officer showed "a clear Saxon eye" and usually wore a smile, which the general described as "pleasant but with a reserve in it" that befitted a man of his rank and responsibility.[4] Another observer described him as "tall, handsome, and very arrogant."[5] Mrs. Perry had quickly gained a reputation as a fine hostess and an excellent cook, and it was apparent to all who knew her that she adored her husband. On the other hand, she apparently lacked the self-discipline and stoical resolve so often found in the wife of a commanding officer, and in this sense she was a liability. One rival described her as "a foolish and hysterical woman."[6]

At face value, Perry appeared to be an excellent choice — if it had been a matter of choice — to lead an expedition against the non-treaty bands. His bearing inspired confidence and generated respect. He had a long record of military service, and he knew what Indian fighting was all about. If he lacked anything, it was a knowledge of the territory. Northern Idaho was new to him, and others would have to provide him with basic information concerning trails and terrain.

Edward Russell Theller of the Twenty-first Infantry had replaced Peter Bomus as the junior officer for Company F. He was a native of Vermont but had gone west at an early age. He eventually ended up in San Francisco, where he entered military service on October 5, 1861. Commissioned as a captain in the California Volunteers, he saw duty at a number of small posts in his home state during the Civil War, and at various times he commanded Forts Gaston

27–28, 36, 64; *Perry Obituary*, ACP; Heitman, *Historical Register*, 1:885; David Perry, "The First and Second Battles in the Lava Beds, and the Capture of Captain Jack," in Brady, *Northwestern Fights*, pp. 291–304.

3. Creek to Assistant Adjutant General, Department of the Columbia, March 27, 1868, letter 1024, Letters Received, 1878, DC.

4. Howard, *Nez Perce Joseph*, p. 88.

5. Account of Angie B. Bowden in McWhorter, *Hear Me*, p. 232n.

6. Brown, *Flight of the Nez Perce*, p. 118.

and Humboldt. On March 13, 1865, he received a brevet, that of major, for faithful and meritorious service.[7]

On September 6, 1865, Theller received orders to report to the Camp on San Pedro River in Arizona Territory, and he remained there for six months before returning to San Francisco to be mustered out on May 4, 1866. While in Arizona, Theller participated in several skirmishes with the Apaches and fought in one major engagement near White Mountain. Finding military life to his liking, Theller applied for a commission in the Regular Army and received it on March 7, 1867. He remained in California as a second lieutenant in the Ninth Infantry, and when his unit prepared to move elsewhere, Theller secured a transfer to the Twenty-first Infantry and a position as Acting Assistant Adjutant General on the staff of Brig. Gen. Edward O. C. Ord, commander of the Department of California. On August 31, 1871, Theller became a first lieutenant, the rank he held at the time of the outbreak. He also served in the Modoc War and saw action in a number of engagements; but of the four officers who rode out from Fort Lapwai, Theller was at the bottom of the list when it came to combat experience.[8]

General Howard described Theller as "a generous, brave man, with a warm heart." The lieutenant and his wife Delia were noted for their hospitality and frequently entertained.[9] Theller apparently lacked the stability and judgment expected of a forty-four-year-old officer. A year before the outbreak, William Boyle, then a first lieutenant on an inspection tour, wrote a confidential letter to Howard in which he recommended that the general transfer Company G of the Twenty-first Infantry to another post, if for no other reason than to separate Theller from his civilian associates, who were not fit companions for an officer. Theller had a love of fast horses, and one writer has surmised that the lieutenant had probably become involved with gamblers in Lewiston.[10] The Thellers were childless.[11]

Alexander M. Baird was the first sergeant of Company F. Born in Glasgow, Scotland, Baird was about thirty-three years old. Blond-haired and blue-eyed, he was about five feet seven and one-

7. "Idaho County Marks Sites of Nez Perce Battleground," *The Idaho Statesman,* September 4, 1927, section 3, p. 2; Theller to Board of Examiners, April 21, 1867, File of Edward Russell Theller, ACP.

8. Heitman, *Historical Register,* 1:952; Theller to Secretary of War W. W. Belknap, May 3, 1870, ACP.

9. Howard, *Nez Perce Joseph,* p. 90.

10. Brown, *Flight of the Nez Perce,* pp. 121–122.

11. *Idaho Tri-Weekly Statesman,* June 23, 1877, p. 1.

half inches in height. Only three other sergeants were available for duty, because Perry had ordered Louis Bollinger to remain at Fort Lapwai to look after the company property. They were Patrick Gunn, Charles Leeman, and Thomas Ryan.[12] Of the three, grey-haired Patrick Gunn probably had the most experience. He had fought the Seminoles in Florida and served in the Mexican War and of course had seen action during the Civil War and in numerous Indian campaigns in the Northwest.[13]

Four corporals completed the contingent of non-commissioned officers: Thomas J. Fanning, Charles W. Fuller, Joseph F. Lytte, and John L. Thompson. The company trumpeters, who held the rank of private, were John M. Jones and Michael Daly.[14] The former was affectionately known as "Jonesy" and was apparently a very likeable young man who nursed a passion for strong drink. A one-time deserter who had returned to the service under a general amnesty act, Jones had been in the guardhouse as a result of his intemperance when Howard tired of the harangues of Chief Toohoolhoolzote at the Indian council in May and clapped the old warrior in irons. A strange friendship developed between the private and the chief, and Jones had remarked to a friend that if they ever did have to fight the Nez Perce, he knew that he would not be harmed: Toohoolhoolzote had promised him as much. Born in Wheeling, Virginia, Jones was about thirty years old. He stood a shade over five feet four inches in height and had hazel eyes, sandy hair, and a ruddy complexion.[15]

The farrier for Company F was John Bressler; but he had also been ordered to stay at Fort Lapwai, where he was to keep the company stables in order. Joseph Schultz was the saddler. The other privates in Company F were Charles Armstrong, Joseph Blaine, Levi L. Buckner, Frank E. Burch, Charles S. Clarke, James C. Colbert, Robert W. Connell, Patrick Connolly, Bartholomew Coughlin, Lawrence Dauch, William Davis, John H. Donne, David M. Fisk, Joel S. Haines, William Harding, William L. Hurlbert, Edward Kenny,

12. Muster Roll of Company F.

13. Registry of Enlistments, 1873; List of Remains of Soldiers and Others Disinterred in Post Cemetery at Fort Lapwai by Second Lieutenant N. F. McClure, c. November 15, 1890, General Correspondence, Military Cemeteries File, Records of the Office of the Quartermaster General, Record Group 92, National Archives.

14. Muster Roll of Company F.

15. Jones to Howard, May 14, 1877, Letters Received, Fort Lapwai, Record Group 98, National Archives (hereafter cited as Letters Received, Fort Lapwai); Account of John Schorr in McWhorter, *Hear Me*, p. 246n; Registry of Enlistments, 1869.

Hewy T. Kidd, James S. Lewis, William Liston, Florence McCarthy, Thomas McLaughlin, Dennis Maher, Willam L. Marriott, John M. Martin, John R. Mosforth, Alexander Ohters, Franklin C. Pratt, David Quinlan, John Rebstock, John Schorr, Peter Schullein, Andrew Shaw, Charles Sullivan, Alexander Tethrow, Louis Warren, James Wilson, and John White. The full strength of the company was fifty-five, excluding officers; in addition to Bollinger and Bressler there were four others missing but accounted for. Pvt. George G. Brown had remained at Fort Lapwai to take care of the company garden. Pvt. Louis Reiss had stayed behind to help Sgt. Bollinger with the stables. Pvt. John Dailey was in bed in the post hospital, and Pvt. Jacob Shaefer languished in the guardhouse.[16] Pvt. Hurlbert was the only enlisted man who had his family with him at Fort Lapwai. He had enlisted in St. Louis on May 8, 1875, in consequence of some "reverses in business." His wife and children had followed him west a year later.[17]

The enlisted men of Company F were a rather cosmopolitan group. Eighteen of them had been born in foreign countries: eight in Ireland, five in Germany, two in England, two in Canada, and one in Scotland. Of those born in the United States, eight were from New York, five from Massachusetts, five from Pennsylvania, four from Ohio, and one each from Virginia, Maryland, Georgia, Illinois, Kentucky, Missouri, and the District of Columbia. Thirty-eight of the men were serving in their first enlistment. Their occupations before entering the Army had been quite varied. Nine of them had been laborers, four had been clerks, and three had been carpenters. Also in the group were two barbers, two sailors, two farmers, two carriers, two saddlers, a roller, a jeweler, a shoemaker, a musician, a wheelwright, a teamster, a machinist, a telegraph operator, a painter, a blacksmith, and a butcher. Generally these men had not had the time to develop into excellent horsemen or good shots. Ten of the men in Company F had previous military experience, and they gave the unit a degree of strength and stability. The average age of the enlisted men in the company was twenty-eight and one-half years. The average height was five feet seven inches.[18]

16. Muster Roll of Company F.

17. The government furnished transportation for Alice Hurlbert and the children. The cost was $400, and the Army made arrangements to deduct $10 per month from Hurlbert's pay until the debt had been satisfied. This meant that Hurlbert received only $3 per month in wages. "Soldiers Life and Death," *New York Times*, July 12, 1877, p. 2; *The Idaho Avalanche* (Silver City), August 4, 1877, p. 2.

18. Registry of Enlistments, 1869; Statements of Parnell and McCarthy, CI, pp. 72,

The commander of Company H was Joel Graham Trimble, the oldest of the four officers. Trimble was born in Philadelphia on September 15, 1832. His family soon moved to Cincinnati, and at the age of seventeen Trimble entered Kenyon College. After the discovery of gold in California, Trimble secured his father's permission to leave school, and he started for the goldfields with four companions. Two of them died of cholera in St. Joseph, Missouri, and the other two decided to return home. Not to be discouraged, Trimble continued the journey and walked sixty miles to Fort Leavenworth, where he obtained employment as a herder for the Mounted Riflemen, then making preparations to depart for Oregon. He reached Oregon City with the regiment in November of 1849. Hiring an Indian guide, the youth traveled by canoe to the mouth of the Columbia River. In the spring of 1851, he joined the command of Maj. Phil Kearny in another civilian capacity and rode with the First Dragoons to California. During the trip Trimble participated in two major Indian engagements in what is commonly referred to as the First Rogue River War. In the initial battle, which took place on June 17, Trimble received an ugly wound in the hand as he attempted to rescue a disabled soldier from a ravine.[19]

On February 5, 1855, Trimble enlisted as a private in Company E of the First Dragoons. His first military engagement as a professional soldier took place on October 31, when Company E and a number of other units began a two-day battle with the Rogue River Indians on Hungry Hill between Grave Creek and Cow Creek in Oregon. On March 27, 1856, he assisted in a rescue at the Cascades of the Columbia in Washington Territory and on the same day received his first promotion. On January 30, 1857, Trimble made sergeant, but he lost his stripes ten months later for some unknown transgression. In 1858 he was back on the war trail and served with conspicuous gallantry in both the Steptoe and Wright campaigns.[20]

After being discharged on February 5, 1860, Trimble decided to return to civilian life and spent a few months as a rider for the Pony Express; but he found that he missed the ways of a soldier and reenlisted on June 16 as a private in Company A of the Second

83. There are no available data on Levi Buckner, and therefore the generalizations are based on the records of forty-eight men.

19. *Obituary of Joel Graham Trimble, Military Order of the Loyal Legion of the United States, Circular No. 33, Series of 1911, San Francisco, California*, File of Joel Graham Trimble, ACP; Will J. Trimble, "A Soldier of the Oregon Frontier," *The Quarterly of the Oregon Historical Society* (1907), 8:42–43.

20. Military History of Joel G. Trimble, April 29, 1879, ACP.

Dragoons, soon to become the Second Cavalry. The beginning of the Civil War found him in Utah, but Company A soon received orders to proceed to Washington, D.C., and arrived in the capital city in October of 1861. The next spring Trimble marched with the Army of the Potomac. On May 5 he saw the first action of the war in the Battle of Williamsburg, and two weeks later he made corporal for the second time. Two months later he was wounded in the Battle of Malvern Hill.[21]

Trimble became a sergeant in the Second Cavalry on New Year's Day in 1863, and in February he received the opportunity he had been waiting for: he was offered an appointment as a second lieutenant in the First Cavalry and quickly accepted. He continued to serve throughout the war and participated in many important engagements, including the Battle of Gettysburg, where he received another wound. Gen. Philip Sheridan personally complimented Trimble after the Battle of Cedar Creek and during the pursuit of the Confederate Army to Appomattox. On January 3, 1864, he made first lieutenant, and he earned two brevets shortly thereafter: the first for gallant and meritorious service in the Battle of Trevilian Station, and the second for gallantry at Cedar Creek. After the war, Bvt. Maj. Trimble accompanied his regiment to Texas and then back to Oregon. He became a captain on December 26, 1868, after having previously declined promotion and transfer to the Ninth Cavalry.[22]

In 1873 Company H rode to California to fight in the Modoc War. While on patrol on July 1, Trimble's scouts encountered a Modoc named Humpy Joe, who led the officer to the refuge of Captain Jack on Willow Creek. There Trimble received the wily warrior, who surrendered his weapon and gave up the fight.[23] After the Modoc War, Trimble commanded Camp Warner and Camp Harney in southeastern Oregon. He reached Fort Lapwai with his company on May 9, 1877.[24]

As one comrade put it, Trimble was "rather spare." He could not

21. Trimble, "Soldier," p. 43; Trimble to Senator John S. Fowler, c. March, 1867, ACP.

22. Military History of Trimble, ACP; Trimble to Fowler, c. March, 1867; Heitman, *Historical Register*, 1:970; Trimble, "Soldier," p. 43.

23. Keith A. Murray, *The Modocs and Their War* (Norman: University of Oklahoma Press, 1959), p. 270. For more information on Trimble in the Modoc War see his accounts "The Country They Marched and Fought Over," "The Killing of the Commissioners," and "Carrying a Stretcher Through the Lava-Beds" in Brady, *Northwestern Fights*, pp. 281–285, 286–290, 314–319.

24. Trimble, "Soldier," p. 44; Muster Roll of Company H.

have weighed more then 140 pounds, and yet he was almost as tall as Perry. He was a fine horseman and had gained the admiration of his men for endurance. "A cup of coffee and a few crackers," wrote his first sergeant, "was [sic] all he ever required for the longest and hardest day's ride."[25] Howard noted that Trimble had a slight cast in one eye because of a wound he had received at Gettysburg. He was in fact partially blind in both eyes.[26]

William Russell Parnell was the junior officer for Company H, and it would have been difficult to find a better one. Born in Dublin, Ireland, on August 13, 1836, Parnell enlisted in the Fourth Hussars of the British Army at the age of eighteen. He later transferred to the Lancers and fought in the Crimean War, participating in the capture of Sebastopol. He was one of the few survivors of the fabled Charge of the Six Hundred at Balaclava.[27]

Parnell immigrated to the United States in 1860, and soon after the start of the Civil War he enlisted in the Fourth New York Cavalry. Probably because of his military experience, his comrades elected him a first lieutenant. In 1861 and 1862 Parnell served with Blenker's Division in the Army of the Potomac in the Shenandoah Valley and West Virginia. He took part in the Battles of Cross Keys, Port Republic, Cedar Mountain, and Second Manassas. With the Cavalry Corps he fought in the Battles of Fredericksburg, Beverly Ford, Brandy Station, Stoneman's Raid, Aldie, and Middleburg. During the Battle of Upperville on June 21, 1863, Parnell fell into Confederate hands after leading an unsuccessful cavalry charge, but in August he eluded his captors and made his way to Petersburg, West Virginia. Reunited with his command, he continued to see action in the Battles of the Wilderness, Spotsylvania, Trevilian Station, Petersburg (Virginia), Lee's Mills, Winchester, and Cedar Creek, and in a number of less important engagements. Before being honorably mustered out on December 5, 1864, Parnell reached the rank of lieutenant colonel and earned one brevet, that of captain, for the gallantry he had displayed at Upperville. Two years after Appomattox, he received a second brevet for general gallantry and meritorious service.[28]

25. Michael McCarthy, Journal, Journals and Papers of Michael McCarthy, p. 102.

26. Brown, *Flight of the Nez Perce*, p. 120; Certificate of Disability, Case of Captain Trimble, October 28, 1877, ACP.

27. *Obituary of William Russell Parnell, Military Order of the Loyal Legion of the United States, Circular No. 29, Series of 1910, San Francisco, August 27, 1910,* File of William Parnell, ACP.

28. Military Record of Captain William Russell Parnell, Appendix B, Proceedings of Retiring Board, April 1, 1885, ACP; Parnell to Secretary of War, February 19,

Parnell applied for a commission in the Regular Army near the end of the war, and on February 3, 1866, he accepted an appointment as a second lieutenant in the First Cavalry, becoming a first lieutenant on October 15. During the summer of 1867, Parnell joined his company from detached service and almost immediately received orders to march to California in order to participate in a campaign against a band of hostiles operating on the Pit River. Lt. Col. George Crook led the punitive expedition, which consisted of Company D of the Twenty-third Infantry, Company H of the First Cavalry (commanded by Parnell), and a group of Boise scouts. Before long the force encountered a band of warriors on the south fork of Pit River. Entrenched behind boulders on a high and almost inaccessible ledge of rock, the Indians were difficult to reach. On September 26 Crook ordered an assault. Parnell led Company H and the Boise scouts up the south bluff, but the warriors drove them back and the troops returned to their camp at the base of the mountain shortly before dark. At daylight Parnell led a second charge. Under heavy fire, the attackers gained ground and were able to enter the stronghold. There they found only twenty dead hostiles, the rest having made their escape through a subterranean passage. Crook recommended Parnell for another brevet for his part in the action, and he soon earned the right to be addressed as lieutenant colonel. During the next decade Parnell continued to serve in the Northwest and fought in a number of Indian campaigns. On March 14, 1868, he was wounded at the Battle of Dunder and Blitzen Creek in Oregon, and like the other officers under Perry's command he saw action in the Modoc War.[29]

Parnell bore the marks of many hard campaigns. At Upperville he had been shot in the left hip, and the bullet had imbedded itself in the bone. His doctor had decided to leave the missile where it was, and the veteran officer still carried it with him. Parnell had also received a number of deep saber cuts at Upperville, and one of them had severed the bone in his nose. As a prisoner of war after battle, he had received no medical attention, and the bone had corroded

1894, Medal of Honor File 3310, Case of Captain William Russell Parnell, Record Group 94, National Archives (hereafter cited as Medal of Honor File); William R. Parnell, "Recollections of 1861," *The United Service* (1885), 13:264–270; *Parnell Obituary*; Heitman, *Historical Register*, 2:771.

29. Statement of Major Thomas McGregor, February 27, 1885, Appendix G, and statement of General George Crook, March 2, 1885, Appendix H, in Retiring Board Proceedings, ACP; Memorandum of the Service of Captain W. R. Parnell in Indian Campaigns, *c.* 1885, ACP; General Orders 32, Department of the Columbia, November 1, 1867, DC; Webb, *List of Engagements*, pp. 33, 36.

and fallen away, leaving a gaping hole in the roof of his mouth and making it difficult for him to articulate. Parnell had a metal plate made to cover the aperture, and although it permitted him to speak intelligibly, it caused his voice to rise in pitch. The plate was fragile, and he lived in constant fear of breaking it — as he did in November of 1869, having to travel to Portland to have a new one made and inserted.[30]

Michael McCarthy described Parnell as "a large fleshy man" who "taxed the powers of his horse quite heavily."[31] Although he called the Irishman a fine soldier, McCarthy declared that he could not measure up to Capt. Trimble in skill or endurance. In his journal McCarthy referred to Parnell obliquely:

> We had the advantage of contrasting . . . [Trimble's] endurance on horseback with that of the first Lt., an ex English dragoon guardsman who claimed a high degree of skill in H. B. M. [Her British Majesty's] service. The ex British dragoon was not in it, when it came to campaigning and physical endurance.[32]

Michael McCarthy was the first sergeant of Company H. Born in St. John's, Newfoundland, he was thirty-two years old. He had apparently enlisted in the Army shortly after the close of the Civil War. He had seen duty on the Mexican border and had fought in the Modoc War, where he had participated in the capture of Captain Jack. Before entering the Army, McCarthy had been a printer. He was five feet seven inches in height. He had reddish brown hair, brown eyes, and a ruddy complexion.[33]

The other non-commissioned officers of Company H were Sgts. Patrick Reilly, Isidor Schneider, Henry Arend, John Conroy, and William Havens; and Cpls. Michael Curran, Roman D. Lee, Michael Milner, and Frank L. Powers. The company had only one trumpeter, Frank A. Marshall, since Albert Reilly had been tapped for detached service at Fort Walla Walla on May 6. John Drugan was the farrier, John Galvin the saddler, and Albert Meyers the company

30. Statement of Assistant Surgeon Ezra Woodruff, March 23, 1885, and statement of Assistant Surgeon G. E. Bushnell, April 1, 1885, Appendix C, Retiring Board Proceedings, ACP; Parnell to Adjutant General USA, January 14, 1871, ACP.

31. McCarthy to Howard, September 10, 1897, Case of First Sergeant Michael McCarthy, Medal of Honor File.

32. McCarthy, Journal, p. 102. It is interesting to note that McCarthy crossed out this passage in his journal and later pasted a newspaper clipping over it. However, the clipping came unglued and exposed the uncomplimentary comment.

33. Registry of Enlistments, 1869, 1874; McCarthy, Army Sketches, Journals and Papers of Michael McCarthy.

blacksmith. Other privates in Company H were Michael Behen, Theodore Bezent, Maier Cohn, Adalaska B. Crawford, Thomas Daly, John S. Davidson, John B. Davis, Valentine Edwards, John Foley, Charles E. Fowler, William Gallagher, Charles O. Hammer, Aman Hartman, Joseph W. Held, William Hellman, Laurence Kavanagh, Joseph Kelly, James Kennedy, Jackson Mardis, James McAndrew, Frank McCullough, Jesse S. Minnerty, James E. Morrisey, John J. Murphy, Henry Neal, Olaf Nielson, George Patrick, Thomas Powderly, Richard Powers, Timothy Quinn, Joseph Renaud, Charles E. Savonell, Michael Seyler, James Shay, John Shea, John Simpson, Henry Staples, Andrew E. Unger, Albert Werner, and Gottfried Zilly. The normal strength of the company was fifty-eight, but in addition to Trumpeter Reilly, Pvts. Burrill, Shafer, and Schultz had been detailed at Fort Walla Walla.[34]

The majority of the men in Company H were foreign-born. Fifteen of them came from Ireland, eight from Germany, three from Canada, and one each from England, Denmark, France, and Austria. Of the twenty-four men born in the United States, eight came from Massachusetts, four from Pennsylvania, two from New York, two from Connecticut, and one each from Maine, Maryland, Tennessee, Texas, Indiana, Ohio, Michigan, and California. Forty-five of the men of Company H were in their first enlistment. Before becoming soldiers, thirteen of them had worked as laborers, five as farmers, three as teamsters, two as blacksmiths, two as bricklayers, and two as tailors. Other occupations represented were bodymaker, shoemaker, boatmaker, peddler, barber, mill hand, gardener, baker, shopman, boilermaker, painter, plasterer, miner, bookkeeper, engineer, stonecutter, machinist, and carpenter. Nine of the men in Company H had previous military experience. In later years Lt. Parnell remembered many of the men in his company had been raw recruits. Actually there were seven that had been in the Army less than a year. About ten of the men in Company H had been in an Indian fight of one kind or another. The horsemanship of the company was generally good. According to Sgt. McCarthy, the men (with a few exceptions) could "stick" a horse bareback and lead another at a gallop. The average age of the men in Company H was twenty-seven and one-half years. The average height was five feet seven and one-half inches.[35]

34. Muster Roll of Company H.

35. Registry of Enlistments, 1869-1876; Statements of Parnell and McCarthy, CI, pp. 64, 83–84.

Two of the enlisted men in Company H were especially worthy, according to McCarthy. Pvt. James Shay had no equal as a soldier when he was sober, which unfortunately was not too often. Shay was five feet eight inches in height. He was born in Tipperary, Ireland, in about 1838. During the Civil War he had received a commission, but before joining his command he got into trouble and had his appointment revoked. McCarthy remarked that Shay had a knack for getting into scrapes, and if there happened to be a "strange" breach of discipline, the Irishman was sure to be involved. Once he rode his horse through the commanding officer's tent. On another occasion he tried to put out a fire by pouring alcohol on the flames. However, in the field and away from whiskey, Shay was a model soldier, noted for his courage and clearheadedness.[36] The other extraordinary enlisted man was Pvt. Charles E. Fowler. Although he had only been in the Army for nine months, Fowler had already demonstrated that he possessed the necessary talents to become a fine soldier. He was brave to the point of recklessness, but, like Shay, he also had a flaw in his personality. He was high-strung and hot-tempered and found himself continually in difficulty because of it. Fowler was about twenty-two years old. He had been born in Jackson, Michigan, but had spent most of his life in California. Grey-eyed and brown-haired, he was five feet six and one-half inches tall.[37]

Relatively speaking, companies F and H were untried in battle. Their officers and a few of their number had experience. The effectiveness of the force would depend in part on the leadership these veterans exercised.

36. Registry of Enlistments, 1873; unnumbered essay on James Shay in McCarthy, Journal.

37. Registry of Enlistments, 1876; McCarthy, Journal, p. 80.

What They Said

I saw at once that if I allowed these Indians to get away with all their plunder without making any effort to overtake and capture them, it would reflect discredit upon the Army and all concerned.

DAVID PERRY

I felt as if I could take forty winks myself even if there were Indians around.

MICHAEL McCARTHY

It would be difficult to convey to the mind of an ordinary reader anything like a correct notion of the state of feeling which takes possession of a man waiting for the commencement of a battle. In the first place, time appears to move on leaden wings; every minute seems an hour, and every hour a day. Then there is a strange commingling of levity and seriousness within him; levity which prompts him to laugh, he knows not why, and a seriousness which urges him ever and anon to lift up a mental prayer to the throne of grace. On such occasions, little or no conversation passes. The privates generally lean on their firelocks, the officers on their swords; and few words, except monosyllables in reply to questions put, are spoken. On these occasions, too, the faces of the bravest often change their color, and the limbs of the most resolute tremble, not with fear, but with anxiety; whilst watches are consulted, til the individuals who consult them grow absolutely weary of the employment. On the whole, it is a situation of higher excitement and darker and deeper agitation then any other in human life, nor can he be said to feel all that man is capable of feeling, who had not filled it. – "Siege of St. Sebastian."

CLIPPING IN THE JOURNAL OF MICHAEL McCARTHY

7

The Approach

Captain Perry had to halt his command at regular intervals in order to permit the pack train of Company H to keep up. The roads were generally muddy and especially bad in sheltered places. The terrain added to the difficulty. Not far from Fort Lapwai, they entered mountainous country where heavy timber and deep ravines retarded progress, and the blackness of the night made it impossible for the men to proceed at a fast pace.[1]

About 1 o'clock in the morning, Lieutenant Parnell took charge of a platoon of skirmishers and put out flankers on both sides. The skirmishers moved ahead of the column about 200 yards, and the flankers kept about 150 yards to the right and left of the main force. There were occasional halts to allow the flankers to maneuver around clumps of thick brush and cross ravines.[2]

They reached the Norton ranch about 10 o'clock in the morning. Under a shed near the house, the men found some wagons loaded with goods that had obviously been disturbed, but generally the scene was a peaceful one that belied the visit of a raiding party. The inside of the house showed few signs of unwelcome visitors.[3] The Indians had apparently made an attempt to set the building on fire by throwing a torch into a trunk filled with papers and clothing; but something had caused the lid to fall shut, and the flames had been smothered before much damage had been done.[4]

The soldiers dismounted in a field behind the house and turned their horses loose to graze inside the fence. Perry stationed pickets at strategic locations around the ranch to warn him of approaching riders. While the cooks prepared breakfast, the rest of the men lay in the grass and tried to catch a few moments of sleep.

After breakfast, about noon, they continued the march toward

1. Perry, CI, p. 115.
2. Parnell, CI, p. 70.
3. McCarthy, Diary, June 16, 1877.
4. Account of Schorr in McWhorter, *Hear Me*, p. 234.

Mount Idaho. Not long afterward they began to see evidence of depredations. Dead horses, abandoned wagons, and burning ranches testified to the violence that had been unleashed on Camas Prairie a few hours before. About 4 o'clock, they reached the wagons owned by Wilmot and Ready. Empty boxes were everywhere. Cigars littered the roadside, and an empty whiskey keg stood nearby. A mile down the road, the pickets noticed a group of men on horseback approaching. The men were from Mount Idaho, and Arthur Inghram Chapman was their leader.[5]

Chapman told Perry that the Nez Perce had crossed the prairie about five hours before, traveling in the direction of Salmon River. He believed that unless the troops pursued the Indians quickly and caught them before another day had passed, it might be too late. They would have their stock and belongings across the river a few hours after dawn the next day, and they would be very hard to find in the mountains on the other side. The citizens informed Perry that they knew the Nez Perce well, that the Indians were cowardly scoundrels, and that they could whip them easily if they only had enough rifles.[6]

The men rode into Grangeville about sunset. While the troopers prepared to spend the night, Perry continued his discussion of the outbreak with the citizens. Perry knew that if he allowed the Nez Perce to escape without making any effort to overtake and punish them, he would be loudly criticized by the settlers. They reported that the Indians had a great many horses that had been taken from them, and they were very anxious to reclaim their property. Howard had given him a certain amount of leeway in his orders so that he need not worry about overstepping his authority in giving chase, but at the same time Perry realized the dangers involved and the fatigue of his men and horses. He finally decided to lay the matter before his officers and summoned Trimble, Parnell, and Theller for a conference. After explaining the situation, Perry asked for their opinions and found them in agreement. They believed the attempt should be made.[7]

In the meantime, the men had been busy making camp. They unsaddled their horses and turned them loose to feed and then prepared their own meager repast — bean soup. Almost all the men lay

5. McCarthy, Diary, June 16, 1877.

6. Perry, CI, pp. 115–116; Howard, *Nez Perce Joseph*, p. 108; Schorr in McWhorter, *Hear Me*, p. 233.

7. Perry to Lt. Col. James W. Forsyth, *c*. October, 1878, letter no. 1024, Letters Received, DC, p. 1; Perry, "Battle," pp. 113–114.

down to rest while the beans boiled, but before supper was ready the order came to saddle up. Some of the men attempted to eat the half-cooked beans, but many did not. "Boots and Saddles" came at 9 o'clock, and a half-hour later the column was ready to move out. Perry left three men to look after the camp and the property that could not be carried with them. He permitted only ammunition and overcoats to be carried as extra items.[8]

Perry had asked Chapman to augment his force with as many volunteers as he could muster and to provide him with a guide. Chapman promised twenty-five or thirty men but later showed up with eleven, including himself.[9]

The commander of the volunteers was about thirty-six years old. Apparently born in Burlington, Iowa, he had been named after his mother's father, Colonel Arthur Inghram. The Chapmans left Iowa in 1847 to make their home in the Pacific Northwest. Arthur's father, William William Chapman, was one of the founders of Portland and in 1861 became Surveyor General of Oregon. As a mere boy, during the Rogue River Indian War of 1855–56, the younger Chapman carried dispatches for the Army from The Dalles to Fort Walla Walla. In 1861 he settled on White Bird Creek near the mouth of the rivulet that now bears his name, and the following year he began raising cattle and horses. For several years he operated a ferry across the Salmon River near the mouth of White Bird Creek, and tradition has it that because of the experience he earned the nickname "Ad," an abbreviation for Admiral.[10] He later moved his ranching headquarters closer to the mouth of White Bird Creek. In 1874 he sold his land and buildings to J. J. Manuel and settled on Cottonwood Creek, about eight miles from Mount Idaho, where he continued to raise horses. At the time of the outbreak, he claimed to own 400 head.[11]

Chapman married an Indian woman, apparently a Umatilla, who

8. McCarthy, Diary, June 16, 1877. The names of the three men left behind are not known.

9. Theodore Swarts to Alonzo Leland, June 21, 1877, *Lewiston Teller*, July 28, 1877, p. 4.

10. The nickname may have been a short term for adjutant. In a letter to A. F. Parker, Frank Fenn referred to "Adjutant Chapman." See *The Idaho Statesman*, September 4, 1927.

11. Chapman, November 23, 1886; Statement of Chapman, March 21, 1890; Statement of David B. Baldwin, December 1, 1886; and Report of Special Agent Stanley, 1890, in Chapman 1102; "Colonel William William Chapman," in Joseph Gaston, *Portland, Oregon: Its History and Builders* (Chicago: S. J. Clarke, 1911), 3:218–223.

bore him a child. Because he had an Indian wife, some of the settlers held him in contempt, and a number of them resented his election as captain of the volunteers. Chapman was apparently rough and ready — easy to anger and quick to strike out. McWhorter named him as a member of the party that had hanged an Indian called Wolf Head, and, according to Many Wounds, Chapman had brutally assaulted two Indian boys whom he had caught stealing his watermelons. He is also supposed to have sold a horse to White Eagle and then taken it from him by force, although Thomas Beal reported that Chapman had been unsuccessful in his attempt to reclaim the animal and the warrior had given him a sound beating. There are reports that Chapman was on the tribal blacklist for selling Nez Perce beef to Chinese miners, but he apparently maintained good relations with some of the Indians despite his shortcomings. Looking Glass was his friend, and there were others.[12]

The other volunteers were George M. Shearer, Frank A. Fenn, Theodore D. Swarts, John Crooks, Charles Crooks, William Bloomer, William Coram, Herman A. Faxon, Vince Tullis, and Johnny Barber. Shearer, a thirty-six-year-old Virginian, was second in command. He had attended Tuscarora Academy in Pennsylvania and in 1854 made his first trip west to California. Returning to Virginia five years later, he joined the Confederate Army and rose to the rank of captain. He served on the staff of Brig. Gen. Bradley Johnson and fell into Union hands on three occasions, but each time he escaped. After the Civil War Shearer headed west again, this time to Idaho, and located near the confluence of Elk Creek with Salmon River, where he operated a ferry. In 1874 he won a seat in the Territorial legislature, but lost it the following year to W. H. Rhett. Shearer was a man of tested courage and combat experience and a good choice to serve as Chapman's lieutenant.[13]

Frank Fenn had probably seen more of the world than most men

12. McWhorter Notes, item 28, packet 150; Many Wounds to McWhorter, November, 1926, item 15, packet 189; and undated statement by Thomas Beal, item 19, packet 189, McWhorter Collection; "Frank D. Vansise," *North Idaho*, p. 506; Howard, *Nez Perce Joseph*, p. 133; Haines, *Nez Perces*, p. 220.

13. Although Shearer was commonly referred to as a major, Union dispatches called him a captain, and he is not listed in *List of Field Officers, Regiments, and Battalions in the Confederate States Army, 1861–1865*, which gives the names of all those holding the rank of major and above. For biographical information on Shearer see *Twenty-seventh Biennial Report of the Secretary of the State of Idaho*, p. 73; Francis Haines, ed., "The Skirmish at Cottonwood: A Previously Unpublished Eyewitness Account of an Engagement of the Nez Perce War by George Shearer," *Idaho Yesterdays* (Spring, 1958), 2:2–7.

his age. He was born in Nevada County, California, on September 11, 1853. His father, Stephen S. Fenn, who was later to attain political prominence in the territory, took his family to Florence in 1862 and opened the first mercantile establishment in the flourishing mining community. Five years later, Fenn moved to Lewiston to become register of the land office. Frank Fenn attended public school in Florence and later graduated from Whitman Academy in Walla Walla. He received an appointment to the United States Naval Academy in 1869, but officials dismissed him in 1873, three months before graduation, for hazing a lower-classman. Next Fenn traveled in Europe. He was shanghaied in Spain but escaped his captors in Rio de Janeiro and worked his way back to the United States aboard a British sailing vessel. Returning to Idaho in 1876, he located on a ranch near Grangeville and taught school at various times. Hill Norton knew Fenn as his schoolmaster.[14]

Theodore Swarts was born in Warren County, Ohio, on March 11, 1847. In 1852 the family traveled to California and, ten years later, to Idaho, settling in Florence. After a few years, the Swartses moved to Oregon and then returned to Idaho to farm on Camas Prairie. Theodore attended public school until he was sixteen and then tried his hand at mining. In 1877 Swarts worked as an expressman and carried mail from Mount Idaho to Warrens. His father, John A. Swarts, was the man who found Lynn Bowers on the morning of June 14.[15]

John and Charles Crooks were the sons of J. W. Crooks, cattle king and Grangeville promoter. Charles was a boy in his teens.[16] William Bloomer was a prominent Granger and the owner of a steam sawmill located about three miles southwest of Grangeville.[17] William Coram had been born in Bristol, England, on March 29, 1844. The family migrated to Canada and in 1864 settled in New York City. A year later they went west to California. Coram worked as a steamboat engineer until 1868, when he moved to Idaho and became a miner and packer. He had been in Florence on June 14 and arrived just in time to join the expedition.[18] Little is known about the early lives of Faxon, Tullis, and Barber. Faxon was

14. Elsensohn, *Idaho County*, 1:470–471; *Eleventh Biennial Report of the Board of Trustees of the State Historical Society of Idaho* (Boise: The Society, 1928), p. 80; "Frank Fenn," *North Idaho*, pp. 457–458; Defenbach, *Idaho*, 1:481n, 3:386.

15. "Theodore Swarts," *North Idaho*, p. 474.

16. McWhorter Notes, item 29, packet 150, McWhorter Collection.

17. Elsensohn, *Idaho County*, 1:131.

18. "William Coram," *North Idaho*, p. 493.

twenty-eight years old, and the others were also apparently young men.[19]

About midnight the command reached the head of White Bird Canyon. Perry told the men to dismount and passed the word to keep awake. He also issued an order prohibiting fires and smoking. The men were starting on their second night without sleep and many of them dozed off. Sgt. McCarthy made continual rounds to rouse the sleeping, and he noted that many of the horses had succumbed to fatigue and lain down by their masters to rest.[20]

Forgetting himself, one of the men struck a match to light his pipe. Parnell, who happened to be standing near the man, reported the incident to Perry. Shortly after the match flamed, Parnell heard a coyote howl. He noted that the last note of the howl was different from anything he had heard before and concluded that the sound emanated from an Indian picket, who was signaling their approach.[21] Pvt. Schorr later described the howl as "a shivering one" and declared that it was "enough to make one's hair stand on end." In the silence that followed the men waited for dawn to break.[22]

19. H. A. Faxon to George W. Webb, *Winners of the West* (February, 1937), 14:7.

20. McCarthy, Diary, June 16, 1877.

21. Parnell, CI, p. 58; Parnell, "The Battle of White Bird Cañon," in Brady, *Northwestern Fights*, pp. 100–101.

22. Schorr in McWhorter, *Hear Me*, p. 235. See also Schorr, "Participant in Whitebird Massacre Recalls Fatal March into Ambush," *The Idaho Statesman*, September 13, 1931, section 2, p. 2; Schorr, "The White Bird Fight," *Winners of the West*, (February 28, 1929), 6:7.

What They Said

Thinking of it afterwards I thought he was surprised at meeting them there.

TRIMBLE OF PERRY

I did attempt to take it, but when I called my men up on the hill they would not come. They ran.

GEORGE SHEARER

My order had been misunderstood and the men evidently understood it an order to retreat. They were getting on their horses and everybody in a perfect panic, with no trumpet and only my voice.

DAVID PERRY

I did all I could, and the other non-commissioned officers, but it seemed impossible to get them to stand.

CHARLES LEEMAN

He came up where I was when they changed their positions. He was dismounted and seemed somewhat confused and excited.

PARNELL OF THELLER

There was a wounded man came out with myself and party. He was given a horse and overcoat put on the horse for him to ride on by one of the men of the company. That was the only man that I saw that could be lifted.

BARTHOLOMEW COUGHLIN

The Sergt. rejoined his party and continued the defense of that flank until the whole command was a mile away and in full rout.

TRIMBLE OF McCARTHY

Captain Trimble subsequently told me that he heard my call and saw me motion but did not comprehend what was wanted.

DAVID PERRY

8

The Battle: White Side

As dawn broke about 4 o'clock on Sunday morning, June 17, Capt. Perry gave the order to mount. Tired legs lifted heavy bodies into the saddle, and the column surged forward, a trickle of blue moving through the mist that rose from rainsoaked ground. A broad horse trail plunged down a narrow gorge that eventually sliced into the canyon proper.[1] Now and then the column crossed a dry creek bed that meandered from one side of the ravine to the other. Clumps of willows and heavy underbrush advanced and retreated as riders pressed by. The rugged terrain and clusters of dense foliage made Perry apprehensive; it was a good place for an ambush. Ad Chapman tried to allay the officer's fears by promising an end to the narrows in another mile or two. He declared that the canyon soon opened into a comparatively smooth valley, a place where cavalry could fight to advantage. Besides, the Nez Perce were probably already making preparations to flee across the Salmon River. Their tasks would keep them preoccupied while troops moved into position.[2]

About a mile from the summit, a woman suddenly appeared on the trail. She held a small child in her arms, and another stood by her side. The wayfarers were Isabella Benedict and her daughters, who had been eluding the hostiles by keeping to the brush and camping without fires. They had eaten little or nothing since Thursday, and they were obviously suffering from exposure. Isabella thanked God for her deliverance and told the story of her escape. Requesting a safeguard, she begged Perry to give up the chase and return to Mount Idaho. She ended her appeal with a prophecy of death and declared that a massacre waited for the command on the valley floor, but Perry was firm in his determination to push ahead.

---

1. McWhorter, *Hear Me*, pp. 236–237.

2. Howard, *Nez Perce Joseph*, p. 6; Perry, CI, p. 117; Perry, "Battle," p. 101; Joel G. Trimble, Report of the Nez Perce Campaign, *c.* December, 1877, letter no. 131, Letters Received, DC, 1878, p. 6 (hereafter cited as Trimble Report).

He offered to send the woman and her children to Mount Idaho by
one of the friendly Nez Perce, but Isabella chose to remain where
she was. Someone might pick her up on the return trip — if there
were one. Not having a man to spare, Perry assented to her wish. He
ordered one of the men to give her a blanket, and Trumpeter Jones
made a gift of his lunch.[3] The pitiful condition of Mrs. Benedict and
her girls did much to strengthen the resolve of the men. Thinking
back to the episode many years later, Lt. Parnell wrote: "It was a
terrible illustration of Indian deviltry and Indian warfare." Suffering of this kind, he continued, called for "sympathy, compassion,
and action."[4]

Perry decided that the time had come to take special precautions.
He detailed Lt. Theller and eight men of Company F to serve as an
advance guard. Among them was Trumpeter Jones. He also sent
Chapman and several of the Indians with the detachment to serve as
scouts. Theller had instructions to halt his command when he
sighted the enemy, deploy his men, and notify Perry immediately.
The detail moved 100 yards ahead of the column, and the march
continued. Perry assumed his position of leadership at the head of
the main force. Behind him rode the volunteers, then Company F
and Company H at forty-yard intervals. A few minutes later, Perry
gave the order to load carbines and remove overcoats.[5]

About two miles from the summit, Perry and his men emerged
from the ravine. Below them was the canyon proper, the place
where danger lay. The trail to the bottom was steep and looped
down the west side of White Bird Hill to reach the valley floor. The
view was breathtaking. The west wall of the canyon was almost perpendicular in places and rose to great heights. It would be difficult
to ascend in case of an emergency. At present White Bird Hill was
the barrier on the left, but it had already started to slope downward,
and in a few miles it would disappear completely. Actually the hill
stood between the east and west walls of the canyon and gave it a
Y-shaped appearance. The east wall was many miles distant and
would not be a factor. On the valley floor a ridge was discernible. It
lifted gracefully upward and seemed to divide the west branch of the
canyon into halves. It ran from north to south, and from high up on

3. Perry, CI, p. 116; Trimble Report, pp. 5–6; Schorr in *Hear Me*, p. 235; McCarthy, Army Sketches, pp. 10–11.

4. William R. Parnell, "The Battle of White Bird Cañon," in Brady, *Northwestern
Fights*, p. 101.

5. Perry, CI, p. 117; Parnell, CI, p. 58; Trimble, CI, p. 26; Trimble Report, p. 6;
Testimony of Frank Husush in Nez Perce Claims, p. 94.

the hillside it looked like a giant wave about to crest and smash against the west wall. It appeared to fade out to the left after several miles, and beyond it rose another ridge. It cut across the route of advance, and a deep ravine separated it in the middle. South of the second ridge, Perry could see the tree-lined banks of White Bird Creek and follow the green line through a cleft in the west wall that permitted the stream to continue its southwesterly course and join the Salmon River.[6] Unknown to Perry, the Indian camp lay behind the second ridge on the creek bottom. Joseph, Ollokot, Two Moons, Yellow Wolf, and a host of others watched from concealed positions as the column began its descent to the canyon floor.[7]

II

The Indians had reached the campsite on White Bird Creek late on Saturday afternoon. As shadows deepened in the canyon, Nez Perce women lifted lodge poles into place and tightened tepee covers around them, and sentinels prepared for an all-night vigil. The camp held about thirty lodges. Perhaps there were as many as 135 fighting men in the village. Many of the warriors, however, were in poor condition to do battle before the night ended. Barrels of whiskey seized on Camas Prairie and at Benedict's store soon opened and emptied, and more then one fighting man drank himself into a stupor.[8]

Not long after the camp quieted in slumber, one of the Nez Perce watchguards, an amputee called No Feet, galloped into the tepee circle with the dreaded news.[9] The soldiers were coming. Joseph, Ollokot, White Bird, and Toohoolhoolzote held a hurried

6. For Perry's description of the terrain see CI, p. 118, and Perry, "Battle," p. 115.

7. McWhorter, *Yellow Wolf*, p. 51.

8. According to Indian sources, there were fifty-five warriors in Joseph's band (Wallowas), fifty in White Bird's band (Lamtamas), and thirty in Toohoolhoolzote's band (Pikunans). However, apparently some of the Wallowas stayed with Looking Glass on the Clearwater, so that the figure may be somewhat smaller. Account of Three Eagles in Curtis, *North American Indian*, 8:25n; Josephy, *Nez Perce Indians*, p. 525; McWhorter, *Hear Me*, pp. 177 ff, 251n.

9. Hand in Hand, Vicious Weasel, Red Raven, and No Feet had been located on the summit of a butte that stood on the east side of Grasshopper Spring, a little more than four miles north of the battleground. Many Wounds showed Lucullus McWhorter the spot in 1932. No Feet had been a slave to the Yakima chief Kamiakin. The chief had purchased him from some tribe farther west, and his tribal origin has never been determined. No Feet had lost both feet and one of his hands when Kamiakin left him outdoors, shackled with traps, one sub-zero night to punish him for stealing. Later Kamiakin gave the Indian his freedom, and he settled among the Nez Perce. Because of his condition, he spent a great deal of time on horseback and became an

conference. All of them still wished to avoid war, but the possibility of doing so appeared remote. At least one chief supported a withdrawal across the Salmon River to the mountains. The Nez Perce would be difficult to find in the jagged maze rising in the west. In the early hours of the morning, the chiefs reached a decision: the Nez Perce would stand their ground. They would send a small party forward to make peace overtures when the soldiers appeared. In the meantime they would prepare to defend themselves in case the emissaries failed in their mission.[10]

Dark shapes moved in the Indian camp. The chiefs directed the young men to bring in the horses. Warriors tethered their best mounts close by and herded the rest together to facilitate a quick departure if necessary. As dawn approached the able-bodied stripped for battle. Some of the finest warriors lay helplessly drunk, oblivious to the sting of the quirt applied by their tribesmen in an effort to revive them.[11] Perhaps not more than seventy men answered the call of the chiefs.[12] Some of them carried only bows and arrows. Others had firearms of all kinds — pistols, trade muskets, shotguns, and modern rifles.[13]

---

excellent rider. McWhorter, *Hear Me*, pp. 236–237; McWhorter, *Yellow Wolf*, pp. 52–53; Yellow Bull in Curtis, *North American Indian*, 8:165; Account of First Red Feather on the Wing, n.d., packet 211-b, McWhorter Collection.

10. Josephy, *Nez Perce Indians*, p. 524; Three Eagles in Curtis, *North American Indian*, 8:26n.

11. Account of About Asleep, n.d., item 49, packet 168, McWhorter Collection; McWhorter, *Yellow Wolf*, p. 51; Wounded Head and Black Feather in *Hear Me*, pp. 239, 241.

12. Participants give varying estimates concerning the number of warriors in the battle. Joseph reported that about sixty Nez Perce fought in the engagement and Yellow Wolf put the number at about seventy. Most white estimates were surprisingly close to Indian figures. Trimble believed that there were about one hundred warriors, although he noted that he had not seen more than thirty or forty at one time. McCarthy, Richard Powers, and George Shearer estimated that there were about sixty Nez Perce. Perry believed that he had encountered about 125. Joseph, "Chief Joseph's Own Story," in Brady, *Northwestern Fights*, p. 64; McWhorter, *Yellow Wolf*, pp. 51, 55; Trimble, CI, p. 87; Shearer, CI, p. 93; Perry to Howard, June 17, 1877, letter no. 1450, Letters Received, DC: Stephen Perry Jocelyn, *Mostly Alkali* (Caldwell, Idaho: Caxton Printers, 1953), p. 225.

13. McWhorter believed that about forty-five of the warriors carried firearms. Three Eagles estimated about fifty guns. McWhorter, *Hear Me*, p. 251n; Three Eagles in Curtis, *North American Indian*, 8:26n. See also Wounded Head and George Comedown in McWhorter, *Hear Me*, pp. 239, 250–251; Robert H. Ruby, "First Account of Nez Perce War by Man who Went: Josiah Red Wolf," *Inland Empire Magazine*, November 17, 1963, p. 3.

When other sentinels reported that the troops were moving down the canyon, the warriors mounted and rode from the camp in small parties. Eventually nearly fifty of them, including Ollokot, gathered behind a loaf-shaped butte on the west side of the canyon. Between the creek bank and the ridge that hid the camp from view there were two small knolls, which had served as burial places for the Nez Perce in years past. Two Moons and fifteen others took a position behind the west knoll and hid their horses behind the east one.[14] By placing themselves between the line of march and their village, the warriors protected it from a cavalry charge. By concentrating forces on either side of the trail leading down to White Bird Creek, the Nez Perce were in a position to flank the column to the right or the left if the soldiers repulsed the peace party. To believe that the Indians had a precise battle plan, however, is to ignore one of the basic precepts of aboriginal warfare. Weyehwahtsistkan, known to the whites as John Miles, put it succinctly: "Unlike the trained white soldier, who is guided by the bugle call, the Indian goes into battle on his mind's own guidance."[15]

On the canyon floor, things looked somewhat different to Perry. The trail led over rolling country, up and down grass-covered knolls, always descending. The column kept to the left of the ridge as it moved down the canyon. Soon the troops reached the place where the wave-like barrier began to dip and angle to the left. Suddenly another ridge came into view. Like the one beyond it, which had been seen from above, it ran diagonally from west to east and cut across the direction of advance. It had not been discernible near Poe Saddle, because its southern slope was a gradual one, and the lip of the parallel ridge — at a point where it curved to the east — lifted high enough to hide its steep northern face from view. By the time Perry reached the first diagonal ridge, the advance guard was already on its way toward the second.[16]

Abraham Brooks and Frank Husush, two of the Nez Perce scouts, rode ahead of the detachment. Signs told them they were nearing the Indian camp, and they reported their discovery to Thel-

14. McWhorter, *Yellow Wolf,* pp. 51–55. Three Eagles claimed that Joseph was in charge of one group of warriors. John Miles reported that while Joseph did some fighting, "he did no leading." Yellow Bull agreed when he stated that Joseph fought like any other warrior. Bow and Arrow Case also confirmed the presence of Joseph in the battle. See Three Eagles and Yellow Bull in Curtis, *North American Indian,* 8:26n, 165; John Miles and Bow and Arrow Case in McWhorter, *Hear Me,* pp. 249, 254.

15. John Miles in McWhorter, *Hear Me,* p. 249.

16. Perry, CI, p. 118; Perry, "Battle," p. 114.

ler. Ad Chapman immediately spurred his horse forward to see for
himself. Reaching the place where the ground sloped downward before rising to form the crest of the ridge, he looked to his right and
saw the peace party coming toward him. Apparently the Indians had
ridden around the west end of the ridge and were angling east in
order to intercept the soldiers before they rode over the divide.
Without a moment's hesitation Chapman opened fire.[17]

The truce team, consisting of Vicious Weasel and five others, had
strict orders not to fire unless fired upon. Chapman shot twice before the Nez Perce sought cover and returned the way they had
come. Continuing due south, the volunteer commander moved up
the ridge to get a view of the creek bottom. Theller and the detachment followed. Topping the rise, they could see the Nez Perce moving along the river bank in small groups in order to occupy positions
directly in front of them. Theller immediately began to deploy his
men as skirmishers, and Trumpeter Jones began to blow the call to
battle which would bring the main force forward; but before he had
time to finish it, a bullet jarred him from the saddle. Fire Body, an
elderly Nez Perce located behind the cemetery knoll with Two
Moons, was the one who fired the lucky shot.[18] Several hundred
yards to the rear, Perry saw his advance guard rein to a halt and
observed Theller dismounting the detachment. Quickly the senior
officer returned to his men. He formed Company F left front into
line and the gave the order to drop carbines and draw pistols, intending to charge the enemy.[19] While Perry was busy with his company, George Shearer led the volunteers forward. Moving around
the east end of the ridge, he galloped toward White Bird Creek.
Several warriors emerged from the thicket bordering the stream,
and the volunteers opened fire. Seeking cover, the Nez Perce retaliated with effective swiftness. Shearer ordered his men to dismount, but only a few obeyed the command; some of the rest turned
tail and fled. With a handful of men, the ex-Confederate officer
knew that he could not advance. In the background he could hear
the report of rifles, and he realized that Theller was under attack.

17. Husush in Nez Perce Claims, p. 94; McWhorter, *Yellow Wolf*, pp. 55–56; Three
Eagles in Curtis, *North American Indian*, 8:26n; Floyd Laird, ed., "Reminiscences of
Francis M. Redfield, Chief Joseph's War," *Pacific Northwest Quarterly* (January, 1936),
27:72.

18. Two Moons and Bow and Arrow Case in McWhorter, *Hear Me*, pp. 246–254;
McWhorter, *Yellow Wolf*, pp. 55–56.

19. Perry, CI, p. 118.

Gathering the remainder of his command, Shearer made a dash for the ridge to rejoin the regulars.[20]

While the volunteers exchanged shots with the Nez Perce on the river bottom, Perry advanced toward the ridge at a trot. Turning to Trumpeter Daly to give the order to charge, the officer received some disheartening news. The man no longer possessed his trumpet; he had lost it somewhere along the way. By this time Company F had reached the crest of the ridge occupied by Theller, and Perry could see the Nez Perce advancing below him. Sizing up the situation, he could only succeed in driving the warriors back into the underbrush on the creek bank, where they would be under cover and his command exposed to fire. He also perceived that the ridge he held was the most defensible position in the vicinity. Perry came to a quick decision: he would make his stand on the ridge.[21]

Inclining slightly to the left, Perry gave the order to dismount and fight on foot. The distance between skirmishers was about three yards, varying somewhat with the terrain. A few rocks and boulders scattered here and there afforded some protection, and the waist-high grass hid most of a man's body. Perry sent the horses to the rear by number fours to a sheltered position in a swale behind the ridge and ordered Daly to ride quickly to Trimble with instructions to look out for his right.[22] At this point in the battle, Company F held a position about midway between the east end of the ridge and the ravine that divided it in half.

Completing his preliminary instructions, Perry told Theller to take command of the line so that he might reconnoiter his position. Looking to his left, he noticed the volunteers posted on a little knoll that was about 100 yards from the end of his line. It was the last high point on the east end of the ridge, and it was a strategic point in the event of a flanking movement because it commanded the position of Company F and the hollow where the horses were. Perry apparently did not realize that Shearer and his men had just returned from the creek bottom and that they had already seen action. Secure in his belief that the volunteers protected his flank, Perry galloped toward Company H, then swinging into line.[23]

Trimble was at least 150 yards to the rear when firing commenced. He formed his company left front into line and deployed

20. Shearer, CI, p. 89.

21. Perry, CI, p. 118; Perry, "Battle," p. 118.

22. Powers, CI, p. 85; Charles Luman, CI, pp. 97–98, 103; Bartholomew Coughlin, CI, pp. 104–105; Perry, CI, p. 118.

23. Perry, CI, p. 119.

his men to the right at five-yard intervals. They remained mounted.
Trimble cautioned the men to remain steady and rode to the front
and to the right of his company. At the same time Lieutenant Parnell moved off to assume a position on the far left of the line. Almost immediately some of the Nez Perce began to move around the
right flank of Company H by riding around and over the west end
of the ridge. They did not pose a threat to Perry, because he was
already on the crest and the ravine protected his right. To some of
the troopers it appeared that the Indians were attempting to drive a
herd of wild horses through their line, and although the ponies
passed to the right at a distance of 100 yards, some of the men retreated from the flank and bunched together in the center of the
company. In truth, however, many of the horses held riders. The
warriors leaned to the opposite sides of their ponies as the party
swept by, hiding their bodies from the view of the cavalrymen, some
of whom were recruits who were not familiar with the ancient Indian tactic. During the next quarter-hour, other warriors followed
the horsemen to press the company on the flank and in the rear.
Shore Crossing, Red Moccasin Tops, and Strong Eagle led the fighting on the right and gained a special place in the memories of their
people.[24]

One of the first men to be wounded in Company H was Cpl.
Roman Lee.[25] He was shot near the groin and dismounted with the
assistance of his comrades. Suffering from shock, he wandered aim-
lessly toward the Indian camp and into the sights of Nez Perce rifles.

To stem the onrush on his flank, Trimble detailed 1st Sgt.
Michael McCarthy and six men to hold a rocky point that commanded the ravine and the west half of the ridge. It was a natural
breastwork fronting the Indian advance, open from the rear except
for a few boulders on the slope. Trimble rode with the detachment
to the bluff and then returned to his company. By this time some of
the men had dismounted in order to fire more accurately.[26]

Capt. Perry headed for Company H with a dual purpose in

24. Trimble, CI, pp. 26, 38, 51; Trimble Report, p. 7; Parnell, CI, pp. 58, 64, 70;
Parnell, "Battle," p. 102; McCarthy, CI, pp. 75, 84; Powers, CI, p. 85; Coughlin, CI,
p. 104; McWhorter, *Yellow Wolf*, p. 57n; Two Moons and John Miles in McWhorter,
Hear Me, pp. 247, 249.

25. Roman Lee was about twenty-six years old. Born in Bloomsburg, Pennsylvania,
he worked as a laborer before enlisting on October 21, 1873. He was five feet five
inches in height and had blue eyes and brown hair. Registry of Enlistments, 1873.

26. Trimble, CI, p. 27; Trimble Report, p. 8; Trimble to the Adjutant General,
April 14, 1897, Berkeley, California, McCarthy, Medal of Honor File; McCarthy, CI,
pp. 76–83; McCarthy, Diary, June 17, 1877; McCarthy, Army Sketches, p. 6.

mind. He wanted to examine Trimble's position, and he wanted to obtain a trumpet. Cavalry had to be able to maneuver quickly when the opportunity presented itself. With his force strung out across the ridge, Perry was desperately in need of means of projecting his commands. His voice carried only a short distance in the din of battle, and the length of time it took to pass the word along the line could prove to be disastrously long. Hand signals were fine for close quarters, but not very useful in this situation. Terrain, smoke, and dust combined to reduce their effectiveness in any event. In short, divested of a trumpet Perry was nearly helpless. As he later put it, "a cavalry command on a battlefield without a trumpet is like a ship at sea without a helm."[27] Perry covered about two thirds of the distance between the companies before he noticed a commotion among the horses in the hollow behind Company F. He saw that the citizens had been driven from the knoll and that it was now in the possession of Nez Perce marksmen.

Two Moons, Yellow Wolf, Fire Body, and the rest of the warriors originally secreted behind the cemetery knoll were responsible for the disaster. When the citizens returned from their abortive foray on the creek bottom, they found the Indians firmly entrenched on a point about fifty yards from their position. Dismounting, the volunteers tried to hold the line, but they refused to advance to the point when Shearer beckoned.[28]

One of the warriors called to Charles Crooks: "You, Charley Crooks: Take your Papa's hoss and go home."[29] Soon Theodore Swarts took a bullet in the hip and Herman Faxon another in the thigh. At the same time, the regulars on the left of the line began to move back in response to the telling fire delivered by the warriors on the point. Seeing the soldiers withdrawing, the volunteers hastily galloped to the rear. Swarts jumped his horse over an Indian to make good his escape.

Perry was too far away to order a charge to retake the hill, so he decided that the only thing to do was to move to a new position near Trimble's company. Dashing back to the line, he ordered the word passed from man to man to move slowly to the right and rear.[30]

27. Perry, CI, p. 119.

28. Shearer, CI, pp. 89, 93; Perry CI, p. 119; Perry, "Battle," p. 115; McWhorter, *Yellow Wolf*, p. 57; Two Moons in McWhorter, *Hear Me*, p. 247.

29. "Old Timers," McWhorter Notes, item 29, packet 150, McWhorter Collection.

30. Perry, CI, p. 119; Perry, "Battle," pp. 114–115; Shearer, CI, p. 89; Trimble, CI, pp. 38–51; Coughlin, CI, p. 103; Parnell, CI, p. 61; Sears, "Mount Idaho"; L. P.

Seeing the order in the process of execution, Perry resumed his journey to Trimble's line. He found Company H in poor order. Some of the men fought on foot, while others fired from horseback. Many of the men huddled close together in the center of the line, among them some from his own company who had gone to the rear without orders after the firing began. A few of the men were having difficulty managing their horses, which were bucking and kicking in cadence with each volley. Continuing to his left, Perry met Trimble, who had just returned from posting McCarthy on the point. He asked Trimble for a trumpet but learned that he had none. The last trumpet had also been lost.[31]

Glancing back at his company, Perry saw that the left of the line had broken completely and the men were scrambling for their horses. After the volunteers fled from the knoll, some of the warriors had moved around the end of the line and fired into the company from a position in the rear. Six men fell in a short time. Suddenly the skirmishers on the left saw the right of the line begin to pull back and move up the ridge to the west to join Company H. Word had not yet reached them of the tactics being employed by Perry, and they interpreted the movement as a signal for a full-scale retreat.

The instinct for survival soon gained the upper hand. Scurrying down the banks of the hollow, terror-stricken soldiers swung into the saddle and galloped to the rear — some of them leaving their weapons behind in their haste. As they sped away the men on the right responded in panic, and in a short time most of the company joined in the unceremonious retreat, including Lieutenant Theller. Perry later remarked that he had not seen anything like it since Gordon's raiders jumped the men of the Eighth Corps in their beds at Cedar Creek in October of 1864.[32]

Once again Perry was off on a race to avoid disaster. He tried to rally the men and reform the line and in part succeeded. He managed to contain scattered segments of the company, and some of the men halted after they reached the position held by Company H.

Brown to Commanding Officer of Fort Lapwai, June 17, 1877, *The Daily Oregonian* (Portland), June 21, 1877, p. 3; "Theodore Swarts," *North Idaho*, p. 474; Swarts to Leland, July 21, 1877.

31. Perry, CI, pp. 119–120; Perry, "Battle," pp. 114–115; Parnell, CI, p. 64; Trimble, CI, p. 38; Trimble Report, p. 8; McCarthy, CI, p. 84.

32. Perry, CI, p. 120; Perry, "Battle," p. 116; Parnell, CI, pp. 59, 62, 73; Leeman, CI, pp. 98–100; Coughlin, CI, pp. 104–105.

Perry returned with the vestige of his company and called Trimble for a quick conference. He told his subordinate that they would have to act quickly or suffer a resounding defeat. Company H was on the verge of bolting. Indeed, a few of them had already departed. Trimble half-heartedly suggested that they might take the remaining men and charge through the Indians to the Salmon River. Perry replied that the result of such a maneuver would be utter annihilation and instructed Trimble to move his company to the rear, where they might find a more defensible position. There was still time to organize an orderly retreat, because the Nez Perce were not advancing rapidly.[33]

Trimble ordered his company to move back by twos from the right, and the men moved out in fairly good order. Several hundred yards to the rear, Trimble encountered Theller. He was on foot and held a carbine in his hand. It was obvious from his appearance that he had lost control of himself. Parnell saw Theller about the same time Trimble did, and together the officers rushed to his assistance. They ordered a horse caught for him. One enlisted man held the head of the animal, while the other gave him a boost up. Clinging to the horse bareback, Theller galloped off down the trail leading back up the canyon. Suddenly Parnell remembered that Sgt. McCarthy and his men were still on the rocky point and brought them to Trimble's attention. Both officers rode back to signal the men to join the command and then returned to their companies.[34]

When McCarthy had reached the point, he had dismounted his detail and sheltered the horses behind some of the bigger boulders. He saw a number of warriors hunting cover on a hillock opposite him, and he opened fire. An exchange of shots followed, apparently with little effect on either side. Presently he observed the right of the line begin to swing near him, and a few men of Company F reached the point and took a position on his left. A few minutes later he heard a voice summon him to the rear. Looking north, McCarthy could see that the command had retreated about 400 yards, and, mounting his detail, he started back at a gallop.[35]

After Trimble returned to his company, he met Ad Chapman,

33. Perry, CI, p. 120; Perry, "Battle," p. 116; Trimble, CI, p. 27; Trimble Report, p. 8; Parnell, CI, p. 64.

34. Trimble, CI, pp. 26–27; Trimble Report, pp. 9–10; Parnell, CI, pp. 61–64; William R. Parnell, "The Nez Perce Indian War — 1877: Battle of White-Bird Cañon," *The United Service*, n.s. (1889), 2:370.

35. McCarthy, Diary, June 17; McCarthy, CI, pp. 76–79; McCarthy to General Howard, September 20, 1897, McCarthy, Medal of Honor File; McCarthy, Army Sketches, p. 10.

who told him that the best place to defend in the present situation was the bluff held by McCarthy. Trimble communicated the information to Perry, and the commander agreed to give it a try. Shouting his intentions to Parnell, Trimble gave the order to move out. As the officer rode ahead of the column, he saw McCarthy galloping toward him. He shouted for the sergeant to return to the point, and McCarthy obeyed. The main body of troops, however, did not reach the bluff or apparently even come close to it. The men became scattered in the charge and the column disintegrated. For the second time, the cavalrymen turned to the rear in hasty retreat.[36]

On the first of the diagonal ridges, which the command had crossed when it entered the valley, Perry made his most strenuous efforts to halt the runaway. He succeeded in rallying a few of the men and had the semblance of a line formed, but when the Nez Perce came within range the left gave way, and most of the rest followed with Trimble and Perry after them. Only Parnell stood his ground with a handful of men.[37]

McCarthy had been able to bring only three men back with him to the rocky point. After taking his position, the sergeant could see the Nez Perce riding up the canyon, taking the offensive from the front as well as from the flank. He noticed several small war parties pass to his right. Another band of warriors rode by on the left under the lip of the ledge he occupied. He would have to ride through them to reach the rest of the company. The men fired about ten rounds apiece before they heard a call to retreat a second time. Showing himself to acknowledge the command, McCarthy noticed fire coming obliquely from either side. Realizing that he was completely cut off, he ordered a rapid withdrawal, leaped into the saddle, and started back with a rush. Hugging the back of his horse, he rode to safety. Two of his men were cut off and killed in the retreat.

When McCarthy reached Parnell, he found the officer about ten yards in advance of his men, urging them forward in an attempt to rescue some of the wounded and dismounted men who had been left behind in the retreat. The wounded seemed to be wandering about in a daze, and little could be done for them because they were under heavy fire. As McCarthy rode up, Parnell shouted: "Sergeant take charge of the line. Try and hold the road and I will ride back and bring you help." The remaining troopers were strung out in

36. Trimble, CI, pp. 28–29; Trimble Report, pp. 8–10; Trimble to the Adjutant General, April 14, 1897; McCarthy, Diary, June 17, 1877; McCarthy, CI, p. 76.

37. Perry, "Battle," p. 116; Parnell, CI, p. 59; Parnell, "Battle," p. 103; Leeman, CI, p. 99.

open order across the trail and blocked the Indian advance. McCarthy did as he was told. He checked the onrush in his front, but the warriors began to ride around his right in the direction taken by the fleeing column. By this time nearly all the dismounted men had reached and passed the little detachment, so McCarthy began to pull back. Suddenly some of his men on the right flank bolted. The sergeant made an attempt to stop them, but a bullet had wounded his horse and it soon gave out. He dismounted and tried to move the animal along, but to no avail. In the meantime the rest of his command had been falling back, and McCarthy saw that he would soon be alone. Abandoning the horse, he broke into a run to catch the rapidly disappearing detachment.

Fortunately for McCarthy, Pvt. Charles Fowler saw his predicament and returned for him. Abraham Brooks also came back to assist McCarthy in mounting behind Fowler, and after the sergeant was in the saddle the three men continued up the trail. At this point, the Nez Perce did not follow the retreating detachment in great numbers. Most of the warriors kept to the west in order to pursue the main force led by Perry and Trimble; McCarthy noticed only four or five warriors in their rear.[38] After a bullet wounded Fowler's horse, McCarthy rode double with Cpl. Michael Curran until he could catch a horse of his own. At intervals they were joined by Cpl. Frank Powers, Pvt. James Shay, and a third man.[39]

The stragglers soon caught up with the detachment, which consisted of 1st Sgt. Alexander Baird of F Company and five or six men of Company H. Parnell had returned to take command of the squad, and he had the men in good order. McCarthy and his companions took a place in the rear, fronting the Indian advance. Parnell was fortunate to have such a preponderance of non-commissioned officers and veteran soldiers in the party, and with them he was able to organize a respectable retreat. The detachment worked its way slowly back up the canyon, passing from one little swell to another — sometimes at a walk — and holding on until the Indians got on the ridges on both flanks and threatened to cut them off. Then they

38. McCarthy, Diary, June 17, 1877; McCarthy, CI, pp. 76–81; McCarthy to Howard, September 20, 1897; McCarthy, Journal, p. 80.

39. Michael Curran was born in Ireland and had previously worked as a laborer before entering the Army on April 12, 1875. About twenty-seven years old, he was almost five feet seven inches in height and had brown hair and brown eyes. Frank Powers was a native of Connecticut. A shoemaker before enlisting in the service, he was five feet seven and one-half inches in height, blond-haired and blue-eyed. He was about twenty-six years old. Registry of Enlistments, 1875, 1876.

moved rapidly to higher ground, came to a halt, and began the slow withdrawal all over again. They waited at every halt for their adversaries to come near enough to receive the contents of their carbines, and once they stopped long enough to tighten up their saddle girths. Under these circumstances, the Nez Perce dared not approach too close, although at one time they were near enough for Parnell to use his pistol.

About one mile from the point where the trail left the canyon floor and began its steep ascent to the summit of White Bird Hill, a bullet crippled McCarthy's horse and he was forced to dismount. He attempted to keep up with the retreating party by running but gradually fell behind. By the time he reached the foot of the steep hill, Parnell and the rest of the detachment were already high above him. Overcome with fatigue, he fell repeatedly in his desperate efforts to gain higher ground. As his pursuers drew close, McCarthy fired one wild shot from his revolver and, in turning about, lost his footing and tumbled down the hillside and then lay still. The warriors swept by him and continued the chase.[40]

Meanwhile, Perry and Trimble had been riding along the base of the west wall on the other side of the canyon, followed by most of the Nez Perce. The only way Perry could make a show of resistance was to gallop in front of a few fleeing soldiers and turn them about. Sometimes he promised to shoot them if they failed to comply, but even under the threat of death they would stand for only a short time, and he had to start all over again with another shaky squad.[41]

The men followed the lead of the volunteers, who knew of a cattle trail that led up the west wall of the canyon to the high plateau above. Nearing the place where the trail began, Perry noticed a point that he believed could be defended if he could reach it before the men rushed by. But his horse failed to respond to his urging, and, realizing that the animal would never make it in time, Perry hailed a passing trooper and requested a lift to the bluff. When he reached the point, he slid to the ground and called to Trimble, whom he saw riding up the trail about fifty yards ahead. Perry ordered his subordinate to post some men on a second point in the vicinity, and Trimble replied that Chapman believed there was a

40. Parnell, CI, pp. 59, 67; Parnell, "Battle," pp. 104–105; McCarthy, Diary, June 17, 1877; McCarthy, CI, pp. 79–80; McCarthy to Howard, September 20, 1897. For what McCarthy referred to as a "glowing account" of his part in the battle see W. F. Beyer and O. F. Keydel, editors, *Deeds of Valor*, 2 vols. (Detroit: Perrin-Keydel Co., 1903), 2:239–243.

41. Perry, CI, p. 120; Perry, "Battle," p. 116; Shearer, CI, pp. 91–92; Coughlin, CI, p. 104; *Idaho Tri-Weekly Statesman*, June 28, 1877, p. 3.

more defensible place higher up. Perry repeated the order and Trimble complied.[42] Turning to Sgt. William Havens of Company H, who occupied a third point close by, Perry told him to hold that position while he attempted to form another squad and find another point above them that commanded the trail and the defenses organized below.[43]

Busying himself with the work at hand, Perry succeeded in stopping a few other cavalrymen. When he glanced back to see how Trimble was doing, Perry discovered much to his dismay that his senior officer had departed along with Sgt. Havens and the rest of the men who had been holding the bluffs a few moments before. Because he was on foot, Perry could only watch the retreat. His shouts and gesticulations were either ignored or misunderstood.[44]

With the few men that were left, Perry made his way up the bluff, keeping under cover as much as possible and steering clear of the trail until near the top of the wall. As the men ascended, they were able to stem the onslaught of the Nez Perce. Higher ground gave them better positions to fire from, and the warriors became wary. Perry broke his tiny command into equal parts; as one retreated to assume a position a short distance in the rear, the other delivered a volley. Repeating the maneuver again and again, the small remnant gained confidence and soon reached the summit. About halfway up the bluff Perry was able to catch a loose horse, which he rode for the rest of the day.[45]

When the troops reached the top, their pursuers were not far behind. Some of the Nez Perce were already making their way along the high ridge and threatening to flank the men in the rear. Others were moving rapidly up the trail to the top and promised to continue the assault at close quarters in a matter of minutes. In the distance, Perry saw Trimble, who was galloping obliquely to the left. Perry was too far away to make himself heard, so he attempted to

42. Perry, CI, p. 119–120; Perry, "Battle," pp. 116–117; Trimble, CI, pp. 29–30; Trimble Report, p. 11.

43. William Havens was born in Lynde, Connecticut, in about 1839. At the time of his first enlistment in 1873, he had given his profession as a "bodymaker." He had dark hair and hazel eyes and was a little over five feet eight inches in height. Registry of Enlistment, 1873.

44. Perry, CI, pp. 121–122; Perry, "Battle," p. 117; Perry to Lt. Col. James W. Forsyth, c. October 22, 1878, pp. 3–4; Trimble, CI, pp. 30–32; Trimble Report, pp. 11–12; Shearer, CI, pp. 90–91.

45. Perry, CI, p. 122. According to Bartholomew Coughlin, the horse belonged to Trumpeter Jones. Coughlin, CI, p. 105.

wave the officer to the right: he believed Theller and Parnell must be coming up the road below, and he hoped to combine forces as soon as they appeared on the summit. But Trimble continued on his course and soon disappeared from sight.[46]

Perry then moved to the right and soon encountered Parnell, who had just emerged from the narrows and stood on the summit of White Bird Hill. Their combined force numbered about two dozen.[47] Theller was nowhere in sight, and Parnell had no knowledge of him. Perry surmised that perhaps he had preceded Trimble and was far ahead of them on the way to Grangeville and Mount Idaho. Immediately in front of them was a deep ravine that had to be crossed. Perry told Parnell to hold the ridge while he moved his men to the other side, and he would do the same for him. Parnell did as ordered, but when Perry's men reached the opposite bank they refused to stop. Parnell crossed the gulch at a gallop with the Indians closing the distance. Halting on the high ground, he ordered a volley, and the Nez Perce reined short.[48]

Perry continued to fall back until he reached the Henry Johnson ranch, about four miles from the head of the canyon. There he dismounted his men and took a position on a high rocky point. To his left were the house and barn. A small creek ran between the bluff and the buildings. Parnell arrived shortly thereafter, and Perry ordered him to deploy his men on the firing line. Perry kept his own men in reserve. In the course of conversation, Perry remarked that he believed that they could defend their position until dark. Astonished, Parnell informed his commander that it was about 7 o'clock in the morning, not evening, and that each of the men had only ten or fifteen rounds of ammunition left.

Presently bullets came flying over their heads from the front and from the right flank. The Indians had taken shelter in a clump of rocks on higher ground about 200 yards from their position and therefore commanded the bluff. At the same time, another party of Nez Perce began to move around to the left. They were hidden by a fence that ran up from the house and was perpendicular to Perry's

46. Perry, CI, p. 122; Perry to Forsyth, c. October 22, 1878, pp. 3–4.

47. In his report of the battle written on June 17, Perry gave the number as twenty-three. Later he said there were twenty-six. Parnell reported the figure as twenty-seven or twenty-eight. Perry to Howard, June 17, 1877, Letters Received, DC; Perry to Forsyth, c. October 22, 1878; Parnell, CI, p. 61.

48. The account of the retreat by Perry and Parnell, unless otherwise noted, is based on Perry, CI, pp. 122–123; Perry, "Battle," p. 181; Parnell, CI, pp. 59–61, 67–68, 71; Parnell, "Battle," pp. 105–108; Parnell, "Indian War," pp. 371–372.

front. Luckily, one of the men discovered them before they got close enough to do any damage. Had they been able to move around the flank, they might have captured the horses. Quickly Perry mounted his command and gave the order to move out. Parnell and his detachment provided cover fire, while Perry and his men got under way. Parnell then ordered his own men to mount, waiting until all of his men were in the saddle before beginning to look for his own horse. While he searched for the animal, his men rode off after Perry, and suddenly Parnell found himself alone and on foot. He shouted to the troops, now more them 100 yards distant, but none heard him.

Bullets whizzed past Parnell from every direction. He looked for a hiding place, but there was little cover to be found. He made up his mind that he would not be taken prisoner. If he had to, he would use his hunting knife and the little derringer that he always carried in his vest pocket. Breaking into a run, he struggled to catch the column. Finally some of his men missed him and reported his absence to Perry. The command halted, and one of the men caught a horse and led it back to him so that he was able to rejoin the column.

After the men covered another quarter of a mile, Perry gave the order "fours left" and directed Parnell to organize the party. The lieutenant divided the men of each company off, threw out the men of Company H as a skirmish line, and asked Perry to keep within a supporting distance of no more than 100 yards. Parnell deployed the line at unusually great intervals; he wanted a broad front, so that flanking movements would be more difficult. After a few words of instruction and caution, Parnell took his place beside the men and awaited the coming of the Nez Perce.

He did not have long to wait. The warriors charged with a yell, but the men remained steady. Not a shot was fired until the Indians were within 100 yards of the line and coming fast. Then Parnell gave the order to fire, and a volley knocked half a dozen Indian ponies to the ground. After the barrage, the command moved to the rear at a walk and halted a short distance away. Another volley kept the Nez Perce back. The Indians made several other attempts to drive the party off to the left toward Rocky Canyon, but every time they charged the right flank, the soldiers repulsed them.

During the retreat the force passed through a marsh, and Parnell noticed a man struggling over the swampy ground about halfway between the column and the Indians. He could just see the man's head bobbing above the tall grass. In a few more minutes, the Nez Perce would surely have him. The man was Pvt. Aman Hartman of Company H, who had lost his horse to an Indian bullet. Parnell de-

tailed a couple of men and charged to the rescue. Hartman mounted
behind one of the men and the little party rode back to the column,
which continued to move toward the settlements on Camas Prairie.[49]
A few miles from Mount Idaho, a band of armed citizens rode out to
meet the men and the Nez Perce finally abandoned the chase. The
weary force rode on to Grangeville and comparative safety. Sleep
was uppermost in the minds of the men. It was 10 o'clock in the
morning when they reached Grange Hall.

In Grangeville, Perry found Trimble and a number of other men
of both companies. The commander greeted the company officer
rather coolly. He had good reason to suspect that Trimble had deserted him. Apparently Perry did not ask Trimble for an explanation but kept his feelings to himself.

But what had happened to Trimble? About eighteen months
later, the officer told his story to a court of inquiry.

IV

TRIMBLE'S ACCOUNT

The bluffs were very high; it was some distance to the top. My
object there was to get on a high point that projected out on our left
and commanded a view of the whole ground. The Commanding Officer hollered out to me two or three times, "Trimble do you know
where you are going?" I hollered back that I was going to try and get
on that high point. I thought that would be the best place to see the
Indians coming in from that direction. As soon as I got high enough
up, I turned in the direction of that point. Some men were still going
further on.

I got on that point. I rode out on it pretty well; it seemed to be the
top of a ridge. A ridge ran right up to it. I saw two Indians riding up
this ridge towards where I was. I thought they were a good distance
off. I got off to adjust my saddle . . . . Two or three men were there
. . . . these Indians rode up quite close, though a little lower down on
the ridge, and I could see them dismount. I knew they would fire in a
minute, but I had not quite cinched up my saddle. I jerked my cinch
quickly. Just then one of them fired. The bullet went just under my
stirrups . . . . As soon as this Indian fired, I jumped on my horse, and
the only man I saw there was a Corporal of F Company. He was back
sitting on his horse. He had a gun. I hollered . . . [for him] to come
out where I was. I thought we could stay there a minute or two. Just
then another shot was fired by the other Indian. I suppose it was fired
at the Corporal. I heard the ball whistle. As it did not come very close
to me, I supposed it was fired at him. We both turned our horses and
galloped to where we saw a larger number of men to be. They were
galloping down from the ridge. They seemed to be all in motion.

I kept somewhat to the left along the edge of the bluffs, and I
looked down from these high bluffs and saw something glittering like

49. Affidavit of Aman Hartman, May 24, 1897, Parnell, Medal of Honor File.

water. I was afterwards told it was Salmon River. I then turned to the right and rode over to where I thought the main position of the men were. I came up to quite a number. They all seemed to be going to the rear . . . . Chapman was there too. I heard Chapman say "The House" [Johnson's ranch] was the only place where we could make a stand. I did not know what house he meant. He (Chapman) rode off very fast. All were galloping to the rear . . . . I kept along in the same direction.

I was going down a slope. In a hollow to the right, I saw a man without a hat, dismounted and running about. Sergeant Havens and myself rode down towards him and told him to hide himself in the bushes. The man ran into the bushes. The horses were jumping around, and it was hard to restrain them.

Two men of F Company rushed past me. Neither of them had guns. One of them was bareback. They seemed to be coming from another direction further to the right. I hollered to them several times to stop. Sergeant Havens remarked that they had no guns anyway. We started on some distance further and found one of these men lying in the road. His horse had thrown him and [he had] broke [n] his neck. I stopped long enough to see that the man was dead; [he] had broken his neck by a fall from his horse. Just then, considerably over to the right, I saw a large body of men galloping down into a ravine [Perry and Parnell]. There seemed to be 40 or 50. They disappeared very quickly. I saw then that there were only five or six men with me, two with guns: Sergeant Havens and Private Powers of H Company. The Sergeant told me he had but one cartridge and that was in his gun.

We seemed to be inclining to the left. Someone remarked we were going toward Craig's Mountain. There were some parties in front of us. Several men could be seen down in the valley, going across the valley. I supposed [they] were going in the direction of Craig's Mountain too. Am not positive. I said then that was not the proper direction to go. We ought to go towards Mount Idaho and turned to the right.

We got down into the lowlands then and went towards a house that was on the right. Going from that house were several men. Among them, was Chapman, a man on a white horse, going across the valley. There was some water near by, and I stopped some of the men. Two went on. We got off our horses and watered them. The men with me reported seeing two or three Indians on our right towards the mountain, and I heard one or two shots fired up in that direction. I mounted up and moved along slowly, and I thought I saw several men up near the timber. I was not positive whether I saw them or not.

After we moved along a mile or two, probably three miles, the men reported seeing a number of men moving along between us and the mountain. I halted them and sent a man, Private Powers of H Company, over to see if they were stragglers and bring them over to where we were. He came back in a little time and said that he could not get to where they were. There were fields and fences, so I moved on with the party towards Grangeville.

I met one man beside the three men left in camp. It was Mr. Crooks, the proprietor of the place. It [Grangeville] consisted of two or three houses, a mill, and a large hall stored with flour. The soldiers had the mules packed up ready to go off to Mount Idaho. Some of the men that had come in before had told them that there was a disaster. Mr. Crooks told me there was no one to defend the place, that he had rather die than lose all his property. It was all he had and asked me to stay and help him. Just then a citizen rode over from Mount Idaho about two miles off and wanted me to go to that place to defend it. I went with Mr. Crooks down to the Hall, and ordered the party down there [and] concluded to stay there. I discovered quite a party of men going along the mountain towards Mount Idaho. I sent two men to where they were to tell them where I was. A short time after Captain Perry came in with quite a large party.[50]

After he talked with Crooks and Trimble, Perry decided to go to Mount Idaho to inspect the fortifications erected there by the citizens. He ordered his men to make camp in Grangeville and departed. During his absence, Trimble and Parnell counted heads. Thirty-eight were missing, including Theller. Among those present, only two were wounded: Pvt. Thomas McLaughlin of Company F and Pvt. Joseph Kelly of Company H. McLaughlin suffered from a bullet wound in the right arm and Kelly from one in the left thigh.[51]

50. Trimble, CI, pp. 32–36.

51. Trimble, CI, pp. 36–37; Trimble, Report, p. 16; Muster Rolls of Companies F and H.

What They Said

They are dropping like hunted birds.

ABOUT ASLEEP

It was a wild, deadly racing with the warriors pressing hard to head them off.

WEYEHWAHTSISTKAN

Look at mangled flesh and shattered bones and see the lifeblood flow.

UPON THE PARAPET (POEM)
Copied in the Journal of Michael McCarthy

A quick keen searching glance makes it patent to him
That his life he can no longer hope to defend;
And so, bracing each muscle, and nerving each limb
For a last gallant effort, he waits for the end.

IN MEMORY OF LIEUTENANT THELLER (POEM)

I kind of thought that was the little girl that belonged to Jack Manuel's house. So I went out on me hands and knees and got her.

PATRICK BRICE

9

Incidents, Escapes, and Rescues

I

Yellow Wolf was one of those who raced ahead in the chase to catch the retreating soldiers. About one mile from the place where the fighting began, he encountered five enlisted men who had taken shelter behind some rocks. He dismounted and ran forward to strike one of them with his bow. The soldier was in the process of reloading when the Indian reached him. Yellow Wolf grabbed the barrel of the weapon and shoved hard, and the cavalryman went over backward. The warrior wrenched the gun free, while another Nez Perce administered the fatal blow. Seeing another soldier below him, Yellow Wolf jumped in an effort to reach him, but he fell short of his goal and, when his feet hit the ground, he slipped and sprawled in the grass. Quickly the soldier turned to fire, but he did not bring the weapon down far enough and the bullet passed over the warrior's shoulder. Up in a flash, Yellow Wolf succeeded in grasping the carbine, and the two men wrestled in desperation until a second Indian came up behind the soldier and fired point-blank. The man slumped to the ground, and Yellow Wolf was free. He noticed that a cavalryman on a distant point was starting to draw a bead on him, so he began to run from side to side up the hill to cover. A friend, seeing his predicament, picked up a rock and threw at the soldier. The missile struck the man just above the ear, and death was instantaneous.[1]

As they continued after the retreating soldiers, Yellow Wolf and the others came upon two dismounted men. The cavalrymen died quickly. North of the place where Perry and Trimble had turned to the left to scale the foothills and ascend the west wall of the canyon, Yellow Wolf and his companions cornered eight men in a dead-end ravine. Thorn bushes grew in the gulch and made it difficult for the

---

1. Yellow Wolf was about twenty-one years old. Well built and a fine athlete, he stood about five feet ten and one-half inches in height. McWhorter, *Yellow Wolf*, pp. 13–16, 58.

Nez Perce to get at them. With their backs to a rocky wall, these
soldiers put up a good fight. They died well.[2]

About Asleep and his brother, No Leggings On, joined in the
chase to the bluffs, but they were only boys and kept behind the
older men. Each time one of the warriors killed a cavalryman, the
young Indians stopped long enough to retrieve the man's pistol, and
in this way they collected a number of good sidearms before the
fighting ended.[3] Two Moons and Fire Body were in the forefront of
those who followed Perry and Trimble to the cattle trail. Not so
young as in other summers, they followed the soldiers only part way
up the mountain.[4] Arthur Simon was another Nez Perce who failed
to make it to the top of the west wall. His horse gave out, and he
decided to lead the animal back to camp. Suddenly he heard a warning call, which told him that a soldier stalked him. He whirled about.
The soldier was unarmed, but the warrior did not have time to use
his weapon before his enemy was upon him. The men grasped each
other and the fight became a simple test of strength, with the soldier
soon beginning to gain the upper hand. Fortunately for the warrior,
a tribesman came to the rescue and succeeded in dispatching his
attacker.[5]

Wounded Head arrived too late to participate in the close
fighting.[6] When he reached the battlefield, however, he did find one
dismounted soldier. The cavalryman leveled his weapon when the
Indian approached, but the warrior was the first to fire. The bullet
hit the soldier between the eyes. Dismounting, Wounded Head took
the carbine from the dead man and placed his own old cap-and-ball
revolver on his chest as a parting gift to a conquered foe.

2. Account of Roaring Eagle in McWhorter, *Hear Me*, p. 251n; McWhorter, *Yellow Wolf*, p. 59; Merrill D. Beal, *"I Will Fight No More Forever": Chief Joseph and the Nez Perce War* (Seattle: University of Washington Press, 1963), p. 56.

3. Account of About Asleep, *c.* 1906, item 49, packet 168, McWhorter Collection.

4. Account of Two Moons in McWhorter, *Hear Me*, p. 247.

5. Account of Arthur Simon as told to Camille Williams, item 19, packet 166, McWhorter Collection.

6. Wounded Head had had too much to drink. Wandering from camp while intoxicated, he had lost consciousness and fallen into some bushes. It was there that his
wife found him the next morning, after most of the men had already left to meet the
enemy. She was able to arouse him, and he quickly looked for his rifle, but it was not
to be seen. Mounting his horse, he rode after the rest of the men. Later he overtook
one of his tribesmen, and, stopping, he asked the man if he had his gun. The warrior
handed him an old pistol with the last powder and cap in place. Thinking that one
shot was better then none, Wounded Head accepted the offering and hurried ahead
to join in the fray. Account of Wounded Head in McWhorter, *Hear Me*, p. 240.

When Wounded Head reached the top of White Bird Hill, the soldiers were already gone, so he joined some other Indians who were rounding up Army horses. It was not long before they discovered two enlisted men who had been left behind in the retreat. The soldiers were brave, but they were soon overwhelmed and killed. The Indians stripped them of their arms and ammunition and then began to make their way back to camp.

As Wounded Head rode down the trail, he heard some of his tribesmen call to him to look on the hillside above him. He saw a white woman running up the bluff in a effort to escape and rode after her. Isabella Benedict made a sign, which he interpreted as a request for mercy.[7] He motioned for her to mount behind him, and she complied. Wounded Head asked the other Indians to take charge of her, but they refused. They did, however, relieve her of her watch, her jewelry, and her money. The warrior then carried his passenger to the bottom of White Bird Hill, where, according to Mrs. Benedict, some Indian women met them and persuaded the warrior to release her.[8] Once again she started for Mount Idaho.

There were many tasks to keep the victorious Nez Perce busy during the rest of the morning and early afternoon. The injured had to be cared for. Apparently there were four warriors who had suffered wounds in the battle, although the non-treaty Indians interviewed in later years mentioned only three:[9] Bow and Arrow Case, who had been shot in the right side during the early stages of

7. During the retreat, Isabella had been given a horse by William Coram and Private John Schorr, but she had been unable to control the frightened animal and had been thrown. Her children also had been placed on horses by the men, but they were more fortunate and returned to Mount Idaho with the retreating party. Benedict to Orchard and Dougherty, June 19, 1877; "William Coram," *North Idaho*, p. 493; Schorr in McWhorter, *Hear Me*, p. 235; Elsensohn, *Idaho County*, 1:528.

8. Wounded Head's version of the release of Mrs. Benedict is slightly different. He stated that he took a circuitous route down the hill, which hid him from the rest of the Nez Perce. Later he halted in a gulch and told the woman to dismount. He knew that she feared for her life, but he soon put her at ease. He told her how to make her way back to safety, and, after shaking hands, he continued back to the village. Account of Wounded Head in McWhorter, *Hear Me*, pp. 240–241; Benedict to Orchard and Dougherty, June 19, 1877; account of Isabella Benedict in Kirkwood, *Indian War*, p. 52.

9. Yuwishakaikt, one of the friendly Nez Perce captured in the battle, reported to an officer shortly after his return to Fort Lapwai that there were four warriors suffering from wounds. H. M. Chase of Lewiston also claimed that there were four wounded Indians, in a letter written on June 22 to the *The Daily Oregonian*. He had spoken with an Indian who had come directly from the Nez Perce camp. See Memorandum of Indian's Statement Relative to Fight with Colonel Perry, Letter no. 1451, Letters Received, DC, 1877; *The Daily Oregonian*, June 26, 1877, p. 3.

the retreat;[10] Land Above, who had been hit in the stomach;[11] and Four Blankets, who had a cut on the wrist received in a fall from his horse.[12] None had been killed.

There was also the matter of what to do with prisoners. All of the wounded cavalrymen had been killed during the fighting, but there were three agency Nez Perce who had been captured unharmed: Yuwishakaikt, Joe Albert, and Robinson Minthon. Yuwishakaikt had been detailed as a horse holder, and when the retreat began he joined in it; but before long his pony gave out, and he was taken into custody.[13] Albert and Minthon probably fell into the hands of the non-treaty Nez Perce for the same reason. However, Albert's father fought with the victors, and he intervened for his son.[14] Yuwishakaikt also had a relative in the village who pleaded in his behalf. The prisoners were secured for the night to await judgment by the chiefs when they convened in council the following day.

The Nez Perce made a careful search of the battleground to pick up arms and ammunition. Yuwishakaikt reported that the Indians recovered thirty-five or thirty-six weapons, but other Nez Perce interviewed in later years gave much higher figures.[15] Yellow Wolf claimed that there were sixty-three guns recovered, and Yellow Bull declared that there were ninety.[16]

After the search on the battlefield had been completed, the Indians returned to the camp to eat and rest. About 3 o'clock in the afternoon, Black Feather stood near the Manuel house on the river bottom. Three other Nez Perce sat on the ground nearby, enjoying a

10. Bow and Arrow Case received the wound about forty feet west of the later White Bird Monument on old U.S. Highway 95, near the end of the first diagonal ridge referred to by Perry. See account of Bow and Arrow Case in McWhorter, *Hear Me*, p. 253.

11. Land Above received the wound when he reached for the gun of a soldier who appeared to be dead. The man had been wounded but was still alive, and when the Indian attempted to obtain the weapon, the soldier pulled the trigger. McWhorter, *Yellow Wolf*, p. 60.

12. Four Blankets fell from the horse when fired at by one of the men in the dead-end ravine. Account of Philip Williams in McWhorter, *Yellow Wolf*, p. 60n.

13. Memorandum of Indian's Statement, Letters Received, DC; Statement of Yuwishakaikt, December 30, 1899, Nez Perce Claims, p. 103.

14. McWhorter, *Yellow Wolf*, p. 65.

15. Memorandum of Indian's Statement, Letters Received, DC.

16. McWhorter, *Yellow Wolf*, p. 61; Account of Yellow Bull in Curtis, *North American Indian*, 8:165. Perhaps the differences can be partially reconciled by considering that Yuwishakaikt may have been speaking of carbines only, while Yellow Wolf and Yellow Bull included revolvers in their estimates.

smoke after the hard day's fighting. Suddenly the warrior heard a rustling in the thicket and saw a white man and a little girl emerge from the underbrush. By the look of his clothes, the man was probably a miner or a farmer. The face was familiar to Black Feather, but the name did not come to him. The man did not carry a gun. The little girl wore a nightgown and was barefooted. The white man addressed him and requested permission to leave unmolested. He explained that he had had nothing to do with the trouble between the whites and Indians, and that his only wish was to reach friends on Camas Prairie, where he could have the girl cared for — she was wounded — and where he could get some food. Black Feather took pity on the man and child, but his companions were not feeling so charitable, and a heated discussion followed. Two Mornings wanted to shoot the white man, but Black Feather countered by asking the old warrior if he would be willing to care for the child once her guardian was dead, and the Indian relented. Finally the Nez Perce gave the refugees permission to leave, and, lifting the little girl into his arms, the white man departed.[17]

Patrick Brice had had some anxious moments while the Indians debated his fate. But he had been without food for five days and had reached the end of his endurance. His anxiety and fear took a back seat to his hunger and fatigue, and of course Maggie Manuel's suffering played heavily on the Irishman's sympathy and compassion. He had found the little girl in the thicket on Saturday morning. Her whimpering drew him to her hiding place. He had tried to comfort her as best he could: he wrapped her in a blanket and fetched water for her, but she was sick in mind as well as in body, and his ministrations had been only temporarily effective. She needed food

17. Account of Black Feather in McWhorter, *Hear Me*, pp. 216–217; Patrick Brice, "Nez Perce Outbreak." Brice mistook Black Feather for White Bird, and in his account of the affair the Irishman credited the chief with saving his life. In later years a story evolved that Brice had gained his freedom by awing the Indians with a cross tattooed on his breast, but that is probably untrue. Brice did not mention it in his first account, which is elaborate in detail. Black Feather denied having seen markings of any kind. Besides, the non-treaty Indians were non-Christians and did not hold the sign in reverence. In any event the story came to be accepted as fact, and, as the years passed, the tale grew to heroic proportions. Apparently it was nurtured and fed by Brice and eagerly swallowed and relished by all who heard it. The story reached the epitome of preposterousness in an article entitled "The Bravest Deed I Ever Knew," written by Charles Stuart Moody for the March, 1911, issue of *Century Magazine* (55:783–784). In it Moody related that Brice made a deal with the Nez Perce to return to the Indian camp after he had taken the girl to Mount Idaho. According to Moody, Brice offered to let the warriors work their will upon him after he had seen the girl placed in good hands. To cap the story, Moody had Brice return as promised and gain his freedom because the Nez Perce were impressed by his courage.

and medical attention and quiet surroundings so that she could re-
cuperate from the terrible shock of the past two days. Maggie told
Brice that during the night her mother had been stabbed to death by
an Indian and that her baby brother had also been killed. Before he
left for Mount Idaho, Brice entered the house and found it empty.
Nor was there any sign of Popham, whom he believed to be somewhere in the vicinity.

Brice was so weakened from his ordeal that he had to stop frequently to rest. By the time they were among the dead on the battlefield, Maggie had begun to realize that the real danger had passed, and she pointed out the fallen cavalrymen to Brice as he
trudged along. Once they came upon a dead man who had been
propped up by a thorn bush. His arms had been placed around the
shurb so that he appeared to be hugging it, and the thorns held his
clothing so that he continued to stand almost upright. A little later
they discovered another whose brains lay exposed. The upper part
of the head had been severed, probably in a fall from a horse.[18]

By nightfall they reached the Harris ranch near the head of
Rocky Canyon. All the doors and windows had been smashed in and
the house had been pillaged, but it provided the shelter they
needed. Brice found some bread, bacon, tea, and sugar and prepared supper. He also discovered an empty dry goods box, which he
fashioned into a chair in order to carry Maggie the rest of the way to
the settlement. In the morning he strapped the apparatus to his back
and the little girl scrambled aboard. They reached Mount Idaho on
Monday evening.[19]

II

But there was one cavalryman who still lived on White Bird battlefield. He was 1st Sgt. Michael McCarthy of Company H. A few
days after the fight occurred, McCarthy wrote an account of his ad-
ventures in his diary. The following excerpt tells the story of his
climb to safety:

> After falling I lay still a few minutes as much to rest myself as from
> fear of attracting attention, for my legs from the knees down were so
> tired that even when I did move I had to trail them after me and drag
> myself along by my hands. I crawled down the bed of a branch [of a

18. Statement of Brice, November 23, 1897, Brice 7427; Brice, "Nez Perce Outbreak."

19. George Popham, "Hostilities"; Account of Maggie Manuel Bowman in Defen-
bach, *Idaho*, 1:418. For other accounts written by Maggie Manuel see the *Walla Walla
Union Bulletin*, January 23, 1944, copy in packet 211-d, McWhorter Collection; and
Idaho County Free Press, April 1, 1903.

creek], wiggling like a snake so as not to disturb the top brush. The little creek had cut quite a deep channel, and in this channel I crawled down in the direction of the battlefield. After gaining about 100 yards in that direction unobserved, I lay perfectly still for about fifteen minutes, allowing the water to flow over my legs, and employing the time planning an escape. It was rather a difficult thing to attempt to leave the creek, for the hills were steep and bare upon both sides, and there was no doubt of there being Indians about. Shots, and some quite close, were heard at intervals and [also] that dreadful yell, which a couple of hours had rendered so familiar and, also, so certain a precursor of death to many.

Not daring to leave the creek I retraced my steps, if crawling back again could be called retracing my steps. I succeeded in getting a short distance above where I had fallen, crawling over a bare spot and into a clump of rose bushes, when I heard the patter of a pony's hoofs on the road above me. Two young warriors returning from the pursuit rode past my hiding place. [They were] so close that I could almost touch the blankets trailing by their pony's side, which they had flung across their saddles. It didn't seem possible that they could avoid seeing me, but they did not [see me], and one of them said as he passed as if addressing me: "Now will shoot your horses," and they passed on. A squaw also mounted came galloping down the road, another following. The first calling the young warriors back and using the chinook [jargon], she told them there was a soldier in the bushes, and she pointed to where I fell, about 75 or a hundred yards below. She described me quite accurately, not even forgetting my stripes and chevrons. She had evidently seen me when I fell in and was watching my hiding place, but I had crawled away from the spot she watched, it seems, unobserved by her. I had also already taken off my coat and hat, fearing the color would betray me and believing that my gray shirt would harmonize more with the color of the rocks, and because I heard of such things being done by others.

I crouched down closer in the channel and managed to conceal the lower part of my body, [with] my head in the thickest part of the bush and my right hand resting on a rock with pistol cocked, determined to have a shot if discovered. I did seriously think of shooting myself and avoid being captured alive, but I found life too sweet to commit suicide. But I was again lucky; the young warriors after firing a couple of shots, as I supposed in the bushes near where I fell, passed on. This gave me hope. I had already escaped death — almost certain death — 3 times that morning.

But as I am flattering myself that they have given up the search, my two squaw friends, accompanied [by] an old man, came riding up the road, passed by, and, arriving at the head of the branch 50 yards above me, came down again, riding in single file and peering into the brush as they went along. I could look into their faces as they leant [sic] down toward the bush in which I was concealed, and I could, if I so wished, grasp the muzzle of the old smoothbore musket that the old reprobate carried, did I dare not make a motion. But keeping him covered and trusting to my miraculous luck, I lay motionless, holding my breath and trying to stifle even the beating of my heart. It didn't

seem possible that I, who can see even the whites of their eyes [and]
note every detail of their dress, could myself remain invisible, but
these three vicious pairs of eyes with all their Indian acuteness again
pass me unobserved, and they disappear down the road. In a few
minutes the squaw so eager to find me rides back again up the road
and stops a little above me, where the bushes end and the road bends
to the right. I lay still a few minutes and looked at my watch. It is half
past six. I must be nearly an hour in the creek.

After mature deliberation, as the Courtsmartial say, I determined
to take up the steep hill behind me and if necessary fight for my life. I
am led to this step by reflecting that, when all the warriors return,
they will search thoroughly, if for nothing else [than] for arms and
ammunition; and again I will not . . . by taking the hill encounter
many, for it is on the other side that they have been fighting; and
again I am convinced that I am going to get out all right. This impression has been upon me from the first. So [I begin] stripping off my
boots; they are very long and heavy and would impede my movements. My limbs by this time, and through immersion no doubt, are as
supple as ever. Rising in the top of the bushes, I take a look down the
road and over the opposite hill and see no one stirring.

I commenced creeping up the hill that rises on the right hand as
one goes into the canyon. [After] arriving at a little bench ½ half way
up and I lay flat, pause for breath, and still see no one moving.
Another burst and I reached the top. Looking down to where I
crawled out of, about 50 yards above [I] see my lady friend lying on a
buffalo robe and her pony grazing by her side. They make a very
pretty picture. She was steeped in reverie. Perhaps she was thinking of
her lover, for she was quite young, or more likely she was enjoying in
anticipation the delights of cutting my humble self in the artistic manner practised by her race.

I turned my eyes in another direction. In the direction taken by
the retreating troops and on a hill overlooking the prairie, I saw a
mounted Indian sitting stationary on his horse; he is fully 500 yards
distant. Back of me rose another hill upon which were growing pine
trees, the advance guard of the forest around Mt. Idaho. Below and to
the left was the battlefield in full view. It looked so still, not a soul
moving on its surface. I looked along the ravines that run back to the
woods and to the creek, expecting to see some other unfortunate trying to escape, and although I was so placed that no movement could
escape me, I saw none. All below me must have ere this been dispatched, and it was barely two hours since the first shot was fired.
How many there were I could only guess.[20]

McCarthy found cover in the woods and after resting began the
trip back to Mount Idaho — which turned out to be much longer

20. McCarthy, Diary, June 17, 1877. This account was probably written on June
20. The narrative has been partially punctuated and paragraphed for greater read-
ability.

than he had anticipated because of an initial mistake in directions. On the morning of June 19, the tired and hungry sergeant made contact with some settlers five miles from Grangeville, and his ordeal was over.

III

The morning after the battle, Rainbow, Five Wounds, and a small party of warriors rode into the Indian camp; they had just returned from hunting buffalo in Montana. Their arrival was cause for rejoicing, because they were experienced in matters of war and the people looked to them for advice and leadership. The fighting Indians joined the chiefs and elders in council to determine the fate of the prisoners and to plan the next move.[21]

The chiefs decided to give the captured Nez Perce their freedom but promised them that if they helped the soldiers again, they would be caught and whipped with hazel switches. Yuwishakaikt left immediately and rode a horse to death before he reached Fort Lapwai on June 19.[22] Joe Albert also returned to his home,[23] but Robinson Minthon decided to remain with the non-treaty bands. Days later, when the caravan reached Kamiah, he took his leave and returned to his people.[24]

The men spent the next hours in careful deliberation. Obviously the blue-coats would soon return in force, and the Nez Perce did not want to fight them unless it was necessary. Rainbow and Five Wounds had a plan, and it satisfied the majority. They proposed removal to the opposite bank of the Salmon River, where they could find shelter in the mountains. If the soldiers chose to follow them, they could double back and recross the stream at another place. They knew that white men had an inordinate amount of trouble in crossing rivers, and they could lead Cut Arm Howard and his men on a merry chase. When the time came to fight, they would fight.[25]

21. McWhorter, *Yellow Wolf*, pp. 61–62. The council took place just within the corporate limits of the town of Whitebird at a point a short distance north of the original route of U.S. Highway 95.

22. Testimony of Yuwishakaikt, December 30, 1899, Nez Perce Claims, p. 103.

23. Albert later rejoined the non-treaty Nez Perce during the Clearwater Battle, after he learned that his father had been killed in the fighting at Cottonwood July 4–5. McWhorter, *Yellow Wolf*, p. 65.

24. Because he stayed with the victors for a short time, Minthon earned the emnity of his agency associates and became an outcast to both sides. McWhorter, *Yellow Wolf*, p. 65.

25. McWhorter, *Yellow Wolf*, pp. 63, 69; Josephy, *Nez Perce Indians*, p. 527.

Later in the day, the women broke camp and the village moved up the Salmon River to Horseshoe Bend. There was a good crossing place nearby. The fortified settlers at Slate Creek noticed the activity and feared that their time had come, but later some of the Nez Perce came to talk with them under a flag of truce. They were friendly. The Indians told them about the battle with the soldiers and related a number of incidents connected with it. A few of the Nez Perce owed small amounts to John Wood for articles purchased in his store, and because of the uncertain future many of them paid their debts. While the Indians were talking, Tolo came out of the stockade, upbraided them for killing her friends, and told them that she intended to stay with the whites. H. W. Cone heard one of the Indians say that Mrs. Manuel had been killed by a warrior who had had too much bad whiskey.[26]

On June 19, the Nez Perce crossed the river. They had only one canoe, but they were able to fashion a number of adequate vessels out of buffalo skins and willows. These were circular in shape, and the men hitched two, three, or four horses to them, depending on the size of the craft. Tepee covers, cooking pots, pans, blankets, and the rest of their paraphernalia filled the boats. Women, children, and old people climbed to the tops of the piles, and the ponies plunged into the swift current. Warriors swam on either side of the boats to steady them, and they reached the opposite bank without incident. Thirty warriors remained behind. Their mission was to watch for the soldiers on Camas Prairie.[27]

IV

After Michael McCarthy awoke on the morning of June 20, he decided to see if he could do something about replacing his footwear. The rubber miner's boots he had found on his way back to Grangeville had served him well, but he needed something sturdier to see him through the campaign that he knew would follow. In Mount Idaho he found what he needed. As a patriotic gesture, storekeeper Rudolph presented the veteran with a pair of good boots, a hat, and a pair of gloves.[28]

26. Cone, "White Bird Battle," pp. 5–6. Robert Bailey erroneously stated that Cone had written that Yellow Bull had bragged to the settlers of Mrs. Manuel's presence in his camp. See Bailey, *River of No Return*, p. 188. Cone's statement is as follows: "She [Tolo] began to talk upbraiding them for killing their friends and hers, and Mrs. Manuel, who we learned from them 'one of them had killed, who was full of bad whiskey.' "

27. McWhorter, *Yellow Wolf*, pp. 62–63.

28. After the war had ended, Rudolph had second thoughts and presented McCarthy with a bill for the items. See note in McCarthy, Diary, June 20, 1877.

The thought of the fate of those left behind lay heavily on the minds of the men and the settlers. Among those still missing and presumed dead were Lt. Theller, Cpl. Lee, Cpl. Curran, Trumpeter Marshall, Saddler Galvin, and Pvts. Crawford, Edwards, Kavanagh, Morrisey, Murphy, Nielson, Shea, Simpson, and Werner of Company H, and Sgt. Gunn, Sgt. Ryan, Cpl. Fuller, Cpl. Thompson, Trumpeter Jones, and Pvts. Armstrong, Blaine, Burch, Colbert, Connolly, Dauch, Donne, Hurlbert, Lewis, Liston, Martin, Mosforth, Quinlan, Schullein, Shaw, Sullivan, and White of Company F.[29] In order to learn the condition and disposition of the dead, the citizens asked Perry if he would be willing to accompany a scouting party to the battlefield. The officer agreed to support the party, and on the morning of June 21 the reconnaissance party left Grangeville and marched toward the scene of disaster. A large body of citizens led the expedition, and most of the remnant of Perry's force followed.

En route they passed a wounded horse and discovered the body of one unfortunate cavalryman. Teams designated by Perry visited outlying ranches as they moved forward and collected items of value. They saw nothing of the hostiles on the prairie or in the foothills.

At Johnson's ranch, Perry halted his men. As previously agreed, the citizens continued forward and apparently reached the head of White Bird Canyon. Along the way they encountered two Chinese, who had just passed through the Indian camp. The men had not been molested. They erroneously reported that the Nez Perce had lost several warriors in the battle. Completing their reconnaissance, the volunteers returned to Perry's camp and the party moved back to Grangeville, reaching it before dark. After reinforcements arrived, they would have the strength they needed to make a careful search of the battleground.[30]

29. Muster Rolls of Companies H and F. See also J. W. Redington, "Battle of White Bird Canyon, Idaho, June 17, 1877," *Winners of the West* (April 30, 1929), 4:2.

30. McCarthy, Diary, June 21, 1877; Perry to Forsyth, *c.* October 21, 1878.

Josiah Red Wolf, last survivor of the Nez Perce War

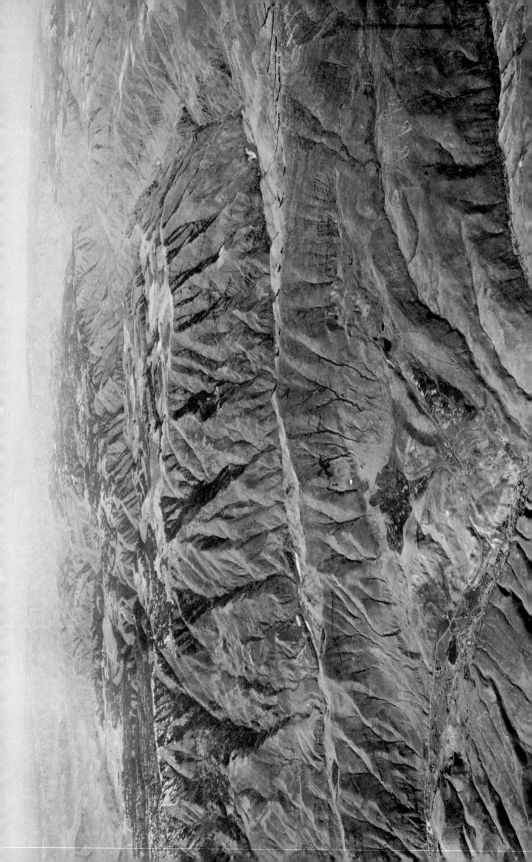

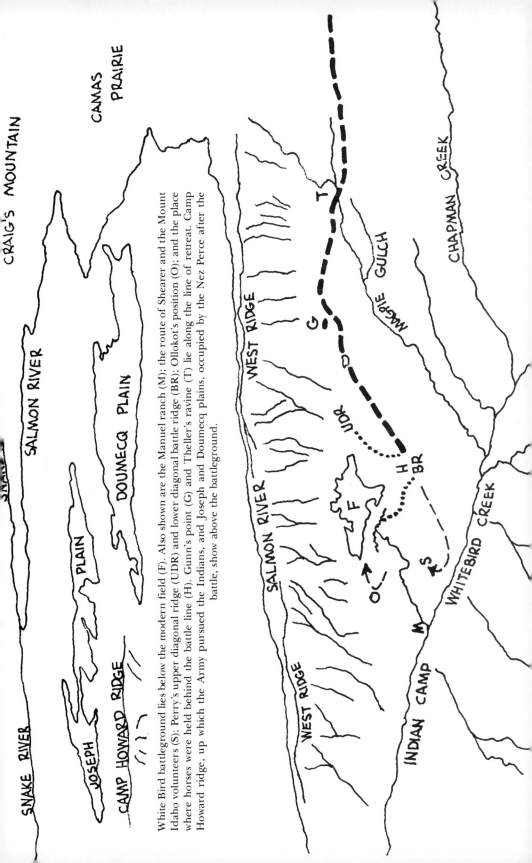

White Bird battleground lies below the modern field (F). Also shown are the Manuel ranch (M); the route of Shearer and the Mount Idaho volunteers (S); Perry's upper diagonal ridge (UDR) and lower diagonal battle ridge (BR); Ollokot's position (O); and the place where horses were held behind the battle line (H). Gunn's point (G) and Theller's ravine (T) lie along the line of retreat. Camp Howard ridge, up which the Army pursued the Indians, and Joseph and Doumecq plains, occupied by the Nez Perce after the battle, show above the battleground.

SNAKE RIVER

CRAIG'S MOUNTAIN

CAMAS PRAIRIE

SALMON RIVER

JOSEPH PLAIN

DOUMECQ PLAIN

CAMP HOWARD RIDGE

WEST RIDGE

SALMON RIVER

WEST RIDGE

MAGPIE GULCH

CHAPMAN CREEK

WHITEBIRD CREEK

INDIAN CAMP

Above: Lapwai, as drawn for *Harper's Weekly,* August 18, 1877

Right: The Benedict ranch. The battleground lay over the ridge to the right.

Below: The hawthorn tree that supported Sgt. Patrick Gunn's body

Arthur Chapman, with an unidentified Indian

Michael McCarthy

Joel G. Trimble

William R. Parnell

Oliver O. Howard

Looking Glass (William Henry Jackson photograph, 1871)

Peo-Peo-Tahlikt

Yellow Bull

Joseph in 1890, when he came to the Nez Perce reservation to meet with U.S. Government allotting agent Alice Fletcher.

NO. 7. SOLDIERS MONUMENT ON NEZ PERCE BATTLEFIELD, WHITEBIRD, IDAHO.
BATTLE OF WHITEBIRD 1877. NORTH AND SOUTH HIGHWAY.

Idaho State Historical Society

The Nez Perce encampment at Lapwai in 1905

What They Said

KEEP COOL GENTLEMEN

Some of our exchanges are sounding a false alarm about probable Indian outbreaks in the different localities. Facts are enough without drawing largely upon the imagination, and making mere possibilities certainties.

LEWISTON TELLER

The almost unanimous opinion among those who live about the seat of war in Mount Idaho and have witnessed its operation, is that the commanding officer is a very pleasant and amiable gentleman, undoubtedly a good military man, according to the doctrines of West Point, but no Indian fighter. Scores of facts are related which have established this belief. The sheep is a very pleasant and amiable animal and has none but sterling qualities, but we do not expect him to chase wolves and coyotes; we assign the task to the dog – also an amiable brute, but better adapted to the purpose.

NORMAN B. WILLEY

Imagine these corpses in an advanced state of decomposition, the flesh falling from their faces, glaring with glazed eyeballs upon us, their comrades.

E. J. BUNKER

Knowing as I do that your columns are always open for any news idea that may enhance the interest of our country and settle the present difficulty with Joseph and his followers, I would with your permission speak of my idea for subduing, capturing and reclaiming our Indian brethren. Some propose that the General and his Aid secure the services of the Tennessee Jubilee Singers and give the poor Indian daily entertainments to be followed with a general outpouring of the soul (not blood). Others propose a protracted meeting. But all these plans consume time. My idea is to set traps in the hills to be baited with a late peace policy, let strings be attached to each trap, the string extended to the Fort (as the Indian Agent is there at present to "Hold the Fort,") and as the struggles of the poor Lo will disturb the string as well as trap, he is readily hauled in, washed, fed, redressed, and can be converted in half the time it will require to organize a Jubilee Band or send to Webbfoot for well broken in female revival material. Hoping you as well as the Head of our Military Department will ponder well before again persecuting the poor Indian.

SCOUT

He who led the young men is dead. It is cold and we have no blankets. The little children are freezing to death. My people, some of them, have run away to the hills and have no blankets, no food; no one knows where they are, perhaps freezing to death. I want time to look for my children and see how many of them I can find. Maybe I shall find them among the dead. Hear me, my chiefs, I am tired; my heart is sick and sad. From where the sun now stands, I will fight no more forever.

JOSEPH

10

Burying the Dead

I

General Howard went to bed early on the evening of June 16. About 10 o'clock, he was awakened by loud talking coming from the front porch of his quarters and went out to investigate. Two Indian women sat on horses, and the larger of the two was the source of the noise. She shouted in her native tongue; and since Howard did not speak the language, he ordered a half-breed to interpret for him. The woman turned out to be the wife of Jonah Hayes, one of the agency Nez Perce who had just come from the Indian village with bad news: Perry and all his men, including Jonah and the rest of the scouts, had been killed by the hostiles. The Indians, she said, laid a trap for the cavalrymen, and they had ridden right into it.[1]

Howard was not disturbed by the report, however. He had already received a message from Grangeville, and he knew that the command had reached the settlement in safety that afternoon. But he did prepare a letter for Perry the next morning in which he cautioned the officer to beware of traps and told him that he might expect reinforcements soon. Howard expected other troops to reach Fort Lapwai in another day.

On the afternoon of June 17, Howard received the stunning news of Perry's defeat. Some of the Indian scouts were the first to return to Fort Lapwai with the story. The first cavalrymen to arrive were Cpl. Charles Fuller and Pvt. John White of Company F, who were apparently among those who had bolted during the early stages of the fight.[2] When they had not appeared at Grangeville after the battle, Perry had given them up for lost. The knowledge of the men was incomplete; they feared that Perry and the rest of their

---

1. Unless otherwise indicated, the material used in this chapter comes from Howard, *Nez Perce Joseph*, pp. 118–146.

2. McCarthy, CI, p. 84. A native of Massachusetts, Fuller had enlisted on October 25, 1873. He was about twenty-six years old. White had been born in Brooklyn, New York, in about 1850. He was one of the few soldiers in the company who had served more than one enlistment. Registry of Enlistments, 1873, 1875.

comrades had been wiped out and that the Nez Perce might be on their way to attack the post.

Acting upon their fears, Howard quickly designated his quarters as a rallying point and had it barricaded with cord wood.[3] Not until the following day did Howard learn the full extent of the disaster. Joe Rabusco came riding in with Perry's report. Before he retired on the evening of June 17, Perry had written:

DEAR GENERAL HOWARD. — I made the reconnaissance foreshadowed in my last letter. I made the attack at 4 a.m. on what was supposed to be only a portion of the main camp, and for the purpose of recapturing some of the large bands of stock taken from settlers in the vicinity of this place, and the possibility of dealing the Indians a telling blow. The camp proved to be the main camp of Joseph's and Whitebird's bands situated on the Salmon or White-bird river at the mouth of the latter. The fight resulted most disastrously to us, in fact scarcely exceeded by the magnitude of the Custer Mas[sacre] in proportion to the numbers engaged. As soon as the Indians made their shots tell, the men were completely demoralized. It was only by the most strenuous efforts of Col Parnell and myself in organizing a party of 22 men, that a single officer or man reached camp. The casualties, are as far as I heard from "F" Co. 1 commissioned officer (Lt. Theller) and 22 enlisted men killed and missing, H company 15 enlisted men killed and missing. Some of the missing will I think come in to-night probably not many. Lt. Theller was killed on the field. The Indians fought us (Parnell and myself with our squad) to within 4 miles of Mt. Idaho and gave it up, on seeing that we would not be driven any farther except at our own gait.

We have been fighting and riding without sleep since leaving Lapwai. We saw about 125 Indians today and they are well armed, a great many of our guns and much ammunition must have fallen into their hands. I think it will require at least 500 men to whip them. All of my friendly Indians left for Lapwai before I got in and in consequence I have been much troubled to procure a messenger. I have promised him a fresh horse from Lapwai to Lewiston. Please see that he gets it. The messenger will return immediately if desired. Please send word to Mrs. Perry that I am safe. Am too tired to write.

Joe Rabusco can be of no further use to me. Please have him discharged. If the Indians emboldened by success return to Camas Prairie it would not be prudent to send the Pack Train. Neither should I like to escort it, [because I only have] the remnant of my two Companies.

The only thing I really need is ammunition as I can with your sanction purchase subsistence stores here. Please break the news of her husband's death to Mrs. Theller.[4]

3. Assistant Surgeon John Fitzgerald, Report for June, 1877, Medical History of Fort Lapwai, Records of the Office of the Surgeon General, Office of the Adjutant General; McCarthy, Diary, June 21, 1877.

4. Perry to Howard, June 17, 1877, Letters Received, DC.

Howard laid the letter aside and went to call on Delia Theller. He endeavored to control himself and break the news gently, but before he could speak Delia read the message in his face. "Oh, my husband!" she cried. After the first shock of the realization of the death of her husband had passed, the widow regressed into a twilight world of false hopes. She maintained a belief that Theller would eventually be found asleep or that he would be rescued from captivity. She kept the lieutenant's uniform neatly pressed in anticipation of his return.[5]

As the news of the defeat spread over the countryside, ranchers, townsfolk, missionaries, agency employees, and friendly Indians flocked to Fort Lapwai for protection. Even the residents of far distant Kamiah, including the lady missionary Miss Kate McBeth, moved to the post under the guardianship of James Lawyer and Black Eagle, a nephew of Chief Joseph.[6]

Panic followed panic as the whites waited for the Nez Perce to sweep down on them. On one occasion, when two Indians rode rapidly toward the post, someone cried out that the hostiles were coming. The result was chaos. Officers scrambled to a nearby hilltop, enlisted men hurriedly barricaded the doors and windows of the most defensible buildings, women clutched rifles they did not know how to use, and children flitted hither and thither among them. It turned out that the Indians were friendly. They were simply trying to escape from some white man who had fired on them in an attempt to get their firearms.

By June 21, eight companies had arrived from various western outposts and were ready to move to the scene of the outbreak. Col. Alfred Sully of the Twenty-first Infantry answered a call to take charge of the defense of the Lewiston area, while Howard prepared to lead the expedition against the hostiles. On June 22, Howard marched out of Fort Lapwai with 227 regulars, 20 civilian volunteers from Walla Walla, and a large number of packers and guides. The military force consisted of Companies E and L of the First Cavalry, Companies B, D, E, H, and I of the Twenty-first Infantry, and Company E of the Fourth Artillery. Two Gatling guns and a mountain howitzer served for armament. More troops were on the way and would join the force later.[7]

5. Robert Pollock to his wife, June 27, 1877, in Robert W. Pollock, *Grandfather, Chief Joseph and Psychodynamics* (Caldwell, Idaho: Caxton Printers, 1964), p. 55.

6. "Blackeagle, Chief Joseph's Nephew, Has Passed Away," *The Nez Perce Indian* (Lapwai Agency) (1918), 14:1.

7. Brown, *Flight of the Nez Perce*, pp. 144–146; Josephy, *Nez Perce Indians*, p. 530.

The expedition left Fort Lapwai about noon and traveled twenty-four miles before going into camp at Junction Trail. Reveille sounded at 4:30 the next morning, and by 1:30 the command had reached Cottonwood House, a distance of forty-three miles from Fort Lapwai. Howard decided to remain in camp in order to gather intelligence concerning the whereabouts of the non-treaty bands. The next day, June 24, Perry arrived from Grangeville to deliver his verbal report. As they talked, Perry conveyed to Howard his dissatisfaction with Trimble's performance. Perry did not believe, however, that the officer's conduct called for disciplinary action. While Trimble's conduct was not above reproach, it had not been vital in determining the outcome of the battle. In Perry's mind the battle had been lost when the left of the line had disintegrated.[8]

Howard decided to send Trimble and Company H to the relief of the settlers at Slate Creek. He needed to protect the settlement in the event that he had to drive the Indians in that direction, and he needed a cover for his left flank as he moved toward the hostiles. Company H had been strengthened on June 23 with the arrival of 2d Lt. Thomas T. Knox and ten men, some of whom had been with him on detached service at Fort Walla Walla and some of whom were apparently recruits. In all there were about thirty well-armed men. Because the Nez Perce stood between them and Slate Creek, the detachment had to circle around the Indians by a little-used and difficult trail. Trimble planned to follow an old mining trail to Florence and then double back to the northeast to reach the settlement. About 6 o'clock in the morning on June 25, Company H rode out of camp.[9]

At the same time, Howard resumed his march. He took the cavalry and rode into Grangeville, sending the infantry ahead to wait for him at Johnson's ranch. After spending about an hour in the little hamlet gathering information and examining supplies that J. W. Crooks made available to the expedition, Howard set out for Mount Idaho.

In the days preceding Howard's arrival, a number of the missing had reached the safety of the settlement. Patrick Brice and Maggie Manuel had been among the first. George Popham had arrived a day later. He had waited until he saw the hostiles burn the Manuel house before attempting to make his way to Camas Prairie. Isabella Benedict had been rescued on Monday by Edward Robie. After it

8. Perry, CI, p. 123.

9. Muster Roll of Company H; McCarthy, Diary, June 24 and 25, 1877; Brown, *Flight of the Nez Perce*, p. 157.

had been reported that Isabella had been left behind in the retreat, Robie went out alone to find the woman whom he had long admired. His search had been rewarded near Johnson's ranch. William George, who had left Mason and Osborn on the night of June 13, had finally reached Mount Idaho. H. C. Brown, his sister, and her husband had been found near Cottonwood House. Isabella Benedict reported that George Woodward and Peter Bertrand had been killed at the Baker ranch, but Woodward walked into Mount Idaho shortly after Howard arrived.[10]

After visiting the fort erected near Mount Idaho in company with H. W. Croasdaile, Howard went to Brown's Hotel to address the principal citizens of the community. In a short speech, he promised them safety and vengeance:

> We have now taken the field in good earnest; more troops are on the way to join us. I propose to take prompt measures for the pursuit and punishment of the hostile Indians, and wish you to help me, in the way of information and supplies, as much as lies in your power. I sympathize deeply with you in the loss of life, and in the outrages to which your families have been subjected, and you may rest assured that no stone will be left unturned to give you redress, and protection in the future.[11]

After the talk, Howard visited the wounded. They were now under the care of Dr. John Morris, the resident physician, who had been in Portland on a trip when news of the outbreak reached him.[12] Dr. Morris had been a busy man since his arrival. Howard learned that Lew Day was dead. Dr. Morris had amputated the scout's leg in an effort to save his life, but the shock had been too much for him. He had been buried in the Masonic cemetery. Joe Moore was still alive but in critical condition. Mrs. Norton and Mrs. Chamberlin were there, as was the Chamberlin girl. Theodore Swarts and Herman Faxon had been badly wounded in the White Bird fight and required continual care. George Shearer had received a shoulder wound, but it was slight and easily treated. William

10. George Popham, "Hostilities"; Kirkwood, *Indian War*, pp. 52–53; Woodward, August 16, 1890, Morris 2718.

11. Howard, *Nez Perce Joseph*, p. 139.

12. John Baker Morris was born in Knoxville, Missouri, on October 1, 1850. A graduate of St. Louis Medical College, he began practicing medicine in Mount Idaho in 1875. Accounts conflict concerning the date of his return to Mount Idaho following the outbreak, but according to his official biography he reached the settlement on June 22. "John Baker Morris, M.D.," in James H. Hawley, editor, *History of Idaho* (Chicago: S. J. Clarke, 1920), 4:9; *Tenth Biennial Report of the Board of Trustees of the State Historical Society of Idaho, 1925–1926* (Boise: The Society, 1926), p. 65.

George, H. C. Brown, Albert Benson, and Maggie Manuel were also on his list of patients, and all were recovering rapidly.[13]

After lunching at Rudolph's with the Croasdailes and some others, Howard left Mount Idaho with the cavalry to join the infantry at Johnson's ranch. At the camp, Howard received a message that his reinforcements were on the way and would reach him in a couple of days.

II

After Trimble and his men reached Florence late on June 25, they halted momentarily to gather the latest information and then covered twelve more miles before stopping for a quick bite to eat. After supper, they resumed their journey. The trail at this point ascended the mountains. It was very steep, and near the summit the snow lay deep. The men traveled along the mountaintop for some distance and then gradually descended toward the Salmon River. It was a clear, moonlit night, and the view was almost worth the effort. "It would take a more eloquent pen than mine," wrote Sgt. McCarthy, "to portray the beautiful scenery it was our privilege to witness."[14]

Trimble reached his destination about 2:30 on the morning of June 26. The settlers welcomed them heartily, and after some confusion the men obtained shelter for themselves and corrals for their animals. The defenses erected by the settlers impressed the soldiers: William Wilson had done his work well.

On June 26, the cavalrymen rested and allowed their horses to shake the fatigue of the hard ride. The next morning, Trimble made a reconnaissance in the direction of White Bird Creek. Many of the settlers trailed after the scouting party and collected stray stock. Some of them found ponies belonging to the Nez Perce which they confiscated. Most of the women and children ventured forth — some of them for the first time in a week. In fact, the cavalrymen saw everyone except Helen Walsh and Elizabeth Osborn. Overcome with shame, the women remained in their quarters.[15] Although the general feeling was one of relief and even gaiety, there was an undercurrent of uneasiness and uncertainty. The Nez Perce were still somewhere in the vicinity. Although the settlers had been told that

13. Elsensohn, *Idaho County*, 2:523; "From the Scene of Hostilities," *Lewiston Teller*, April 13, 1878, p. 2; Sears, "Mount Idaho."

14. McCarthy, Diary, June 25, 1877.

15. *Ibid.*, June 26, 27, 1877.

Howard was in the field, there had been no reports of his movements.

III

At 6:30 on the morning of June 26, Howard broke camp and led his men toward White Bird Canyon. His purpose in going there was twofold. First, he hoped to determine the location of the hostiles. He did not, however, wish to engage them; only after he had been properly reinforced would he be willing to venture an attack. Perry's defeat had given him respect for his foe. His other reason concerned a matter of honor. The dead had to be buried; they had been almost nine days in the sun.

Howard tapped the Walla Walla volunteers for the scouting mission. With Ad Chapman as their guide, the citizens moved along the top of the west wall of the canyon, retracing in part the route taken by Perry in the retreat. Eventually they reached a vantage point that permitted them a good view of the Salmon River. Looking down the canyon, they saw Nez Perce on distant hills across the stream.

In the meantime, Howard made arrangements to recover the dead. He left the artillery and a company of cavalry on White Bird Hill to cover his advance and then ordered the rest of his command to descend to the site of the encounter. Capt. Marcus Miller led the advance guard, and a company of cavalry under Capt. Henry Winters followed close behind.[16] Perry organized the search for the bodies.

The men moved cautiously over the valley floor. They never forgot what they saw. Here and there were decaying bodies, blackened by sun and swollen into unrecognizable shapes. The smell of putrefying flesh filled the air. The men who had been detailed as the burial party dug shallow graves with bayonets. The bodies were unmanageable. The ripe flesh had lost its tensility; a pull on an arm disengaged it from its torso. After some grisly experimentation, the men discovered that the best way to manipulate a corpse was to roll it into a hole dug as close to it as possible. The men had to seek relief from the stench as the work progressed. Occasionally a man dropped his entrenchment tool and sped for fresher air and then returned to renew the task.[17]

16. A native of Massachusetts, Miller graduated from West Point in 1858. He attained the rank of captain in the Fourth Artillery on May 11, 1864. Winters served in the Ohio Infantry in 1861–1862 and rose to the rank of captain. In 1864 he enlisted in the First Cavalry and rose through the ranks to become an officer on March 13, 1865. He was promoted to captain on June 25, 1876. Heitman, *Historical Register*, 1: 711, 1051.

17. Lt. Harry Lee Bailey to his parents, June 27, 1877, item 108, packet 180, McWhor-

Many of the bodies had been stripped of outer clothing, but some had not been touched. No firearms were found on the field. Other hands held them now. To some of the men, it looked as if some of the cavalrymen had been scalped, but the Nez Perce later denied mutilation. One officer later remarked that although there was an appearance of scalping in some cases, it had been caused by decay rather than by violent ripping or tearing of the skin.[18]

The men were ever on the lookout for the return of the enemy, and there were a few anxious moments. As they proceeded down the canyon, they discovered the body of the trooper in the hawthorn tree. From a distance it appeared so lifelike that it was mistaken for an Indian and approached with weapons cocked. The corpse was identified as Sgt. Patrick Gunn. One man remembered that the gray-haired veteran had been badly wounded in the retreat, and although a horse had been brought for him he had been unable to mount it. The body had been ripped and torn by bullets, and there were other indications that the sergeant had been long in dying.[19]

Later in the day, while the men were busy at their work, the sky darkened as a great cloud moved overhead. Suddenly, two or three sheets of flame shot from the cloud and struck one of the buttes. The roar of the thunder sounded like a series of rifle volleys. The men dropped to their knees and prepared for the attack they believed was coming, but they soon realized that it was only thunder. To one soldier, in retrospect, "it seemed like the burial volley for the honorable dead."[20]

The burial party interred eighteen men before rain forced them

---

ter Collection; George Francis Brimlow, editor, "Nez Perce War Diary — 1877 of Private Frederick Mayer of Troop L, 1st United States Cavalry," in *Seventeenth Biennial Report of the Board of Trustees of the Idaho Historical Society, 1939–1940* (Boise: The Society, 1940), p. 48; E. J. Bunker in Kirkwood, *Indian War*, p. 5; George Hunter, *Reminiscences of an Old Timer* (San Francisco: H. S. Crocker and Co., 1887), p. 306.

18. Account of Lieutenant Bailey in McWhorter, *Hear Me*, p. 259; See also Memorandum of Indian's Statement, Letters Received, DC; *Idaho Tri-Weekly Statesman*, July 3, 1877; Account of John Schorr in McWhorter, *Hear Me*, p. 257.

19. Bailey to McWhorter, December 7, 1930, item 4, packet 180, McWhorter Collection; Coughlin, CI, p. 104; H. W. Cone in Bailey, *River of No Return*, p. 187. Frank Fenn claimed Gunn died in as "fair a duel as ever was fought." Civilians Fenn and Faxon were the last two volunteers in the line of retreat. They were perhaps fifty yards from Gunn when he and a Nez Perce warrior, also on foot, began their duel. The men were probably fifteen paces apart. Each fired four or five shots before the sergeant was hit and fell. Frank Fenn in the *Kooskia Mountaineer*, September 3, 1925.

20. Bailey to McWhorter, December 7, 1930.

to abandon their work. The graves were shallow and the bodies barely covered with earth. Stones stacked on top of the burials promised to keep coyotes from disturbing the graves. Some of the men drove stakes into the ground at the head of the trenches and hung the hats of the deceased upon them. But there were several bodies that the men did not have time to bury, so they were covered with blankets and left for another day. The troops were not able to find the body of Lieutenant Theller.[21]

While the dead found a resting place, some of the command rode all the way down the canyon to White Bird Creek. In an outhouse not far from the charred remains of the Manuel house, they discovered its owner. Jack Manuel possessed a will to live. For thirteen days he had endured suffering and privation that would have defeated most men. He had been shot through both hips, and his hands were his only means of propulsion. He had lain in the brush for days before dragging himself to the shed. With the aid of a hunting knife, Manuel had been able to extract the four-inch barb from his neck, and he had made a compress for the wound out of horseradish leaves. Haws and other wild berries had been his only fare, and he had reached the point in starvation where hunger no longer gnawed at his belly. The men fashioned a litter from a broken buggy and carried him back to the camp. The next day, they sent him back to Mount Idaho. In time he would regain the power to walk and work, but he would never be the same.[22]

Ad Chapman examined what was left of the ranch house to see if he could find a trace of the remains of Jennet Manuel and her son. He found some bones in the embers, but they appeared to be of animal rather than human origin.[23]

After Howard returned to camp, he wrote a letter to E. C. Watkins at the agency. In it he gave his analysis of the White Bird Battle:

> White Bird is a wide, rough valley, narrow at the mouth, with an ascent of at least two miles of steep trail to get out of it. The superiority of the Indian ponies in climbing the mountain gave the Indians great advantage after the first break of our cavalry, and nothing but the

21. Bailey to parents, June 27, 1877; Brimlow, "Nez Perce War Diary," p. 28; *Idaho Tri-Weekly Statesman*, July 3, 1877, p. 1; Brown, *Flight of the Nez Perce*, p. 160.

22. Statement of Manuel, February 6, 1878, Morris 2718; account of Maggie Manuel in Defenbach, *Idaho*, 1:419; Bailey to parents, June 27, 1877; Sears, "Mount Idaho."

23. Sears, "Mount Idaho."

courage, resolution, and persistence of clear-headed officers saved a single life. Had all behaved as well as the few who remained together, the Indians might, I think, have been beaten, though we cannot despise the fighting of savages.[24]

On the morning of June 27, the troops returned to the canyon, marched down White Bird Creek to its mouth, and continued up the Salmon River a mile or two to establish another camp, which Howard named after Theller. Companies A, D, G, and M of the Fourth Artillery and Company C of the Twenty-first Infantry united with the command before the day's end. Apparently a volunteer unit from Dayton accompanied the reinforcements. The men continued to search for the dead, but rain made the task a difficult one. Finally Lt. Sevier M. Rains located the bodies of Edward Theller and the seven men who died with him in the dead-end ravine.[25] A bullet in the brain caused the death of the officer. Many empty cartridge cases lay on the ground near the corpses in testimony to the length of their stand. The men buried the dead where they found them and returned to Camp Theller.[26]

IV

On June 29, Howard received some intelligence that Looking Glass and the Alpowai, who were camped on the Clearwater just above Kooskia, were showing evidence of hostility. Distrusting the professed neutrality of the band, Howard sent Capt. Stephen Whipple with two companies of cavalry to arrest the chief and contain his followers, while he made ready to cross the Salmon River and pursue Joseph, White Bird, and Toohoolhoolzote.[27] He also sent Perry and Company F back to Fort Lapwai with the pack train for more supplies. Whipple attacked the Indian camp on July 1 but only succeeded in killing one warrior and wounding two. The most impor-

24. Howard to Watkins, June 27, 1877, Letters Sent, DC.

25. Born in Michigan, Sevier McClellan Rains graduated from West Point on June 15, 1876. Heitman, *Historical Register*, 1:813.

26. "Indian Status Since Our Last Issue," *Lewiston Teller*, July 7, 1877, p. 4; Sears, "Mount Idaho"; Brown, *Flight of the Nez Perce*, p. 161.

27. Born in Vermont, Stephen Girard Whipple served with the California Infantry during the Civil War. He received a commission as a captain in the Thirty-second Infantry on January 22, 1867. He transferred to the First Cavalry on December 15, 1870. Heitman, *Historical Register*, 1:1025.

tant result of the conflict was that the Alpowai joined the other bands and made the task of the Army that much more difficult.[28]

While Whipple attacked Looking Glass, Howard crossed the Salmon in pursuit of his foe. High water made the crossing perilous, and the work occupied most of the day. On July 2 Trimble and Company H crossed the stream and joined Howard on the left bank, and all began the ascent to the top of the Salmon River Mountains. In the meantime, the Nez Perce recrossed the Salmon at Craig's Ferry and headed back toward Camas Prairie. On July 5, Howard reached the place where the Indians had crossed but failed in an attempt to duplicate the feat. Returning to the mouth of White Bird Creek, Howard and his men were successful in crossing the river, and on July 8 the general rode into Grangeville with an advance party.

After the attack on Looking Glass's camp, Whipple had taken a position near Cottonwood House. On July 3, he sent two civilians, William Foster and Charles Blewett, in the direction of Craig's Ferry on a scouting mission. The men encountered a group of Nez Perce warriors who preceded the main body of the non-treaty force. Blewett was shot, but Foster made it back to Cottonwood. Whipple immediately sent Lt. Rains, Foster, and ten men to determine the strength of the force and to aid Blewett if he were still alive. Rains met a war party led by Five Wounds, Rainbow, and Two Moons. In a desperate fight, the Nez Perce wiped them out.

Perry returned to Cottonwood on the afternoon of July 4 and assumed command of the troops. Fearing an attack, he and Whipple improved their defenses. The following afternoon, seventeen volunteers from Mount Idaho, led by D. B. Randall, attempted to reach Cottonwood House, but the Nez Perce pinned them down about one and one half miles west of their destination. Perry refused to leave his position to aid the men. Although his decision was the best one in view of the superiority of the Nez Perce force, he earned the lasting enmity of the volunteers. After about twenty-five minutes had elapsed and the firing had decreased, George Shearer, who was with Perry, rode out to join the Randall party. Shortly afterward, Perry dispatched Whipple and 2nd Lt. Edwin A. Shelton with about forty-two men to bring in the volunteers. They were successful in their

28. For good detailed accounts of the rest of the Nez Perce Campaign see Beal, "*I Will Fight No More Forever*," chapters 6–23; Brown, *Flight of the Nez Perce*, chapters 11–25; Haines, *The Nez Perces*, chapters 27–31; Howard, *Saga of Chief Joseph*, chapters 13–23; Josephy, *Nez Perce Indians*, chapters 13–14; and McWhorter, *Hear Me*, chapters 15–28.

mission, since most of the Nez Perce had withdrawn. Two of the volunteers were dead and three wounded, one of them mortally.

Perry and Whipple joined Howard as he moved eastward after the Nez Perce. By the evening of July 10, Howard and his forces assembled at Walls, four miles beyond Jackson's Bridge on the east side of the Clearwater. The Nez Perce camp stood just above the juncture of the south and middle forks of the river, about five miles north. Howard engaged the Indians in battle the following day, and it was not until the afternoon that the Army forced the Nez Perce to withdraw across the stream. The cavalry under Perry hesitated in crossing the river, and the delay enabled the non-treaty band to escape. They moved downstream and encamped on a bluff beyond the mouth of Cottonwood Creek, near present-day Kamiah. Howard did not pursue them immediately.

Following the Clearwater battle, Hahtalekin and the Palouse united with the other non-treaty bands. According to Indian sources, the five bands numbered about 700, among whom were 155 fighting men. With Howard moving after them at a leisurely pace, the Nez Perce had little difficulty in keeping ahead of their pursuers. On July 14 they reached Weippe meadows. In council the chiefs decided to cross the Lolo Trail and find refuge in the land of the Crow in Montana, and on July 16 they began their journey.

During the next three months, military forces continued to pursue the Nez Perce across the Bitterroot Mountains and across Montana. Ten separate United States commands engaged them in fighting at one stage or another, but the Nez Perce fought them to a standstill in four major battles and a number of skirmishes. They continued to resist until they were surrounded by Col. Nelson A. Miles and his men forty-two miles south of the Canadian border. On October 5, after some made good their escape into Canada, about 418 Nez Perce submitted to the will of the military, and what General Sherman called "one of the most extraordinary Indian wars of which there is any record" came to an end.[29] Military records show that the war had cost the United States Army $931,329.02 beyond normal expenses. One hundred twenty-seven soldiers and approximately fifty civilians had been killed, and the cream of Nez Perce manhood was gone. About 151 Nez Perce men, women, and children died in the campaign and about 88 of them were wounded.

Companies F and H of the First Cavalry were not there to see the end. Both of them remained in Idaho while Howard and the rest of

29. Beal, "*I Will Fight No More Forever*," p. 266.

his men pushed after the fugitives. It was Miles who actually captured the Nez Perce, and he took his prisoners to Fort Keogh. In November General Sherman ordered them to Fort Leavenworth, and in July, 1878, the government exiled them to the Quapaw reserve in Indian Territory.

V

After the scene of battle shifted to the ruggedness of Montana, quiet returned to north central Idaho. Life went on much as it had before, except that death held a larger place in the minds of many. The realization of the death of Edward Theller had been slow in coming to Delia, but it had come, and consequently the news that the lieutenant had been found and buried came as a relief to the widow.[30]

Theller had carried some mementos on his person that Delia wished to have, but they had not been found at the time the body had been buried. Delia believed that the Nez Perce had taken the articles with them. In hopes of eventually recovering some of them, she placed an advertisement in the *Lewiston Teller:*

TO THE OFFICERS OF THE
UNITED STATES ARMY AND OTHERS

1st Lieut. Edward R. Theller, 21st Infantry, was killed and his body robbed by Nez Perce Indians under Looking Glass and Joseph, near Mount Idaho, Idaho Territory, June 17, 1877.

He had upon his person at that time the following articles of jewelry, which will probably, sooner or later, fall into the hands of white persons, and which his widow would be grateful to be informed of, or to have forwarded to her.

One large gold watch-hunting case with inscription.

PRESENTED TO
DR. E. A. THELLER

and possibly stating that it was a present by the trustees of Public Schools in San Francisco.

Also attached to the watch was a heavy gold chain composed of very large links, with round gold ball at the free end.

Also a gold ring set with large plain moss agate.

Also sleeve buttons the size of ½ dollar gold piece, chased around the edge and plain in the centre.

The watch, above described, is a family heirloom, having belonged to Capt. Theller's father, and is the more valuable on that account.

Any information concerning articles herein enumerated will be thankfully received by Mrs. E. R. Theller, 2125 Brush Street, San Francisco, California.[31]

30. Brown, *Flight of the Nez Perce*, p. 161.

31. *Lewiston Teller*, September 1, 1877, p. 2.

It was Delia's wish that her husband's remains be transported to San Francisco for reburial, and General Howard asked that it be done. The request went through channels to the Secretary of War, who granted permission for the reinterment at government expense.[32]

Early in December, a Mr. Pickett of Walla Walla, apparently the contracting undertaker, made the journey to the battlefield to disinter the body. Soldiers from Fort Lapwai provided the labor. Pickett found the grave without difficulty. Theller's feet lay uncovered, but the rest of the body had not been disturbed. The flesh had nearly rotted away from the bone, leaving the skeleton enveloped in loose clothing. In the pocket of the lieutenant's uniform, Pickett found the missing watch. It had stopped at 9 o'clock. Soldiers placed the remains in a casket and returned to Fort Lapwai.[33]

The Oregon Steam Navigation Company volunteered to transport the remains without cost to an appropriate railhead. Howard detailed 1st Lt. Melville Wilkinson, his aide-de-camp, to accompany the body to San Francisco. The funeral took place at 2 o'clock on January 3, 1878. The Reverend Dr. Beers conducted the service, held in the Trinity Episcopal Church. Dr. Beers characterized Theller as a faithful, brave soldier, who died as a soldier wanted to die — in the execution of his duty. The church choir sang the funeral anthem "Lord, Let Me Know Mine End" and the hymn "Hark from the Tombs." After the ceremony, attendants carried the casket to the hearse and escorted it to Laurel Hill Cemetery, where interment followed. Officers of the First Cavalry, the Fourth Artillery, and the Twelfth Infantry acted as pallbearers. Company F and the regimental band of the Twelfth Infantry were in attendance, and Maj. Gen. Irwin McDowell, commander of the Division of the Pacific, conveyed the sympathy of the Army to the widow.[34]

32. Howard to Assistant Adjutant General, Division of the Pacific, December 14, 1877, Letters Sent, DC.

33. Lt. Melville Wilkinson to Commander of the District of the Clearwater, December 14, 1877, Letters Sent, DC; "Theller's Remains," *Lewiston Teller*, December 15, 1877, p. 2; Kirkwood, *Indian War*, p. 7.

34. Adjutant General, DC, to Commanding Officer (telegram), December 20, 1877, and Howard to Wilkinson, December 24, 1877, Letters Sent, DC; *San Francisco Chronicle*, January 3, 1878, p. 4, and January 4, 1878, p. 1; "Idaho County Marks Site of Nez Perce Battleground," *The Idaho Statesman*, September 4, 1927, section 3, p. 2. Theller was buried in lot 2110, grave 1318.

VI

General Howard and his men had been in a hurry when they buried the dead at White Bird battlefield. In fact, some of the bodies had not been buried at all but shrouded in blankets. Under the circumstances, it is not surprising that J. W. Poe found the bones of many cavalrymen bleaching in the sun and other signs of the furtive work of scavengers in abundance when he visited the battleground late in July of 1877. "It is a shame," he wrote in a letter to the editor of the *Lewiston Teller*, "that our government should give to her heroic dead no better burial than this."[35]

About two months after Poe wrote his letter, a detachment of First Cavalry returned to White Bird and reburied the remains in deeper graves. Not until December, 1879, did the Assistant Adjutant General of the Department of the Columbia issue the order that eventually brought the remains to Fort Lapwai. The work was delayed by cold weather until spring of the following year. Late in May, the commanding officer of Fort Lapwai visited the site in company with Theodore Swarts, who now homesteaded at the north end of the canyon not far from the place where Perry and his men had ascended the west wall during the retreat. The former volunteer helped locate the scattered graves. A detail collected the bones and put them in two big boxes. Wagons carried the containers back to Fort Lapwai, where they were placed in a single grave.[36]

35. J. W. Poe, "Letter from Mount Idaho," *Lewiston Teller*, July 28, 1877, p. 1.

36. *Idaho County Free Press*, July 22, 1887, p. 1; Acting Assistant Inspector General to Assistant Adjutant General of the Department of the Columbia, December 5, 1879, letter no. 4546, Letters Received, DC.

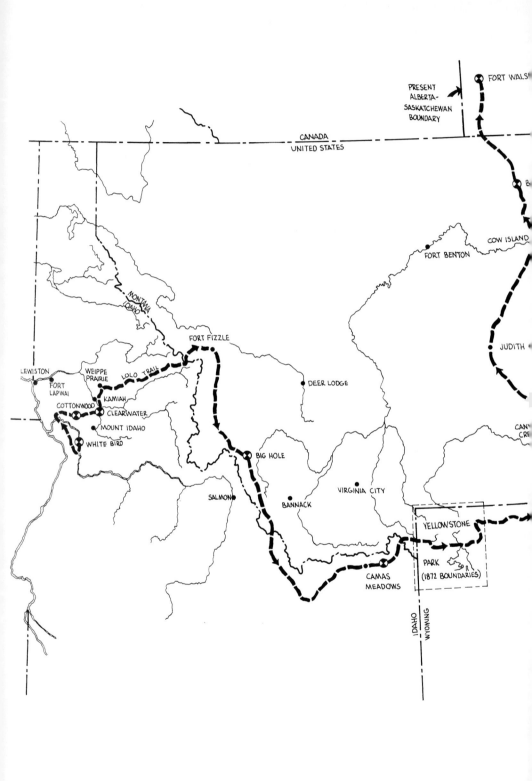

What They Said

It is reported that General Howard said "there is something wrong with the cavalry. I don't know what it is. I wish their horses would die or be killed and then I would know whether it is the fault of the horses or the men."

JUSTICE

If any volunteers show white feathers in these times, let them come to the rear where the women and old men can protect them.

LEWISTON TELLER

I had intended to enter quite extensively into the subject of the cavalry and its equipment, in the report which I am now preparing with a view to supplement mine from Henry Lake. I shall therefore gladly comply with General McDowell's directions sending forward my own special views together with the reports from subordinates, which he required.

O. O. HOWARD

It is due Captain Perry; it is due Captains Whipple, Trimble and Winters; it is due all the Commissioned officers of the 1st Cavalry and above all it is due the Non Commissioned officers and Enlisted men of the 1st Cavalry that these statements be probed to the bottom. If the Enlisted men of this regiment were cowards and abandoned their officers and comrades in the hour of danger and of battle this fact should be established and spread upon the record. If however upon a critical investigation these charges can not be made good then those who have attempted to destroy their reputation should be brought to justice.

JAMES W. FORSYTH

I learned it through two or three officers.

JOEL TRIMBLE

In my opinion he did all a man could to rally the men.

GEORGE SHEARER

11

Court of Inquiry

Following the Nez Perce campaign, the Army began to assess its performance. Generally, it had been a poor one. The cavalry in particular had been inadequate, and in some cases it had performed terribly. In order to reach some conclusions concerning its failure and to develop successful new ways of handling future situations, Gen. McDowell ordered cavalry officers in his Division to comment on the battles in which they had participated and to elaborate on any apparent deficiencies they had noted.[1]

Joel Trimble was at Fort Walla Walla when he received the order. In late December of 1877, he prepared a report as requested and forwarded it to Department headquarters. It was a bombshell. It contained a number of insinuations and denunciations concerning the conduct of Capt. Perry in the Nez Perce campaign and particularly in the Battle of White Bird Canyon. Trimble was apparently fighting mad. He believed that his courage had been questioned and his honor stained. The report was his chance to get even. Midway through the thirty-four-page document, he indicated, in part, his motivation when he wrote that he had been privately assailed by Capt. Perry in a communication to the Departmental Commander following the Battle of White Bird Canyon. He went on to state that he had applied for a copy of the report but had been told that none had been made.[2]

His first criticism of Perry, in effect a criticism of General Howard, was veiled. Trimble noted that troops had left Fort Lapwai twenty-four hours after the attitude of the Indians had been determined and twelve hours after the killings on the Salmon River had been reported. "I mention this not to question or criticize the wisdom of orders," he wrote, "but to show that if a sooner departure had been made, the Indians would have been encountered on the

1. Howard to Asst. Adj. Gen. John C. Kelton, Division of the Pacific, December 13, 1877, Letters Sent, DC.

2. Trimble Report, p. 19.

133

plain, instead of in the Canyon or rough country." The feeble attempt to rationalize the relevancy of the information in an uncritical context was not a successful one. He had most certainly raised a question, and it was a valid one: Why hadn't Howard acted immediately? Trimble then noted that Perry had entered the canyon without first reconnoitering it, leaving him without knowledge of the disposition of the enemy. Another telling point had been made.[3]

Near the end of his account, Trimble made a statement about Perry which he had been suggesting in his descriptions of a number of incidents that had occurred during the battle. Putting it precisely, he wrote: "I firmly believe that after being a few moments under fire it was his settled determination to retreat and that rapidly." Previously, Trimble had mentioned that after he had posted Sgt. McCarthy on the bluff and returned to his men, he had encountered Perry in the rear of Company H. He had quoted the officer as saying, "we had better get our men together or we . . . [will] be whipped out of this." According to Trimble, he had then asked Perry if they might not go on to the Salmon River and, in reply, had been told that the attempt would result in their annihilation, and that they must retreat. The implication, of course, was that it had not been necessary to retreat, but that in fact there had been an opportunity to advance. As further evidence of Perry's inclination toward haste in getting to the rear, Trimble reported that the officer had mounted behind an enlisted man, after his own horse had tired.[4]

Trimble concluded his criticism of Perry by recounting two incidents, both of which had occurred during the week that followed the engagement. On June 21, Perry and thirty-five men under his command had accompanied twenty-five citizen volunteers on a scouting expedition to view the battlefield and determine the whereabouts of the hostiles. Perry and his men had remained at Johnson's ranch, while the citizens completed the reconnaissance. Trimble insinuated that Perry had shown the white feather again, and he remarked that the officer's failure to order his men to go with the volunteers had caused much comment in that part of the country. Second, Howard had sent Perry back to Fort Lapwai on June 26 for more ammunition and supplies. Trimble considered the departure another sign of timidity and stated that Perry had voluntarily separated himself from the rest of the cavalry. In attempting to explain the charge, he implied that Perry had arranged the duty and hinted that Howard had always been partial in matters concerning that officer. Ending

3. *Ibid.*, pp. 4, 30.

4. *Ibid.*, pp. 8–9, 28–29.

the section of the report dealing with Perry, Trimble observed: "These things probably can be classed among the non-effective actions of the Cavalry."[5]

Gen. Howard must have been surprised: he had not expected these things to be included. He must also have been chagrined to find that one of the statements made by Trimble reflected upon his judgment. The delay in leaving Fort Lapwai — the way Trimble had presented it — did not add luster to his image, which had already been tarnished by his failure to corral the Nez Perce until after Nelson Miles had entered the picture and, in fact, stolen the show. Before he forwarded the report to Division headquarters, Howard asked his adjutant general, Maj. H. Clay Wood, to write a letter to the officer and request that he amplify his remarks concerning this particular point. Trimble replied on January 29, going into more detail to show how and when the information had been received and to clarify his own interpretations of the intelligence. He did correct his statement concerning the length of time that had passed before the troops had departed, based on data obtained from Lt. Parnell and Sgt. McCarthy, both of whom kept diaries. He stated that the men had started twenty-six hours after the first letter from L. P. Brown and nine hours after the killings had been reported.[6]

After Trimble's addendum had been received, Howard sent the paper to Gen. McDowell. The Division commander was probably more surprised than his subordinate had been. Howard had had nothing but good to say of Perry at White Bird. But Trimble was not alone in believing the officer had been derelict in his duty during the campaign. The reports written by Capt. Whipple and Capt. Winters contained further criticism of Perry's conduct during the Battle of the Clearwater, and the officer had already been severely criticized for refusing to send troops to the immediate assistance of a group of volunteers during the fighting at Cottonwood on July 5.[7] In fact, the uproar among the settlers had been so great that Perry had demanded and received permission to air the subject at a court of inquiry. On November 30, 1877, the court had rendered a judgment in which it stated that not a word of the testimony had reflected upon the personal courage of the officer, and that he had acted wisely in view of the fact that he had been surrounded by

5. Ibid., pp. 30–31.

6. Trimble to Wood, January 29, 1878.

7. Report of Captain S. G. Whipple, December 30, 1877, and Report of Captain W. H. Winters, January 2, 1878, letter packet 131, Letters Received, DC, 1878.

Indians who had outnumbered his command.[8] But, as always in cases of that kind, the doubt of courage lingered. In any event, Trimble had a great deal to say in his report that made sense, and his charges were serious enough that they could not be ignored.

On April 10, 1878, wheels began to turn. Lt. Col. John C. Kelton, Assistant Adjutant General of the Division of the Pacific, addressed a letter to Gen. Howard. After noting that the reports submitted by Trimble, Whipple, and Winters had traveled far outside the bounds prescribed in the order requesting them, Kelton observed that the ability of Perry as a commanding officer had been impugned, and that Gen. McDowell wanted an investigation conducted to determine the merit of the charges. Howard quickly forwarded the reports and correspondence to Col. Cuvier Grover, the regimental commander of the First Cavalry at Fort Walla Walla, with a note to investigate and reply. However, Grover could not act. Perry had been granted a leave of absence following his exoneration by the court of inquiry, and according to regulations he had to be confronted with the charges and given a chance to reply to the allegations before other steps could be taken.[9]

Perry did not return to Fort Walla Walla until mid-October. After reading Trimble's report and excerpts furnished him from the accounts of Whipple and Winters, Perry began to write his own story of the campaign. His account of the Battle of White Bird Canyon was very straightforward, and, although there were a number of statements that obviously conflicted with Trimble's, Perry did not stop to comment on the difference. Only when he reached the concluding paragraph of his report did Perry show signs of anger and question the wisdom and propriety of Trimble's behavior during the retreat. Bristling a bit, Perry wrote:

> When we reached Grangeville we found Trimble already there, having been to Mt. Idaho and returned a distance of 5 miles, so that he must have been back some time. Under the circumstances, it seems to me that his proper course, having arrived so much in advance, would have been to gather what assistance he could and come to our relief. To go back a little, I had expected, on reaching the summit of the ridge [to find] that Capt. Trimble had collected a party of the stragglers and [was] holding the position which he had said Chapman had

8. Proceedings of a Court of Inquiry which convened at Lewiston, Idaho Territory, on September 3, 1877, to investigate certain charges brought against Captain David Perry, 1st Cavalry by citizens of the Territory of Idaho, packet no. 2521, Letters Received, DC.

9. Kelton to Howard, April 10, 1878, letter no. 1024, Grover to Assistant Adjutant General of the Department of the Columbia, July 13, 1878, Letters Received, DC.

informed him he would find further up, and thus [would have] afforded us invaluable assistance. This he could easily have done, as he
was so far to the rear that quite a number of men were between us.[10]

To accompany his report, Perry prepared an answer to Trimble's
charges. He had shown surprising reserve in his account of the battle — considering what was at stake — but his rebuttal was another
matter. In it he was furious. Perry wrote: "I desire to call attention to
the evident unfairness which Capt. Trimble treats every thing with
which my name is connected."[11] Then he attempted to refute the
report point by point.

Perry denied that he had assailed Trimble in a private communication to Howard and declared that the only remarks that he had
ever made concerning him were oral and made only at the general's
request. He stated that after he had reached Cottonwood on June
24, Howard had asked him why it was that some had believed Trimble had been killed. Perry had replied that perhaps it was because he
had not mentioned him in his early dispatches. He had not mentioned Trimble, he said, because there had been no particular
reason for doing so; his service had been undistinguished. He had
then related the substance of his knowledge and opinions concerning the officer and his conduct.[12]

Perry explained the reasoning behind what Trimble had regarded as a late departure from Fort Lapwai: L. P. Brown had not
been alarmed in the beginning, and the best information at hand
indicated that the early killings had been committed in connection
with a private quarrel. Then he turned to a discussion of the circumstances surrounding his decision to leave Grangeville and attempt to
catch the Nez Perce before they had a chance to cross the Salmon
River. In his report, Trimble gave the impression that Perry had
kept his own counsel, and the officer wanted to set the record
straight. He stated that he had laid the matter before his officers and
obtained their unanimous consent before he gave the order to move
out. If his decision had been the wrong one, Perry wanted the Division commander to know that he had had lots of support in reaching
it.[13]

10. Perry, Detailed Account of the Affair in White Bird Canyon, June 17th 1877,
October 22, 1878, letter no. 1024, Letters Received, DC. Except for the paragraph
reproduced above, this account is identical with that which appears as Perry's statement in CI, pp. 112–123.

11. Perry to Lt. Col. James W. Forsyth, c. October 22, 1878, p. 1.

12. Ibid., pp. 4–5.

13. Trimble Report, p. 5; Perry to Forsyth, c. October 22, 1878, pp. 1–2.

Perry also challenged some of Trimble's statements of fact. In his report, the officer wrote that Perry had been one of the first to start up the trail to the top of the west wall. According to Trimble, Perry took some men to a bluff about 1000 yards in the rear, after stationing him on a point that commanded the approach to the trail. Trimble claimed that after a short time he had seen Perry riding very fast up the bluff and heard him call to the men, "Now for the Canyon." It was then, Trimble stated, that he began his own journey to the top. Perry, however, contended that Trimble had made another grievous error. "The 1000 yards in the rear," he wrote, "should have been front, as that was my position, only not so distant," and the calling had been to the men who were following Trimble away.[14]

There were to other misstatements of fact that Perry wanted to correct. Trimble had noted that he had talked with Perry after he reached the top of the west wall. Perry countered that Trimble had not been close enough to understand what it was that he had been shouting, and in fact Trimble had told him as much after they were reunited at Grangeville. Indeed, Perry declared, Trimble had been so far in the rear at the time Parnell reached the summit of White Bird Hill that the lieutenant had not been able to recognize him. Perry stated that Parnell had inquired who was retreating so rapidly in the distance. Trimble had also reported that Perry had returned to Grangeville with forty-five men; Perry said the number was twenty-six.[15]

Generally, Perry chided Trimble for his haste in getting back to Grangeville. Trimble had remarked that Chapman was well mounted and had been influential in leading many men to the rear. Perry noted that Trimble must also have been well mounted, because the officer told him that he had seen Chapman change horses at Johnson's ranch, four miles from the battlefield. Perry went on to say that not only had Trimble reached the settlement before he and Parnell had arrived, but his subordinate had been there long enough to ride to Mount Idaho and back, a round-trip distance of five miles.[16]

Concerning the charge that he had been determined to retreat rapidly from the outset, Perry declared that he had entered the canyon with the intention of whipping the Indians, and that it was only after his line had completely disintegrated and he had been unable to control the men, in part because he had no trumpet, that he had

14. Trimble Report, pp. 11–12; Perry to Forsyth, c. October 22, 1878, p. 3.

15. Trimble Report, p. 13; Perry to Forsyth, c. October 22, 1878, pp. 3–4.

16. Perry to Forsyth, c. October 22, 1878, p. 4.

decided to retreat. At the time some Indians were already in his rear, and he implied that the retreat was perhaps the only thing that had saved them all from being killed. He also declared that if he had not mounted behind a trooper in the retreat, he would not have been close enough to Trimble to order him to stop and momentarily halt his ascent up the canyon wall. Concluding his rebuttal, Perry stated that the volunteers who had performed the reconnaissance on June 21 had merely asked him to support their action, and that he had simply done what he had been requested to do.[17]

Lt. Col. James W. Forsyth, who acted as the regimental commander of the First Cavalry in the absence of Col. Grover, received the report and the reply to charges written by Capt. Perry. After reviewing them, he forwarded the documents to Maj. Wood with a recommendation. He believed that the only way to investigate the allegations was to take the sworn testimony of the men involved in the controversy and of other eyewitnesses. If Trimble, Whipple, and Winters were correct in their statements, then Perry should be brought to trial. If they were not, then the officers should suffer the consequences.[18]

A little more than a week later, Perry made it easy for his superiors. In a communication addressed to Department headquarters, Perry demanded a court of inquiry to clear his name. On November 27, Howard obliged him and issued the order. It directed the court to convene in Portland on December 16 or as soon thereafter as possible. The purpose of the inquiry was to evaluate the statements contained in the reports and to investigate the propriety of Perry's conduct during the Nez Perce campaign. It was the duty of the court to determine the facts and give its opinion concerning them.[19]

The Court of Inquiry convened at 10 o'clock on the morning of December 18, 1878. Lt. Col. Alexander Chambers of the Twenty-first Infantry, Maj. David P. Hancock of the Second Infantry, and Maj. George B. Dandy of the Quartermaster Department were its members. Capt. Joseph S. Conrad of the Second Infantry was its recorder or chief counsel.

To begin the proceedings, the President of the Court, Col.

---

17. *Ibid.*, pp. 8–10.

18. Forsyth to Assistant Adjutant General, Department of the Columbia, November 14, 1878, Fort Walla Walla, letter no. 1024, Letters Received, DC.

19. Telegram from Perry to Maj. Azor Nickerson, November 23, 1878, letter no. 3675, Letters Received, DC; Special Orders No. 142, Department of the Columbia, November 27, 1878, DC.

Chambers, read the order that authorized the inquiry. Perry had the right to challenge any member of the body, and Chambers gave him the opportunity, but the officer apparently found its composition to his liking. Conrad then swore in the members of the court and in turn took the oath from Chambers. To complete the formalities, Perry introduced his counsel, Maj. Lawrence S. Babbitt of the Ordnance Department. Babbitt had been with Perry at Cottonwood and had provided him with a statement to use in his defense.

Chambers and his colleagues spent the rest of the day examining the written evidence, and they extracted portions of the reports that pertained to Perry in order to append them to the proceedings. By 2:45 the work had been completed, and the court adjourned.

The following day, the recording of testimony began. The first witness was Capt. Stephen G. Whipple, who testified on the engagement at Cottonwood and on the Battle of the Clearwater. He concluded his remarks on December 20. The next day, 1st Lt. Edwin H. Shelton of the First Cavalry continued the discussion of the Clearwater fight, and it was not until late in the afternoon that the court turned to the Battle of White Bird Canyon and Capt. Joel Trimble took the stand.

Trimble's testimony took two days to complete: he began on Friday afternoon and finished on Tuesday morning. First he gave his account of the battle, beginning at the point where the command entered White Bird Canyon. Trimble repeated the criticisms made in his written report: that Perry gave the order to retreat too quickly and that he had not provided the necessary leadership that the occasion demanded. In concluding his opening statement, Trimble declared that he had not gone to Mount Idaho after he returned to Grangeville on June 17, as Perry had stated, but that he had remained with Mr. Crooks in Grange Hall.[20]

The court questioned Trimble on a number of points and asked for additional information concerning others. In the course of the probing, it became apparent that Trimble had little evidence to support some of his accusations and that some of his statements of fact were based on second-hand information delivered out of context. Under oath Trimble modified and qualified many of his declarations to the point that they lost their pungency and, in some cases, their relevancy.

The court learned, for example, that Trimble had been told by a friend who had been told by another officer that Perry had criticized him in a private communication. Trimble did not bother to get the

20. Trimble, CI, pp. 26–37.

story from its source, and he was unaware of the nature of the criticism, if there was any. When the court asked Trimble to state when it was that Perry had mounted behind an enlisted man in the retreat, he replied, "I do not know when it was; I did not see the transaction." When the court asked him if Perry had been ordered to escort the pack train back to Fort Lapwai on June 26, Trimble answered, "I do not know; I suppose he must have been ordered. I was not anywhere in the vicinity." If Perry had been ordered, the court wanted to know, would the action have reflected upon his conduct as an officer? "No, sir," Trimble replied, "I suppose that it would not, officially." When Trimble was asked to explain why it was that Perry left Fort Lapwai about twenty-six hours after the first letter from L. P. Brown had been received, he replied that he could not answer positively. "I believe there was some doubt in the minds of the General or Commanding Officer concerning hostilities," he said. Because Howard had been present at the time, Trimble concluded, he could not say that Perry had been responsible for the delay.[21]

Perry had his chance to question the witness, and he took advantage of the occasion to ask Trimble to clarify the meaning of some of his statements. Trimble had implied in his reports that there had been an opportunity to advance in the early stages of the fight, and Perry asked his antagonist to be explicit:

> Perry: You say you suggested going to the Salmon River. Could this have been done excepting by charging the Indians?
> Trimble: No, sir, it could not. I did not consider it as offering a suggestion. I only made it as a remark in reply. Had I been asked for a suggestion, I do not think I would have stated so.[22]

Although Trimble backed off on the question of the possible advance, he steadily maintained throughout the inquiry that it had not been necessary to retreat. In response to a question by Capt. Conrad concerning the order to withdraw, Trimble declared that it had taken him by surprise, because he knew that "you can't retreat in the presence of Indians." He also remarked that the fact that the Nez Perce had flanked them should not have disturbed Perry. Indians always did that, he said, and Perry should have been prepared for it. At the time Perry had given the order to retreat, Trimble remembered, only a few men had been lost. He did agree, however, that some of the men panicked, and that many of them had difficulty in managing their horses. When it came to the matter of proving that

21. *Ibid.*, pp. 50–51, 53–55.
22. *Ibid.*

Perry had intended to retreat from the outset, Trimble had little to offer in the way of evidence. He could only say that the hesitating manner and the general appearance of the officer told him as much.[23]

After Trimble's testimony, it became apparent that the only real issue that had developed was whether the retreat had been justified at the time Perry gave the order. Trimble had not been properly prepared to answer the inquiries concerning some of the other questions that had been raised, and the court did not pursue them with vigor. Perry had not pressed charges against Trimble or indicated that he should be censured for his conduct, and therefore the court did not spend much time in investigating his behavior. Capt. Conrad did ask Trimble how it was that he had become separated from Perry during the retreat to Grangeville. Trimble answered that the separation occurred when he rode to his left after he had reached the top of the west wall. He said that he had later seen Perry going off to the right. When Conrad asked him if he should not have changed his course at that point and made an attempt to join his commanding officer, Trimble replied: "Considering the condition of the command, I don't think it [would have] made any difference." The court was apparently satisfied with the answer.[24]

Lt. Parnell was the next witness, and he was followed by 1st Sgt. McCarthy of Company H, Sgt. Richard Powers of Company H, George Shearer of the volunteers, Capt. James Jackson of the First Cavalry, 1st Sgt. Charles Leeman of Company F, Sgt. Bartholomew Coughlin of Company F, and Maj. Babbitt. Capt. Jackson and Maj. Babbitt gave testimony on the Clearwater fight; the rest gave evidence relating to the Battle of White Bird Canyon. It required four full days to record the testimony, and they must have been distressing ones for Capt. Trimble.

Sgt. McCarthy appears to have been the only witness who was sympathetic to Trimble, and who shared his conviction that Perry lost his nerve at White Bird. In 1905, McCarthy wrote a letter to J. W. Redington in which he expressed his opinion of Perry. He mentioned that Trimble had been his friend for many years and that had Trimble commanded at White Bird instead of Perry, disaster would have been averted. "Perry was determined," he wrote, "to make that break and sacrifice all that were foolish enough to do their duty, self included." He declared that the cause of the defeat was the stampede led by Perry. The officer showed "cold feet" in the Lava Beds,

23. *Ibid.*, pp. 38, 47, 51–52.

24. *Ibid.*, p. 41.

he continued, and evidenced a lack of courage throughout his varied career. In another letter to Redington, McCarthy simply referred to Perry as "that coward."[25]

However disposed McCarthy may have been to defend Trimble, he could do little to aid him. His personal knowledge of the officer's conduct ended at the time he reached the rocky ledge that commanded the ravine on the right. He did, however, get a chance to agree with Trimble that Perry could have successfully charged the Indian village. "In the first formation," he declared, "I think we could have advanced down the canyon with complete success in five minutes." But McCarthy's was the only affirmative voice.[26]

Parnell and Shearer supported Perry's contention that it would have been imprudent to advance beyond the ridge on which the line had been formed. Parnell, Shearer, Leeman, and Coughlin agreed that the departure of the volunteers left Company F completely exposed to a devastating fire, and that its position had been an untenable one. Parnell stated that it would have been possible to maintain the position held by Company H a bit longer, but, on the other hand, it would not have been wise to do so. The men would have been out of ammunition in a short time, and they would have lost many horses, which would have put them in a desperate situation.[27]

Most of the witnesses agreed that a great number of the enlisted men panicked. Asked if he thought the exodus could have been controlled, Parnell replied, "I did all I could and could not succeed. I don't think we could have done it." He attributed the disaster to the lack of discipline among the men. He noted that there had been a high percentage of recruits in his company and that the horses were green and flighty. Sgt. Powers remarked that the officers did everything in their power to rally the men. Shearer was of the same opinion and testified that he heard Perry repeatedly threaten to shoot men who attempted to ride past him. According to Sgt. Leeman, Perry had been active in stemming the initial retreat, and he noted that his commander had seemed perfectly calm.[28]

25. McCarthy to J. W. Redington, April 26, 1904, and June 14, 1905, Walla Walla, packet 211-b, McWhorter Collection.

26. McCarthy, CI, p. 78.

27. Parnell, CI, pp. 61, 63–65, 67, 73; Shearer, CI, pp. 93–94; Leeman, CI, pp. 98–99; Coughlin, CI, p. 103.

28. Parnell, CI, pp. 64, 73; Powers, CI, p. 87; Shearer, CI, pp. 90–92; Leeman, CI, pp. 100–101. Chapman also defended Perry on this count; in the *Idaho Tri-Weekly Statesman* (July 28, 1877, p. 3), he was reported as saying that "Col. Perry fought bravely to the last and that he did his best to rally his troops, threatening with pistol in hand to shoot the first man to retire, but that it was impossible to hold the men."

Parnell attributed much of the confusion that had existed in his own company to the fact that the men had remained mounted after the firing began. When asked who should have given the order to dismount, he replied that he supposed Trimble should have given it; he had been in command of the company. Commenting further, Parnell declared that if he had been in charge, he would have given the order to dismount; it was the proper thing to do under the circumstances. If the men of Company H had dismounted, the court inquired, could not the Indians have been beaten at the first point of attack? "It is very hard to say," Parnell replied, "they were pretty tough customers as we found out afterward."[29]

Shearer and Parnell also sided with Perry when it came to the matter of Trimble's position in the retreat. Shearer stated that Trimble had been about fifty or sixty yards ahead of Perry in the race for the trail that led up the west wall. He had heard Perry call to Trimble to stop at the top of a hill. Trimble had replied that Chapman had said there was a better place to defend on the summit, but Perry had repeated his order to hold the point. A short time later, according to Shearer, Trimble moved on up the hill, and he saw nothing more of him during the flight. In reply to a question concerning the whereabouts of Trimble during the retreat, Parnell commented:

> I saw nothing of him after the line commenced to fall back until I arrived at Grangeville. I saw a party of men after I got to the top of the hill, after I joined Captain Perry. I saw 6 or 7 men down on the prairie going to Mount Idaho. It must have been three miles off. I afterwards found out that it was Chapman and Captain Trimble and some of the enlisted men of both companies, who were following Chapman back to Mount Idaho.[30]

On January 30, Perry took the stand and read the reports that he had already submitted. In the case of the White Bird fight, he omitted the concluding paragraph of his report in which he had stated that Trimble had gone to Mount Idaho and back before he and Parnell had reached Grangeville. Perry accepted Trimble's statement that he had not done so.

The cross examination was brief and to the point. Perry was given the opportunity to call Trimble to account and to recommend that his conduct be investigated, but he chose to lay the matter to rest.

29. Parnell, CI, pp. 71–74.

30. Shearer, CI, p. 90; Parnell, CI, p. 63.

Court: Did all the officers in your command obey your instructions as given them and behave properly or were they panic stricken as well as the men?

Perry: I saw Lieutenant Theller, he seemed much excited and did not seem to know what he was doing. Captain Trimble failed to obey my orders on the retreat and seemed to be in a hurry to get away.

Court: Did you take any official action in regard to Captain Trimble's conduct, by preferring charges or arresting him?

Perry: No, I merely stated it verbally to the General when I saw him.

Court: Was the disaster at White Bird due to the misconduct of either of the officers named in your evidence?

Perry: No, I do not think it was. A panic was caused by the Indians getting on my left flank, by the citizens abandoning the knoll, thus exposing my whole line and lead horses.[31]

On February 1 the court delivered its opinion and laid the written document before Gen. Howard, who was the reviewing officer. The court stated that Perry apparently took every precaution which good judgment had dictated up to the time the conflict occurred, except that there was no evidence to indicate that a suitable quantity of ammunition had been provided in case of an emergency. His disposition of the troops on the battlefield had been judicious and proper, except that he had trusted citizens to protect his left; the court noted that soon after the fight started, the volunteers had abandoned their position, an act that had engendered a panic among nearly all of the troops. The court further stated that it believed Perry did all in his power to collect and organize the men for a defense. His failure was due, in part, to the fact that the troops lacked experience in firing mounted. Its findings regarding the Cottonwood Fight and Battle of the Clearwater were unqualified. Perry did all that had been expected of him; his conduct had been prudent and proper. In referring to the charges made by Trimble, Whipple, and Winters, the court declared that it appeared that the written statements of some of the officers of the 1st Cavalry were colored by insinuations that were prejudicial and unwarranted by the evidence.[32]

Howard agreed with the findings of the court, except that he noted that it did not appear to him that Perry was answerable for the limited quantity of ammunition on hand, and that it was not clear to him that the citizens had been misplaced on his left; their subsequent conduct could not have been foreseen. The opinion of the

31. CI, p. 125.

32. *Ibid.*, pp. 127–128.

court and Howard's comments were published on February 5 as General Orders No. 1 of the Department of the Columbia. Perry had been vindicated.[33]

33. The opinion of the court and Howard's revision of it are reproduced below, pp. 167–203.

What They Said

They are poor Cavalrymen and d – d bad Infantry. Their horses won't stand fire, and the men are poor shots.

JUSTICE

The present force of our regular army is entirely inadequate to the frontier duty it may at any time be called upon to perform.

F. WHITTAKER

The result of the different encounters of this band with troops are forcible illustration of the entire revolution in Indian warfare occasioned by their acquiring not only arms of precision, but skill in using them.

G. W. BAIRD

I could be fighting Day After Tomorrow [General Howard] yet, but I couln't lick the whole country.

JOSEPH

The toll of human life — wantonly taken — will never justify the purpose of the memorable outbreak.

JENNIE NORTON BUNKER

12

The Reasons Why

The Battle of White Bird Canyon was one of the worst defeats suffered by the United States Army during the period 1865 to 1890. Perhaps only the Fetterman disaster in Wyoming in 1866 and the Custer disaster in Montana ten years later rival it in ignominy, and in both those cases the Indians outnumbered the military units in great proportion. The reasons for the defeat are many. Where men are involved there are always variables, such as courage and fear, knowledge and ignorance, resolution and uncertainty, that are often difficult to document and more difficult to measure. Yet they play a part in every confrontation, and they played a part in the Battle of White Bird Canyon. Chance also seems to have had its day. The loss of all the trumpets in the command could hardly have been anticipated. Certainly there were errors in judgment.

One can debate whether if Howard had sent forces to Mount Idaho at the first sign of restlessness, it would have made much difference, because the killings on the Salmon River and on Camas Prairie had already taken place (except for the murder of Charles Horton) when the first letter from L. P. Brown reached Fort Lapwai. At least Perry might have had the opportunity to engage the Nez Perce on the prairie rather than in the canyon. Perry committed a major error when he did not reconnoiter the enemy and trusted to Chapman for his information. He blundered again by trusting the volunteers to cover his left. In view of the fact that he knew absolutely nothing about them, he was remiss in placing them in a critical position. He erred a third time by not providing cover for his rear, once he had decided not to advance to the Indian camp. From that moment he fought defensively, and he should have prepared for it. It is evident that Perry exercised little control over Chapman and the volunteers at any time. Shearer and his men acted independently of the rest of the force in the beginning when they rushed to the creek bottom; Chapman apparently was influential in leading men to the rear, and generally in confusing and confounding any attempt to halt the runaway by continually suggesting better places to defend.

It is also evident that the volunteers turned tail, the cavalrymen panicked, Theller lost control of himself momentarily, and Trimble simply gave up after the retreat began.

Basic to the failure was the military system itself. A good cavalryman had to excel in both horsemanship and marksmanship, and many of the men who rode into White Bird Canyon on the morning of June 17 did not possess proficiency in either skill. Their ineptitude can be traced to background and training.

In his report of the Nez Perce campaign, Capt. Trimble wrote that, in his opinion, it took from fifteen to twenty years to make a truly fine horse-soldier. He observed that the men furnished the cavalry were generally green, and that they had grown to manhood in an environment which was radically different from the one they were destined to know. Guns and horses were foreign to most of them, and it took years of training to familiarize them with the tools of their trade. Many of those who testified at the Court of Inquiry mentioned that a large portion of the men in both companies had been relatively new to the service. Only a handful had fought Indians before. Some of them had been fresh from the recruiting depots; they had not had the chance to become adept in the necessary skills. But, on the other hand, the performance had been generally poor, and the problem obviously extended to men who theoretically had had the time to improve.[1]

Although Sgt. McCarthy noted that most of the men in Company H could ride a horse bareback and lead another at a gallop, Capt. Trimble referred to them as poor riders, and Lt. Parnell remembered that many of them had trouble in managing their horses under fire. Both officers considered them deficient in drill. The truth of the matter was that a frontier cavalryman did not have much time to spend on such things. The United States Army had a vast country to police, and it had only a few men to do it with.[2] Speaking generally of the problem in 1878, Lt. Gen. Philip Sheridan commented:

> No other nation in the world would have attempted reduction of these wild tribes and occupation of their country with less than 60,000 or 70,000 men, while the whole force employed and scattered over this enormous region . . . never numbered more than 14,000, and nearly one-third of this force has been confined to the line of the Rio Grande to protect the Mexican frontier. The consequence was that every en-

1. Trimble Report, pp. 3–4, 32; Parnell, CI, p. 72; McCarthy, CI, pp. 83–84.

2. Trimble Report, p. 3; Trimble, CI, pp. 43–52; Parnell, CI, pp. 72–73; McCarthy, CI, p. 84; F. Whittaker, "The American Army," *The Galaxy* (1877), 24:397.

gagement was a forlorn hope, and was attended with a loss of life unparalleled in warfare.[3]

The size of the Army's responsibility and the paucity of its man-power dictated its approach to the problem. Its answer was the one- and two-company military post.

The amount of routine work that had to be done at these tiny garrisons varied little with the size of its complement. For example, every military post had to be watched, and this meant incessant guard duty; whether there were six companies or one on the grounds, the number of men that were necessary to secure it re-mained approximately the same. Sgt. McCarthy noted that Company F had been stationed at Fort Lapwai for some time, and, as was the case in those days, about half of the enlisted men had been em-ployed on daily duty almost continually. They had functioned as clerks, carpenters, blacksmiths, and officers' servants and performed many other duties that had nothing to do with soldiering in the pro-fessional sense. Few of the men had been able to attend drill, and target practice had not been encouraged.[4]

Company H had fared somewhat better. It had traveled from Fort Walla Walla in early May, and it had not been officially stationed at the post but attached to it. The march and the five or six weeks of field service gave the men a chance to become acquainted with their professional duties. There had been some time for mounted drill, and during the first week in June the men had been able to practice every morning. Chief White Bird, whom McCarthy described as "a grand looking Indian," watched the performances and must have found them of interest, because the sergeant noted that the old warrior had been very punctual in his attendance. On June 11, apparently both companies maneuvered on the parade ground at Fort Lapwai before an audience composed mostly of laundresses. In his diary, McCarthy recorded that they charged the hospital as a finale, "penetrating even to the backyard and with the loss of only one trooper."[5]

3. *Report of the Secretary of War, 1878* (Washington, D.C., 1878), 1:36. The actual strength of the entire United States Army in 1877 was 24,000 men. "Statistics of the Army," *Frank Leslie's Illustrated Newspaper* (New York), February 8, 1879, p. 415.

4. James S. Hutchins, "Mounted Riflemen: The Real Role of Cavalry in the Indian Wars," in K. Ross Toole, editor, *Probing the American West* (Santa Fe: Museum of New Mexico Press, 1962), p. 81; Perry to Forsyth, *c.* October 22, 1878, p. 2; McCarthy, Army Sketches, p. 18. Company F had arrived at Fort Lapwai on November 11, 1875. See Muster Roll of Company F, October–December, 1875.

5. Trimble Report, p. 3; McCarthy, CI, p. 84; McCarthy, Diary, June 11–12, 1877.

The few hours of training, however, were hardly compensation for the days spent in erecting and maintaining buildings, constructing bridges and roads, tending gardens, cutting hay, gathering wood, drawing water, keeping books, and the like. When Company H left Fort Lapwai, McCarthy still considered it "in a measure raw," and it is evident that the men had not had the opportunity to accustom their horses to the sound of rifle fire. Trimble wrote in his report that horses had to be drilled continually for some years to make them thoroughly manageable in combat, and Parnell described the mounts as green and flighty. Gen. Howard personally believed that the disaster was caused in large part by the unsteadiness of the horses under fire. But perhaps the most important fact of all was that Company H had not had target practice since the preceding winter. Not only were the horses unaccustomed to the sound of rifle fire, but apparently so were many of the men.[6]

In 1877 a cavalryman who was more than a mediocre shot at any range was a rarity in the United States Army. The experience of Company H was not unique, it was the norm: training in the use and maintenance of weapons was universally neglected. Impecunity was part of the reason. For example, in 1874 the Army could issue only 120 cartridges to each man for target practice because of the lack of funds. Target practice — when the men had it — was conducted in a haphazard fashion, and its value was minimal. Not until after the Nez Perce War did enlisted men receive any instruction whatsoever in the theory of marksmanship. In 1893 Capt. James Parker of the Fourth Cavalry observed that the lack of success of his branch of the service in the Indian wars had often been rationalized on the grounds that the enemy had possessed superior weapons. The truth was that the Model 1873 Springfield was the best military rifle in the world. The Indian was simply a better shot. When he fired his weapon, he fired it to kill. Ammunition was scarce, and each cartridge represented a life. Trimble's assessment of the Springfield was the same. In his report, he wrote that it was as good a weapon as the cavalry had ever been issued, and only a few of them malfunctioned in rapid firing. But the rumor was that many of the weapons had become disabled during the Battle of White Bird Canyon. Years later Sgt. McCarthy supplied the answer. Many of the guns had been

6. Trimble Report, p. 3; Parnell, CI, p. 64; McCarthy, CI, p. 84; McCarthy, Army Sketches, p. 18; Lt. M. C. Wilkinson to the Commanding Officer of Fort Cabrille, June 30, 1877, Fort Lapwai, Letters Sent, DC.

rusty and foul; the men had not cared for them properly. Human ignorance and negligence had caused them to jam.[7]

The fact that there were, at the most, only two or three warriors wounded from rifle fire in the Battle of White Bird Canyon is the best evidence to support the contention of poor marksmanship. The piles of cartridge cases found near some of the bodies did not show — as some have claimed — that the men sold their lives dearly. It showed that they did not possess skill in using a carbine. Because the men were poor shots and because the horses were untrained, the decision to leave the men of Company H mounted and to permit them to fire from horseback was indeed a blunder. Parnell knew it; Trimble should have. It rendered an ineffective force almost useless. Accuracy on horseback is difficult to achieve, and it is certainly not the province of the novice. Ammunition had been limited in supply: Company H carried sixty rounds per man, and Company F had forty. McCarthy stated that green men fired recklessly, and many lost the ammunition carried in their saddle bags when their horses broke away from them or from the horseholders.[8]

In contrast to the white soldier, the Indian was a marvel. That he excelled in horsemanship there was no doubt. Practically every cavalry officer who commented on the subject sang his praises. His horse was well-trained and obeyed its master almost without fail. Trimble noted that an Indian pony would stand and eat grass while its owner fought. A cavalry mount had to be held or it would soon depart, and the normal procedure was to detail every fourth man to hold his horse and the horses of three others. In order to compensate for the lack of training, a company of cavalry that wanted to fight on foot had to reduce its fighting power by one quarter.[9]

Knowing that it was very difficult to fire from horseback with accuracy, the Nez Perce rarely attempted to do so. Trimble stated that, contrary to popular belief, the Indian always dismounted to fire unless his purpose was to stampede stock. In a reminiscence Sgt. McCarthy described one technique that the Nez Perce employed: "When a warrior wanted to fire," he explained, "he rolled off the pony to the ground, took deliberate aim, and crawled on again —

7. Oliver Knight, *Following the Indian Wars* (Norman: University of Oklahoma Press, 1960), p. 19; Hutchins, "Mounted Riflemen," p. 83; Chief Joseph, "Own Story," p. 64; Trimble Report, p. 32; McCarthy, Army Sketches, p. 18; G. W. Baird, "The Capture of Chief Joseph and the Nez Perce," *The International Review* (1879), 7:214.

8. Parnell, CI, p. 74; McCarthy, Army Sketches, pp. 9, 18.

9. Trimble Report, p. 32.

the pony remaining quiet and patient during the firing, lying by the roadside." Man and beast were compatible; together they made a splendid fighting unit.[10]

To be able to cope with such a skillful enemy, the men of Companies F and H had to be at their best. They were not. Years later McCarthy wrote:

> We were in no condition to go to White Bird on the night of the 16th. We had been in the saddle for nearly 24 hours, and the men and horses were tired and in bad shape for a fight.[11]

He was right. Perry overestimated the stamina of his men and horses, and, what is more important, he underestimated the ability of his adversary. The settlers told him that the Nez Perce were cowardly scoundrels, and he apparently believed them. It did not take him long to change his mind. In a letter to Lt. Col. Forsyth, Perry wrote that the Nez Perce were "the best mounted and hardest fighting . . . Indians on the continent."[12] Perhaps he overstated the case, but they were opponents worthy of the highest respect.

The Battle of White Bird Canyon had several results. It undoubtedly made those who won it more bold and those who lost it more cautious. It gave the victors a forlorn hope, as it turned out, and it continued a struggle for freedom that, however noble, brought suffering and death to those who participated in it. Like almost all disasters, the Battle of White Bird Canyon was not completely disastrous. The United States Army gained knowledge from it, and the reforms that were to come in later years came, in a measure, because of it. But it was a painful way to learn.

10. Trimble Report, p. 32; McCarthy, Army Sketches, p. 24.

11. McCarthy, Army Sketches, p. 18.

12. Perry to Forsyth, c. October 22, 1878, p. 13. Nelson Miles was equally impressed with the abilities of the Nez Perce. He wrote: "The Nez Perce are the boldest men and the best marksmen of any Indians I have ever encountered." See C. A. Woodruff, "Battle of the Big Hole," Contributions to the Historical Society of Montana (1910), 7:102.

What They Said

In all accounts of conflicts with the Indians it is a noticeable fact that the non-commissioned officers of the regular service have suffered much more than their proportionate percentage in point of numbers would lead one to expect. In the list of killed and wounded the Sergeants and Corporals appear frequently and prominently. Their share in the pomp and circumstance of glorious war is small at best. There is not much glory to be achieved in obscure encounters, but the record shows that these humble and devoted soldiers, with little or no hopes of recognition or promotion, have been regardless of personal sacrifice, ever ready in the discharge of every duty. Their conduct merits the recognition and appreciation of the country, and they should receive the consideration and reward which is due to heroism and self-sacrifice.

IDAHO TRI-WEEKLY STATESMAN

Indeed your action at White Bird was the only one worthy of praise; you fulfilled your orders completely.

TRIMBLE TO McCARTHY

For continuous pluck, good sense, clear headedness under fire, and for the salvation of one-half of the command, I think he is deserving a medal of honor.

HOWARD OF PARNELL

[The] identical thorn tree where the soldier was mutilated and fastened to the limbs is still standing, and Mr. Swarts intends always to preserve it. It is very noticeable that the tree is no larger today than twenty-six years ago when the horrible act occurred.

BIOGRAPHICAL SKETCH OF THEODORE SWARTS

All of these returning redskins were dressed in eastern style. At Lewiston a company of well-mounted soldiers met and escorted them to the reservation. I stood on the porch of the Raymond Hotel, and saw the Indians file by. Among others, there passed an old savage, "Scar-faced Charley," who, fearing that he might be shot, and wishing to conceal his identity, had tied a handkerchief over his face. There was quite a feeling of bitterness displayed. I heard one man on the street call out, "Ben, where is your gun?"

CHARLOTTE KIRKWOOD

Long shall old comrades delight;
When they speak of heroic deeds done in the past,
To tell the youngsters the tale of the fight.

IN MEMORY OF LIEUTENANT THELLER (Poem)

13

Laid to Rest

The disappearance and death of Jennet Manuel and her son continued to be a source of speculation during the days and months and years that followed the outbreak. Rumor fed on rumor. Some claimed that the Nez Perce had taken the woman with them; others declared that she had been murdered in the Manuel house, and that her body and that of the baby had been consumed in the flames.

Maggie Manuel swore until her death that her mother and brother had been murdered in the house on the night of June 15. The accounts written by her in later years vary little in detail. According to Maggie, an Indian, whom she identified as Chief Joseph, entered the house and stabbed her mother in the breast with a knife. After the attack, the Indian took Maggie into an adjoining room, where she fell asleep. When she awoke, the house was quiet. She opened the door to the main room, and there on the floor was the naked body of her mother, lying in a pool of blood. Near her head lay John; he was also dead. Later Maggie left the house and hid in the brush, where Patrick Brice found her the next morning. According to Maggie, she and the Irishman returned to the house to view the bodies before leaving for Mount Idaho.[1]

Two of the statements made by Maggie Manuel bear comment at this point. First, both white and Indian historians agree that Joseph could not have been in the house on the night of June 15. He was in camp on Cottonwood Creek. Second, in his account of the adventure, published on September 14, 1877, Brice stated that he went back to the house after being given his freedom and found it empty.[2]

Apparently the first man to examine the remains of the Manuel house was Ad Chapman, and we have already noted that he was convinced the bones he found in the rubble were those of an

1. Accounts of Maggie Manuel Bowman in *Idaho County Free Press*, April 1, 1903; *Walla Walla Union Bulletin*, January 23, 1944; Defenbach, *Idaho*, 1:415–419; and *North Idaho*, pp. 54–55, 529–530.

2. Brice, "Nez Perce Outbreak."

animal.[3] James Conely was of the same opinion. Probably at a later date, he and some others carefully raked the ashes but failed to find any human bones.[4] But there were those who disagreed. In a letter to the editor of the *Lewiston Teller* dated July 19, 1877, J. W. Poe wrote: "It was currently believed that Mrs. Manuel and the child were still alive until I had examined the ruins and found positive evidence to the contrary."[5] H. C. Brown, who visited the site on the way back to the remains of his store, made a similar declaration.[6] The nature of the evidence that Poe and Brown discovered has never been determined. Perhaps they were earrings. Maggie Manuel came into possession of the pair that her mother wore that day. They had been unearthed in probing the site.[7]

It will be remembered that Harry Cone, one of the settlers in the stockade at Slate Creek, wrote in a reminiscence that he had heard one of the Nez Perce say on July 18 that Mrs. Manuel had been killed by an Indian who was under the influence of liquor.[8] Yet on July 28, the *Lewiston Teller* carried a short news item that read: "Squaws still report that Mrs. Manual [*sic*] is living and a prisoner,"[9] and years later a settler reported that he had seen a white woman with the Nez Perce when they passed up the Bitterroot Valley.[10]

It was not until 1900 that one of the Indian participants commented on the fate of Mrs. Manuel. Yellow Bull told the story to C. P. Stranahan but swore his listener to secrecy. However, he did give his friend permission to publish the account after his death. Yellow Bull stated that Mrs. Manuel was taken prisoner and kept in the custody of a certain Indian, whose name he would not divulge. After they had crossed the divide, her keeper and another warrior had an argument over her, and the next morning she was missing. Yellow Bull believed that she had been killed and her body hidden in the brush.[11]

3. Sears, "Mount Idaho."

4. Howard, *Saga of Chief Joseph*, pp. 156–157.

5. Poe to Alonzo Leland, July 19, 1877, *Lewiston Teller*, July 28, 1877, p. 1.

6. Brown, *Flight of the Nez Perce*, p. 113.

7. Howard, *Saga of Chief Joseph*, p. 156n.

8. Cone, "White Bird Battle," p. 6.

9. *Lewiston Teller*, July 28, 1877, p. 4.

10. Henry Buck, "The Nez Perce Indian War of 1877," Montana Historical Society, Helena, Montana.

11. C. P. Stranahan, "Taciturn Chief Joseph Refuses to Discuss War," *The Idaho Statesman*, June 18, 1933, section 2, p. 4; Bailey, *River of No Return*, p. 190.

There is other corroboration for the statement that Mrs. Manuel did become a captive. In 1935, Peo-Peo Tahlikt was an impoverished old man. He looked on the world with a jaundiced eye; life had the taste of a copper penny. He had seen the white man take the land of his people. He had fought for it and lost. Defeat was not bad, but he had been left without honor. His culture had been ridiculed and supressed; his beliefs had been belittled and banned. Bitterness bubbled over and saturated his being, and when Many Wounds offered to record his story, the old warrior consented. He would tell the white man about the way it really was. The product was a thin document — about twenty typewritten pages — but it was full of insights and interpretations not usually found in accounts of this kind. Indian talked to Indian, and although Many Wounds was not a master of the English language, he knew it well enough to communicate. Many Wounds began the interview by asking Peo-Peo Tahlikt to describe the trophies strewn about his cabin and to relate their significance. One of the first mementos taken in hand was a human scalp and hairlock. "Hair of white woman, Mrs. Manuel," said the warrior. He went on to relate that the woman had been taken prisoner and started with them to Montana. Before long, however, she took sick and died. The Indians buried her body under some rocks by the Lolo Trail. He said that Joseph was the one who took the scalp; the hair was nice. Peo-Peo Tahlikt fell heir to it. He knew that Joseph was sorry, and he was sorry.[12]

Some historians have pointed to the statement of George Popham in support of the contention that Mrs. Manuel and her son died in the house. In a letter published on June 30, 1877, Popham declared that the home had been burned on Sunday, and that his daughter and grandson had been burned in it. He did not say that he saw the bodies. In later accounts written by him, it becomes clear that Popham did not have personal knowledge; his information came from his granddaughter, with whom he had been reunited before he wrote the first version of the affair. He had been hiding in the timber at the time the alleged murders occurred, and he had not been able to return to the house after he left it for the last time on June 15.[13]

12. "Stories about Indians as told by Chief Peo-Peo Tah-likt [translated variously Birds Alighting and Bands of Geese] to Sam Lott (Many Wounds), February 25, 1935," typed carbon, Washington State University Archives, Pullman, Washington.

13. Popham, "Hostilities"; statements of George Popham, October 23, 1888, and August 13, 1890, Manuel 3496.

The only other man who could have been an eyewitness to the fact of death was Jack Manuel, but he was physically unable to reach the house. In one of the few statements he ever made concerning the matter, Manuel simply said that his wife and youngest child had been captured by the Nez Perce and "doubtless killed as they were never found afterwards."[14] Obviously Manuel had his doubts about the cremation theory.

No one has ever questioned the integrity of Maggie Manuel. Those who talked with her were convinced that she believed her story. Some have suggested that the little girl may have suffered hallucinations.[15] The assumption is not an unreasonable one in view of the age of the girl and the emotional turmoil created by the attack on her parents, the killing of James Baker, and the hours of fear and suffering that followed.

There is one way of reconciling all points of view without resorting to the hallucination theory. Perhaps Maggie Manuel did see an Indian stab her mother. Perhaps she did see her lying in a pool of blood. Perhaps she appeared to be dead. Perhaps she was not. The testimony of Harry Cone is easy to pass over. An Indian may have told the whites at Slate Creek that Mrs. Manuel was dead because he did not want them to know that she was alive. The remains found in the ashes may also be dismissed. Earrings are not proof of death. The identification of charred bone fragments is not an easy task even with modern equipment and techniques. On the other hand, it is more difficult to discount the stories told by Yellow Bull and Peo-Peo Tahlikt. Why would they lie? They had nothing to gain by it. The mystery is an intriguing one. Perhaps sometime it may be solved conclusively. Presently the evidence indicates that Jennet Manuel died not in the house but days later somewhere in the mountains.

And what of the others? Joe Moore died two months and three days after receiving his wounds. The rest of the wounded eventually recovered. Jack Manuel lived until 1889, but he was never the same. Catherine Elfers, Isabella Benedict, and Jennie Norton all remarried: Catherine to Philip Cleary on April 13, 1884; Isabella to Edward Robie on April 19, 1880; and Jennie to Thomas J. Bunker in 1883. Neither Isabella nor Jennie ever returned to her former home, but Catherine Elfers continued to live in the house near John Day Creek. She had four children to care for. The last, Marie

---

14. Statement of Manuel, May 26, 1888, Manuel 3496.

15. For example, see Bailey, *River of No Return*, p. 188.

Elizabeth, was born on January 1, 1878. Helen Walsh was reunited with her husband in Lewiston about six weeks after the beginning of the outbreak. In 1906 she met Gen. Howard in Roseburg, Oregon, and told him the story of her experiences. Patrick Brice continued to pursue his trade as a miner. In 1897 he was living in Anaconda, Montana.[16]

Arthur Chapman went with Howard as a scout and served throughout the Nez Perce campaign. At the request of Col. Miles, he accompanied the captured Nez Perce to Fort Keogh, then to Fort Leavenworth, and finally to Indian Territory, where they were ex-iled. He left them in the fall of 1879. Eleven years later, he was still in the employ of the Army, working at Fort Vancouver.[17]

Frank Fenn went on to have a distinguished public career. From 1901 to 1921 he was a supervisor for the United States Forest Service at Kooskia, Idaho. One day an Indian came into his office at Kooskia and introduced himself as Philip Evans. "You shot me," he said. Fenn recalled that he had noticed a warrior gaining on him during the retreat and had fired at him but did not wait to see the results. This time he and Bow and Arrow Case parted friends. Frank Fenn died on June 19, 1927.[18]

Theodore Swarts continued to live near the scene of the battle. On August 21, 1877, he married Electa Brown. They were blessed with nine children. George Shearer died on January 2, 1890, from war injuries. Herman Faxon was still alive in 1937. Eighty-eight years old, he had only a pension of $50 a month, paid to him by the government in compensation for the wound he received in the Bat-tle of White Bird Canyon. Concerned about the cost of his burial, he wrote a letter to the *Winners of the West*, the official organ of the National Indian War Veterans, to inquire if his relatives would re-ceive a burial allowance for him after his death. He must have been pleased to learn that the government would pay $100 and present his survivors with a $7 flag.[19]

Some of the Nez Perce who fought in the Battle of White Bird

16. Greenburg, "Victim,"; Popham, August 13, 1890, Manuel 3496; "Elfers," *North Idaho*, p. 451; Cleary, April 16, 1888, Cleary 2723; Robie, November 9, 1889, Robie 10557; Elsensohn, *Idaho County*, 1:528; Bunker, July 20, 1898, Bunker 9816; Brice, November 23, 1897, Brice 7427.

17. Chapman, November 23, 1886, and March 21, 1890, Chapman 1102.

18. Defenbach, *Idaho*, 3:386; Elsensohn, *Idaho County*, 1:273–274.

19. "Theodore Swarts," *North Idaho*, p. 474; *Twenty-Seventh Biennial Report of the Secretary of the State of Idaho*, p. 73; H. A. Faxon, "Survivor of Nez Perce War," *Winners of the West* (February, 1937), 14:7.

Canyon did not survive succeeding engagements. Among them were Shore Crossing and Red Moccasin Tops, both of whom died in the Battle of the Big Hole on August 9, 1877, and Ollokot and Toohoolhoolzote, who died in the Battle of the Bear Paws on October 1. White Bird and No Feet were among those who escaped into Canada. A tribesman murdered White Bird there in about 1882. No Feet continued to live with the Sioux and eventually married into the tribe. A few, like Four Blankets, succumbed to disease in Indian Territory. Others lived to return to the Northwest in 1885, when the government settled the remnant of the captured bands on the Lapwai and Colville reservations.[20]

Joseph spent his remaining years on the Colville Indian Reservation in Washington. He died on September 21, 1904. The agency physician said that he died of a broken heart. In 1905 the Washington State Historical Society erected an appropriate monument to mark his resting place in the Nespelem cemetery. Wounded Head died in about 1912 at his home on the Lapwai reservation. Swan Necklace also survived the war and later returned to his native land. Because they feared reprisals the Nez Perce kept Swan Necklace's true identity a secret. To the whites he was known as John Minthon. The last of the avengers died in the late 1920's. Bow and Arrow Case apparently lived into the middle of the 1930's. Yellow Wolf died on the Colville Indian Reservation on August 21, 1935, but not before he had given Lucullus McWhorter his life story. Josiah Red Wolf, a small child at the time of the battle and the last survivor, died on March 23, 1971. His grave may be seen at Spalding, Idaho.[21]

Thomas McLaughlin of Company F recovered from his wound and returned to active duty. Florence McCarthy deserted on September 3, 1878. Joseph Lytte deserted on July 13, 1878, but was apprehended on May 12, 1880. He completed his enlistment on July 10, 1882. Written on his discharge papers were the words, "Drunkard, worthless." Maier Cohn of Company H died in the Battle of the Clearwater on July 12, 1877. Joseph Kelly eventually recovered, but he was incapacitated for military service and retired on disability on December 11, 1877. Charles Fowler deserted on June 3, 1879. James

20. McWhorter, *Hear Me*, pp. 255, 374, 524; A. I. Chapman, "More of the Murderers," *Lewiston Teller*, February 23, 1878, p. 2; Beal, *"I Will Fight No More Forever,"* p. 216.

21. William J. Ghent, "Joseph," DAB, 10:219; McWhorter, *Hear Me*, pp. 230n, 241; McWhorter, *Yellow Wolf*, pp. 18, 44n; Ruby, "First Account," pp. 2–3; "Death Comes to Josiah Red Wolf, Last Nez Perce Flight Survivor," *Montana Post* (May–June, 1971), 9:6.

Shay completed thirty years of service and then retired. Michael McCarthy saw him for the last time in Walla Walla, Washington. He was drunk, and a crowd of boys was having fun at his expense.[22]

On November 17, 1885, the United States Army officially abandoned Fort Lapwai but made provision to maintain the cemetery. On August 1, 1890, the Secretary of War approved the disinterment of the White Bird dead in order to ship them to Fort Walla Walla for burial. Second Lt. Nathaniel F. McClure superintended the removal. He reached Fort Lapwai on October 30, and laborers began the work of disinterment the following day. McClure examined the remains carefully and made a full report. He found twenty-six skulls and the fragments of others. Several of the skulls had bullet holes in them, and one showed evidence of having been damaged by a hatchet. On November 6, the dead wagon lumbered into Lewiston. The coffin traveled by rail to Fort Walla Walla and reached the military post on November 12. Reinterment took place the same day.[23]

After Michael McCarthy heard of the transfer of the remains to Fort Walla Walla, he began writing letters to raise enough money for a suitable monument to mark the grave. The men of Company H responded with $155, and Joel Trimble added $5. McCarthy immediately contracted for a monument. Made of Vermont marble, it stood fifteen feet high. Workmen placed the shaft over the grave on December 19, 1891. The total cost of the memorial was $225, and McCarthy made up the difference. David Perry later donated $20, which McCarthy used to build a fence around the monument. Construction workers uncovered the skeleton of another cavalryman in September of 1919, and reburial took place a short distance away. A monument marks the spot at the southern base of White Bird Hill.[24]

William Parnell reached the rank of captain on April 27, 1879. Eight years later he retired on disability. He was promoted to major on the retired list on April 23, 1904. He spent the last ten years of his life as a military instructor at St. Matthew's School in San Mateo, California. He died on August 20, 1910. Parnell received the Medal

22. Muster Rolls of Companies F and H, 1877–1879; Registry of Enlistments, 1875, 1876; "Jim Shay," in McCarthy, Journal.

23. E. Beck to Secretary of War, March 15, 1890; McClure to Chief Quartermaster of the Department of the Columbia, November 15, 1890; and List of Remains, Military Cemeteries File.

24. McCarthy, "White Bird Monument," in Journal, pp. 123–124; *Eleventh Biennial Report . . . State Historical Society of Idaho*, p. 65.

of Honor for rescuing Aman Hartman during the retreat to Grangeville on September 16, 1897.[25]

Joel Trimble went on sick leave on April 2, 1878, and retired on disability on August 21, 1879. He had lost the sight in his right eye and most of the vision in his left. Trimble died on November 16, 1911, in Berkeley, California. He left three sons and two daughters.[26]

David Perry became a major in the Sixth Cavalry on April 27, 1879. Twelve years later he was promoted to lieutenant colonel in the Tenth Cavalry, and on December 11, 1896, he reached the rank of colonel in the Ninth. Promoted to brigadier general on the retired list, he died on May 18, 1908, in Washington, D.C. He was buried in Arlington National Cemetery.[27]

Michael McCarthy became the Quartermaster Sergeant of the 1st Cavalry on June 10, 1878. He completed his military service in the Regular Army on May 24, 1879. Entering the Washington National Guard, he rose to the rank of colonel before his death in 1907. McCarthy received the Medal of Honor for his part in the Battle of White Bird Canyon in 1897.[28]

Delia Theller continued to live in San Francisco. A Maltese cat and a fine bird dog, which had been a special favorite of her husband, were her only companions. She was laid to rest beside Edward Theller on January 4, 1888.[29]

25. Lt. Col. Medical Corps to Adjutant General USA, August 20, 1910, File of William Russell Parnell, ACP.

26. Records of Proceedings of a Board to Retire Disabled Officers, Case of Captain J. G. Trimble, 1st Cavalry, August 6, 1879, Presidio of San Francisco; *Obituary of Joel Graham Trimble, Military Order of the Loyal Legion of the United States, Circular No. 33, Series of 1911, San Francisco, California,* File of Joel Graham Trimble, ACP.

27. Heitman, *Historical Register,* 1:785; Capt. M. A. DeLaney to Adjutant General USA, May 18, 1908, File of David Perry, ACP.

28. Registry of Enlistments, 1874; McCarthy to Secretary of War, March 22, 1880, Medal of Honor File, Case of Michael McCarthy; biographical notes on inside cover of McCarthy, Journal.

29. Kirkwood, *Indian War,* p. 7; "Idaho County Marks Site."

Appendix 1

SPECIAL ORDERS NO. 142

IV. Upon the demand of Captain David Perry 1st Cavalry, a Court of Inquiry is constituted to assemble at Portland, Oregon, at 10 o'clock a.m., December 16th, proximo, or as soon thereafter as practicable to investigate the statements contained in the reports of several officers of the Army, and which Captain Perry believes to reflect upon his conduct during the Nez Perce Indian Campaign of 1877. The Court will also investigate and inquire of so much of Captain Perry's conduct, generally, during the said campaign as has not been already made the subject of inquiry by the Court instituted by Special Field Orders No. 42, Headquarters Department of the Columbia, series of 1877.

The Court will report the facts, and give its opinion on the merits of the whole case.[1]

[*December 21, 1878*]

Captain Joel G. Trimble 1st Cavalry, a witness, was then called before the Court and having been duly sworn testified as follows:

Q. (by Recorder) Please state your name, rank, and regiment.

A. J. G. Trimble, Captain 1st Cavalry.

Q. Were you present at what is known as the "Fight at White Bird Cañon" with the Nez Perce Indians during the summer of 1877?

A. I was.

Q. In what month did it take place?

A. In the month of June.

Q. Please state to the Court what your position was at the time and what transpired.

A. I was second officer in command. The command consisted of two companies of the 1st Cavalry "F" and "H" and about a dozen citizens I think, all under the command of Captain Perry 1st Cavalry. The Command moved

---

1. The Proceedings of the Court of Inquiry, pursuant to Special Orders No. 142 issued from Headquarters, Department of the Columbia, Fort Vancouver, W.T., on November 27, 1878, are found in Records of the Office of the Judge Advocate General, Record Group 153, National Archives. That portion of the Proceedings bearing upon the Battle of White Bird Canyon is reproduced here. The Court was unable to begin its formal hearings until December 18 because of lack of a quorum of members; it did not begin to hear testimony on the events at and near White Bird Canyon until December 21, when Captain Trimble began his testimony.

down into the cañon of White Bird Creek a little before daylight. The citizens and "F" company and "H" company in that order. After proceeding some distance down the cañon and getting into the open space where the cañon widens out, an orderly brought me the order to take off overcoats and load. I observed them as we approached a high rocky ridge. "F" company formed left front into line, and the Indians were advancing. I received this order by a trumpeter. Having every reason to believe that the Indians were advancing in force, I formed left front into line and deployed by the right flank at five paces interval and advanced to the ridge, taking post on the right of "F" Company — some several hundred yards on the right, 200 or more yards. Just as I was advancing into position I could see quite a number of men of "F" Company firing from horseback. After taking position, I discovered and it was reported to me, that the Indians were moving around on our right and driving stock. Several of my men had commenced firing them off their horses. I cautioned the men to remain steady as they were and detailed a 1st Sergeant and six men to take post on a high point on the right and went with them to this point, a high point commanding the whole situation. As soon as they took post, they commenced firing upon the Indians moving to our right. Then I came at once back to the balance of my company where I found several men dismounted and firing. In the rear of my company I saw the Commanding Officer of the Expedition. He told me we would have to get out of that or we would be whipped. I told him I had just taken that position on the right there and stationed those men. I could see then the citizens, who were stationed on the extreme left, had given away, appeared to have given away. I could not see accurately, and a few men of "F" Company seemed to be on foot firing from where they were irregularly. Quite a number of them were in rear and in among my men. After I had been spoken to by the Commanding Officer, I remarked I thought we ought to go through to the Salmon river, that we could go through that way I thought. He remarked, "That would be utter annihilation" and said we would have to retreat from where we were. I asked him then if he intended to march the command to the rear, that the Indians were getting around us there. He said yes, to march the command to the rear. I had the men form in column of twos, rather irregularly, told those to mount up who were dismounted, moved the command to the rear. Lieut. Parnell being in front and conducting the column. After the command had moved a little to the rear I observed Lieutenant Theller dismounted with a carbine in his hand. I think Lieut. Parnell observed him at the same time. He didn't appear to be wounded. I saw a horse running at large kicking, appeared to be getting his saddle under his heels. I hollered to a man, and so did Lieut. Parnell to catch him and hold him by the head, and get the saddle off him, so that Lieut. Theller could get the horse. The man held him by the head and another man got the saddle off him. Lieut. Theller got on the horse bareback and rode off toward the main trail I supposed, where I had seen several men going previously, and then Lieut. Parnell remarked to me are you going to leave those men out on that point. I said if we had to abandon that place we would have to call them back to go with the command. We both rode out of the column and hollered to them a number of times to join their command. Then Lieut. Parnell went to the lead of the column that was moving to the rear. Just then I saw the Commanding Officer and told him I heard Chapman, over the citizens, remark that the point I had selected there was a good point, and it was his opinion that we could hold it against all the Indians in the country, and that I was in favor of holding it, the ridge that the Sergeant and party was stationed on being high and much above the advancing Indians. He explained that we might try, or words to that effect, and I hollered to turn the head of the column to the left. I did so several times and moved up on to this point at a gallop. I supposed that we would dismount there and take this position. Going up there the men became very much scattered and there was considerable firing. The men after arriving up at this point were very much scattered, some going one way and some another. Quite a number of orders were given. I don't know who by, and I told a trumpeter to tell Captain Perry to let the command dismount. I never saw the trumpeter afterwards. I think he was shot. I saw quite a number of the men galloping off towards what I supposed the main trail. The Indians then, I think, were getting pretty well around in every direction, judging by the firing. Quite a number of men went along the bluffs, myself among the number, and quite a number of men rallied or halted on another bluff to the rear and fired at the Indians riding in on the flank. One man by the name of Shea of "H" Company was off his horse trying to get a shell out of his gun that had got fastened. He remarked he could hardly see the use of trying to hang on when the command seemed to have gone all to pieces. I told him we would have to do the best we could. I thought we could make a halt. The men rode off that point. I rode down into a ravine and up the side of a hill on the side of the line. I came up with the Commanding Officer who pointed out, he made the remark he saw a man shot off his horse, he said one man would have to be left behind. He pointed out some men on a ridge and told me to go and take charge of them in person. I went to where these men were and dismounted off my horse. The men were firing on the Indians getting around on the bank. I just ordered all the men to get off their horses. One man was off his horse, Sergeant Havens of "H" Company. Just at that time a trumpeter came down and told me the Commanding Officer told him that I should send half my men to him.

[December 23, 1878]

I did as ordered. At the time I went to this party, Chapman, a citizen, was with the party. He rode rapidly away after I got there up the hill. This party that was sent to report to the Commanding Officer were sent up the bluff and were posted on a high bluff to the East. I think about a thousand yards distant. Shortly afterwards the Commanding Officer rode down towards my position and turned up the bluffs hollering out several times "now for the cañon" I supposed it meant the cañon through which the main trail ran. I was led to that supposition, as I had remarked to the Commanding Officer if we could get a good place somewhere, we could defend it, where we could concentrate. Some of the men remarked he was waving his pistol, suppose as a signal. Several of the men who were with me rode up towards him and the party on the high bluff all started down and proceeded to ascend the main bluff. They had to ride down off this point in order to ascend this main bluff. The Sergeant and myself started up after them. All the men that were within my sight seemed to be ascending the bluffs. I came up with the Commanding Officer on the side of the bluff and he remarked to me "Trimble we will get off our horses and die right here. We must stay here."

We both got off our horses and I saw a man just down in front, off his horse with a gun. I left my horse and ran down to him a few steps and told him to fire on those Indians who were advancing to give them a shot. The Commanding Officer hollered out, "Don't let him shoot he will waste the ammunition." He hollered once or twice. I turned to look up towards him. He got on his horse and moved up the hill. I got on mine and moved up the hill too. Just after I started my horse fell down, his head down hill. I dismounted off him. He had his bits buried in the mud. The saddle had got loose and the overcoat broke from the strap and rolled down the hill. I had to take the saddle off and help him get on his feet, and saddled him on again. I got on him and started up the hill in a winding manner and in going up I got above the Commanding Officer and several men, where they had halted on the side hill. The bluffs were very high; it was some distance to the top. My object there was to get on a high point that projected out on our left and commanded a view of the whole ground. The Commanding Officer hollered out to me two or three times, "Trimble do you know where you are going?" I hollered back that I was going to try and get on that high point. I thought that would be the best place to see the Indians coming in from that direction. As soon as I got high enough up I turned in the direction of that point, some men were still going further on. I got on the point. I rode out on it pretty well; it seemed to be the top of a ridge. A ridge ran right up to it. I saw two Indians riding up this ridge towards this point where I was. I thought they were a good distance off. I got off to adjust my saddle. The Commanding Officer came right up there from another direction, and said that was a good place to hold. Two or three men were there and he rode off to another high ridge or point there seemed to be quite a number of men about it. Just at the time these Indians rode up quite close though a little lower down on the ridge, and I could see them dismount. I knew they would fire in a minute but I had not quite cinched up my saddle. I jerked my cinch quickly. Just then one of them fired. The bullet went just under my stirrup. I believe that I remarked to the Commanding Officer that the Indians were coming up or keeping even with us, or something like that — I am not positive. As soon as this Indian fired I jumped on my horse and the only man I saw there was a Corporal of "F" Company. He was back sitting on his horse. He had a gun. I hollered to come out, for him (the Corporal), to come out where I was. I thought we could stay there a minute or two. Just then another shot was fired by the other Indian. I suppose it was fired at the Corporal. I heard the ball whistle. As it did not come very close to me I supposed it was fired at him. We both turned our horses and galloped to where we saw a larger number of men to be. They were galloping down the ridge. They seemed to be all in motion. I kept somewhat to the left along the edge of the high bluffs, and I looked down from these high bluffs and saw something glittering like water. I was afterwards told it was Salmon river. I then turned to the right and rode over to where I thought the main position of the men were. I came up to quite a number. They all seemed to be going to the rear. I saw the Commanding Officer there. Chapman was there too. I heard Chapman say "The house" was the only place where we could make a stand. I did not know what house he meant. He (Chapman) rode off very fast. All were galloping to the rear. The Com-

manding Officer rode off to the right. I kept along in the same direction. I
was going down a slope. I saw a hollow to the right. I saw a man without a
hat, dismounted and running about. Sergeant Havens and myself rode
down towards him and told him to hide himself in the bushes. The man ran
into the bushes. The horses were jumping around and it was hard to restrain them. Two men of "F" Company rushed past me. Neither of them
had guns. One of them was bareback. They seemed to be coming from
another direction further to the right. I hollered to them several times to
stop. Sergeant Havens remarked that they had no guns anyhow. We started
on some distance further and found one of these men lying in the road. His
horse had thrown him and broke his neck. I stopped long enough to see
that the man was dead, had broken his neck by a fall from his horse. Just
then, considerably over to the right, I saw a large body of men galloping
down into a ravine. There seemed to be 40 or 50. They disappeared very
quickly. I saw then that there were only five or six men with me, two with
guns. Sergeant Havens and Private Powers of "H" Company. The Sergeant
told me he had one cartridge and that was in his gun. We seemed to be
inclining to the left. Someone remarked we were going toward Craigs
Mountain. There were some parties in front of us. Several men could be
seen down in the valley, going across the valley, I supposed going in the
direction of Craigs Mountain too. Am not positive. I said then that was not
the proper direction to go. We ought to go towards Mount Idaho and
turned to the right. We got down into the lowland then and went towards a
house that was on the right. Going from that house were several men among
them I think was Chapman, the man on a white horse, going across the
valley. There was some water near by and I stopped some of the men. Two
went on. We got off our horses and watered them. The men with me reported seeing two or three Indians on our right towards the mountain and I
heard one or two shots fired up in that direction. I mounted up and moved
along slowly and thought I saw several men up near the timber. I was not
positive whether I saw them or not. After we moved along a mile or two,
probably three miles, the men reported seeing a number of men moving
along between us and the mountain. I halted them and sent a man, Private
Powers of "H" Company, over to see if they were stragglers and bring them
over to where we were. He came back in a little time and said that he could
not get to where they were. There were fields and fences, so I moved on
with the party towards Grangeville. I met one man beside the three men left
in camp. It was Mr. Crooks the proprietor of the place. It consisted of two
or three houses, a mill and a large hall stored with flour. The soldiers had
the mules packed up ready to go off to Mount Idaho. Some of the men that
had come in before had told them that there was a disaster. Mr. Crooks told
me there was no one to defend that place, that he had rather die than lose
all his property. It was all he had and asked me to stay and help him. Just
then a citizen rode over from Mount Idaho about two miles off and wanted
me to go to that place to defend it. I went with Mr. Crooks down to the Hall,
and ordered the party down there, concluded to stay there. I discovered
quite a party of men going along the mountain towards Mount Idaho. I sent
two men to where they were to tell them where I was a short time after
Captain Perry came in with quite a large party. I suppose 40 or 50 men. I
told him what Mr. Crooks had said to me and he (Captain Perry) said he
thought we had better go to Mount Idaho as that was the best place to

defend. I said that there was a fort there and about 200 people. He then ordered a party to ascertain the situation. The command unsaddled and remained there. He (Captain Perry) went to Mount Idaho and returned after dark sometime with some citizens.

Q. (by Recorder) In what order did the column of troops enter the "White Bird Cañon"?

A. I think there was an advance guard of 6 or 8 men under the command of Lieut. Theller, then the citizens and "F" Company and "H" Company one or two citizens and three or four friendly Indians were on the flanks of the columns.

Q. How far had the column proceeded [when] the Indians were encountered?

A. I think it was about three miles from the head of the cañon.

Q. What commands were given by Captain Perry for the disposition of the troops?

A. I received an order by a trumpeter to form front into line.

Q. Was that a proper order under the circumstances?

A. I think it was a proper preliminary order.

Q. After the fight opened, did Captain Perry exercise a supervision of the whole command?

A. I did not hear him give any orders except what I have related in his conversation with me.

Q. You have stated that soon after the fight commenced the troop began to get mixed up. What was that due to?

A. I think it was the going away of "F" Company where they were and the citizen who was on a knoll. Two of them were wounded, and the remaining mounted, many of the horses becoming unmanageable.

Q. How long after the first firing commenced did "F" Company give away?

A. From the time I went to post the Sergeant and party on the point and got back there, it did not seem more than five minutes.

Q. Where was Captain Perry at this time? Was he trying to keep his men in order?

A. I met him in rear of my company. Quite a number of "F" Company were among my company and mixed up with it. I saw no demonstration of that kind.

Q. How far in front of your company was "F" Company, when the firing commenced?

A. Well, I think they were probably about 150 or 200 yards.

Q. Was the firing from the Indians severe?

A. No sir. It did not appear to be severe at that time.

Q. How long was it from the commencement of the firing that Captain Perry said, "you would have to get out of that"?

A. Well, I do not think it could have been quite a few minutes.

Q. What was the nature of the ground in your front then?

A. It seemed to be broken but rather lower than that the line was formed on.

Q. Could the Indians envelop the flanks of the troop easily in that position?

A. Yes, sir. They rode around the flanks by riding up a ravine on one side and up a creek on the other.

Q. How many Indians were there?

A. I should judge from my knowledge of the band there were about 100. I saw thirty or forty myself.

Q. How many soldiers and citizens were there in the command?

A. I think there were about 86 soldiers and about a dozen citizens.

Q. Was the withdrawal of the troops commenced in good order?

A. Well, a portion of them in good order. Quite a number of them had gone back without orders.

Q. Did Captain Perry have any other officer with his company beside himself?

A. Lieut. Theller 21st Infantry was with his company.

Q. Did the advance party give any warning of the proximity of the Indians, or did they (the Indians) fire into the column without any information being given of their presence?

A. I do not know what warning the advance gave. I understood the Indians were advancing before I saw any of the parties in the front formed. I did not see them fire into the head of the column, but the firing commenced in front after the troops formed in line. There might have been one or two shots before, but I do not know who commenced it, whether the troops or the Indians.

Q. Could you not see the head of the column from where you were?

A. A part of the time advancing down I could see them, a part of the time a little obscured.

Q. Was it due to the nature of the ground that you could not see it?

A. I do not think it was. As soon as I heard it, I started at a trot. The men had fallen behind strapping their overcoats.

Q. Did there seem to be a panic among the troops in front of you?

A. No, sir, there did not seem to be a panic, while I was forming my company I did not see any. I was busy with my company.

Q. In your opinion did you think that the point where you stationed the Sergeant and party could have been successfully defended had this whole command taken station there?

A. I think that point and the ridge where my company formed could have been held. It was the highest position of the ground.

Q. Did your company remain intact up to the time the order to withdraw was given?

A. Yes, except the portion that was detached.

Q. You have said that you became separated from the rest of the command with but a few men. How did that occur?

A. After we made the attempt to go up on the ridge and halt, the men broke in all directions.

Q. After the retreat commenced did Captain Perry take the necessary precaution to station the troops in an advantageous position to resist the enemy?

A. I saw him station one of the parties on a high point where he took some of the men I had. There seemed to be very few in hand. Well, it seemed to be an advantageous position to see, but there were but a few places that were advantageous after the retreat commenced, but where the men were exposed while mounted.

Q. How did you happen to become separated from the main column?

A. I think by going to the left when I left that point I spoke of. If I had gone to the right I think I would have come up with the main party going over the hill, the largest portion of the men.

Q. Did you not know where the Commanding Officer was at the time?

A. No, not after I saw him going to the right.

Q. Should you not have gone in that direction then, while you were retreating?

A. Considering the condition of the command I don't think it made any difference.

Q. Did you see anything of the Commanding Officer after that time until you arrived at Grangeville?

A. No, sir.

Q. What was the condition of the troops as to drill and discipline previous to the commencement of the "White Bird Cañon" fight?

A. I believe that "F" Company was quite well drilled. "H" Company had been drilled very little, was quite deficient in drill. I think the discipline was very good.

Q. To what then do you attribute to [sic] the early disorganization of the troops after the commencement of the fight?

A. To the attempt to fall back in the presence of the enemy and no disposition to remain. I mean no disposition for defense and the order to retreat.

[Trimble was then asked several questions about the battle at Clearwater.]

Q. You say in your "report" that you were under the impression that it was the firm purpose of Captain Perry to retreat a few minutes after the fight had commenced at "White Bird Cañon." What were your reasons for so thinking?

A. The hesitating manner and the general appearance conveyed that impression to me. It took me as much by surprise, knowing you can't retreat in the presence of Indians.

Cross Examination

(Questioned by Captain Perry.)

Q. Did you, or not, receive an order from me, when you first formed line, to look out for my right at "White Bird"?

A. No, sir, I received no order of that kind.

Q. Did I not ask you for a trumpeter when I came up to you on the right and was it not for that purpose that I was there?

A. I have no recollection of his asking for a trumpeter.

Q. Did the giving way of the citizens on my left threaten the integrity of your line?

A. I did not consider it so. I expected the Indians to ride around us. I knew they always do.

Q. You say you suggested going to Salmon river. Could this have been done except by charging the Indians?

A. No sir, it could not. I did not consider it as offering a suggestion. I only made it as a remark in reply. Had I been asked for a suggestion, I do not think I would have stated so.

Q. At the time you and the Sergeant joined Captain Perry on the bluff how many men had he with him?

A. They were going up the hill so fast, I think there were about a dozen men about there, where we got off our horses. I don't think there were more than three or four men immediately about us. I think there were but one or two between the enemy and ourselves.

Q. During the time you were helping your horse to his feet and unsaddling, were the Indians advancing so as to reach the bluffs?

A. I could see one or two down the bluffs. One or two bullets came up near us. They were a long way off. Those immediately in front of us did not advance quick.

Q. Did you make any effort to halt the men you saw going on beyond you to the high point you mentioned?

A. Yes. I called to several to come out to me on that point.

Q. After coming up with Captain Perry and Chapman and after as you state Captain Perry rode off to the right did you see Captain Perry again before you saw him at Grangeville?

A. Yes Sir. The last time I saw him go off to the right, we were all galloping to the rear. I did not see him any more after that.

Q. Did you hear any firing after, and about the time you discovered the man with a broken neck in the road? If so in which direction was it heard?

A. No. I did not hear any firing at the time. It was some distance beyond that that I heard some few shots to the right.

Q. How long after you arrived at Grangeville was it before Captain Perry arrived?

A. Well I should judge it to be 20 or 25 minutes. About 20 minutes when I first saw the column and between 20 and 30 when they arrived down. I supposed there was a number of men moving abreast of me all the time.

Q. Did your men break up at the time you attempted to take a point at which Captain Perry had told you to try to make a stand in White Bird Cañon?

A. Yes. They broke up after advancing to the ridge at a gallop. There was some firing there by both sides.

Q. What caused your command to break up at that time?

A. I think that it was the indiscriminate firing, by the men staying on their horses and the confusion of orders.

Q. Was [sic] these orders causing confusion given by Captain Perry?

A. I have no recollection of hearing him giving any orders. Chapman was of the party and he hollered a good deal. I can't say Captain Perry gave any orders.

Q. Was the retreat at White Bird Cañon ordered before you noticed a confusion on the left of the line?

A. No sir. There seemed to be some confusion down there before.

[More questioning about the Clearwater battle followed, including the following exchange:]

Q. You say Captain Perry made unjust and unfair criticism upon your conduct. What were they and in what manner were they made?

A. I do not know how they were made. I learned it through two or three officers. I was told by one of them he had seen the letter containing them. The officers were Lieut. Knox 1st Cavalry, Captain Summer 1st Cavalry and Lieut. Wilkinson 3rd Infantry.

Q. Did you learn this before making your official report upon the operations of the Cavalry?

A. Yes sir. Some length of time before.
(Questioned by Court.)

Q. When you received the order from Captain Perry to retreat a few minutes after the attack, what was his manner and bearing?

A. He seemed to be dejected. Thinking of it afterwards I thought he was somewhat surprised at meeting them there.

Q. At this time had the troops met with a reverse or lost heavily?

A. I do not think they had lost many. Just about that time I think that two of the citizens were wounded.

Q. At what distance were the Indians from your right? How many? How many driving stock?

A. There was a herd of stock and half a dozen Indians driving them and half a dozen more with them. I could see a dozen riding up the creek to get around that flank.

Q. You say that the troops were well disciplined. How do you explain their conduct in this fight if they behaved in the manner you have described?

A. I never witnessed their behavior in a fight before. I suppose some of them were panic stricken. Some had as much as they could do to manage their horses. They were poor riders.

Q. Was there a position of safety for the horses of the command in the vicinity and could not a successful fight have been made on foot?

A. A successful fight could have been made on foot, but the horses would have to be removed to the bluffs. There was no security of the horses to the rear.

Q. From your statement you were the first to reach Grangeville. Was there a chance for a delay and rally before reaching there? Were the enemy in hot pursuit?

A. No sir. I don't think the enemy were in hot pursuit. I heard that a portion of the main command had been rallied somewhere in the vicinity of Grangeville. I should imagine it was 4 or 5 miles from the point of attack.

Q. Did you hear of this rally before reaching Grangeville?

A. No sir. I heard it spoken after reaching Grangeville by the officers.

Q. What were the casualties among the troops up to the time of your reaching Grangeville?

A. I did not learn all the casualties. I suppose a dozen or more had been shot between the ridge and the bluffs.

[*December 24, 1878*]

Q. Is the Court to understand that you were the first individual to reach Grangeville from the White Bird fight or the first officer?

A. I was the first officer. I learned there were several citizens and soldiers had passed on to Mount Idaho before I got there I saw one man there out of the command.

Q. Was this command of two companies of Cavalry, citizens and Indian scouts properly supplied with ammunition, and thoroughly prepared for a fight when they left Grangeville?

A. I don't think they had quite ammunition enough. My company had about 60 rounds per man. I suppose "F" Company had about the same. I don't know. I believe "F" Company was armed with pistols besides their carbines. "H" Company had a pistol to each noncommissioned officer and trumpeter. They had no rations, except some of them had something in their haversacks.

Q. What was the cause of the delay of the troops in leaving Fort Lapwai?

A. I cannot state positively. I believe there was some doubt in the minds of the General or Commanding Officer concerning hostilities. The General commanding the Department was present at Fort Lapwai. I cannot state that Captain Perry was responsible for the delay.

Q. You say in your report that Chapman was instrumental in leading many men to the rear. Did you or any other officer endeavor to prevent this?

A. I spoke to him on one occasion about making a good deal of excitement. I don't think I spoke to him very authoritatively though. I did not hear any other officer speak to him at all.

Q. You report that Captain Perry after being under fire for a few moments was settled in his determination to retreat and that rapidly as shown by the incident of his mounting behind a trooper in the retreat. What time of day was this and was it not at the time the first order to retreat was given?

A. It was not when the first order to retreat was given. I do not know at what time of the day it was. I did not see the transaction.

Q. This part of your report is not made then from your own knowledge?

A. No sir.

Q. When you say in your report he Captain Perry voluntarily separated himself from his command, do you refer to his going to Mount Idaho from Grangeville?

A. No sir.

Q. State what occasion you do refer to.

A. I refer to the occasion on which he went back to Lapwai escorting a pack train after General Howard arrived with other troops.

Q. Was this done on his application for this duty or was he so ordered?

A. I do not know, I supposed he must have been ordered. I was not anywhere in the vicinity.

Q. If he was ordered would it affect his conduct as an officer?

A. No sir. I suppose it would not, officially.

Q. Did you or did you not report this fact to bring Captain Perry into discredit?

A. No sir, not to injure him individually, but to show the mismanagement of the Cavalry. I have never spoken of his conduct until I was called to make a report. I asked officially for a communication but had received none concerning myself. The campaign had progressed considerably before I asked, and was about drawn to a close.

(Question by Captain Perry.)

Q. Referring to your testimony on the subject of Captain Perry's criticism of your official conduct, will you please state whether or not you were informed by any officer that he (the officer) had seen Captain Perry's letter on the subject. If so, give the name of the officer?

A. No sir. I was not informed by any officer that he saw the letter, but I was informed by an officer that he had been told by another officer that he had seen the letter or report.

Q. Does or does not your report so far as it relates to Captain Perry's separating himself from his command, reflect upon his conduct as an officer, while you know nothing as to what orders he may have received governing this action?

A. I supposed he had orders for everything, I have always been led to believe in the Army that an officer should seek the highest command his rank would give him in action operations. It does reflect upon him.

1st Lieutenant W. R. Parnell, 1st Cavalry, a witness was then called before the Court and having been duly sworn testified as follows:

Ques. by Recorder: Please state your name, rank, and regiment.

A. W. R. Parnell, 1st Lieutenant 1st Cavalry.

Question by Capt. Perry. Were you at Fort Lapwai at the time of the Nez Perce outbreak?

A. I was.

Q. After receiving news of the massacre by the Indians was due diligence used in getting a command off to the scene of hostilities?

A. In my opinion, yes. The first news that came in was rambling, disconnected information as far as I could learn and General Howard was I think at the Agency with the Inspector Mr. Watkins, and Captain Trimble and myself went from our camp to the post for instruction from Captain Perry, and we found he had gone down to the Agency to consult with General Howard. As soon as the news from the prairie was confirmed we moved out as soon as "F" Company was ready. We ("H"Company) were all ready in the morning but "F" Company was scattered around the garrison in various duties. The Agency is 3½ miles from the post of Fort Lapwai.

Q. Was due diligence used in reaching the Indians after starting out?

A. Yes I think we got out there as soon as any command could have got there with a view of using our animals after we got there. We could have gone quicker. If we had gone much quicker our horses would have been considerably used up which would have embarrassed us in the action. The horses were very soft and fat having had very little drill or exercise for some time before.

Q. Who was in command of this expedition?

A. Captain Perry.

Q. Did you accompany the expedition to White Bird Cañon? If so, give a brief account of the fight which took place there.

A. I did. After leaving Grangeville we moved across the prairie and halted, as we understood, at the head of White Bird Cañon, about 1 o'clock a.m. on the 17th of June 1877. The Commanding Officer gave orders prohibiting lights or fires of any kind. During our halt one of the men of "F" Company struck a match to light his pipe. I found out who it was happening to be near him and reported it to Captain Perry, Commanding Officer. Almost immediately after lighting his match I heard the howl of a "coyote" but noticed the last note of the howl was different from anything I had ever heard before. I thought then, I think still, it was one of the Indians on picket. At dawn we moved on down the Cañon, "F" Company in advance. About half way down we received the order to take our overcoats off and the men to load their carbines. After moving down 3 or 4 miles the Cañon opens out pretty wide (what is known as the Indian Graveyard). I noticed "F" Company form line, Captain Trimble then moved to the right and also formed line. Our company "H" took possession of a high ridge crossing the cañon at right angles with a line of bluffs on the right. The order then was

"H" Company in low ground on our left and about half a dozen citizens on the graveyard knoll on the extreme left. In the meantime, the Indians had come out of their camp and attacked us before we got this position. Almost the first thing they did where I was, they drove a big band of horses into the right of our line. Caused some confusion among the men. Some went to the right and some huddled into where the centre of the company was. There was considerable skirmishing then for about 20 minutes and I found the left of Perry's Company moving up toward the ridge we were on, passing to the right and falling back. Several men of both companies were dismounted and some horses running loose. Captain Trimble gave an order to form "twos" or "fours," I don't remember which, and fall back. This order was only partially executed as some of "H" Company men were some distance off on a rocky point, and I kept some of the men back until they got down from that position. I saw then Captain Perry with portions of two companies some distance to my right and from what I supposed trying to gain the high bluffs to the right of the cañon. I was too far off to follow as the Indians had gotten between the two parties, and I thought the best thing I could do was to follow by going back on the road we came down, which I did, losing several men while falling back. I moved back very slowly, passing from one little ridge to another at a walk and holding on until the Indians got on the ridges on both flanks, picking off the men. On arriving at the head of the cañon I found Captain Perry with about the same number of men I had, 12 or 14. We continued falling back in the order in which we joined forces, until we reached Johnson's Ranch about 4 miles from the head of the cañon. Captain Perry had arrived there before I did, had dismounted his men, tied his horses and taken position on a high rocky point in the vicinity. He ordered me to do the same as soon as I arrived and said we could hold there until dark. I told him it was very little after 6 o'clock, and that our men had only 10 to 15 rounds of ammunition each and I thought it too dangerous to try it. He had forgotten, I think, that it was morning instead of evening. I suggested falling back to Grangeville as a party of Indians had taken possession of a knoll, higher than the one we had and about 200 yards off, while another party of Indians were coming down on our left under cover of a fence by a corn field. If they had come much farther, they would have captured our horses and covered us. Captain then told the command down and mounted. I followed as soon as I was in the saddle with the balance. We moved back in columns of four for about a quarter of a mile and Captain Perry gave the order "fours left" and directed me to organize the party. I divided the men of each company off, threw out the men of "H" Company as a skirmish line and requested Captain Perry to keep within supporting distance with the men of his own company. The Indians, in the meantime were watching our movements and trying to drive our party off to the left, towards what is known as "Rocky Cañon." They made repeated charges on our right flank and on our line of skirmishes, but were met every time by strong opposition. We moved back very slowly halting every few minutes returning the fire of the Indians. About four miles from Johnson's Ranch the Indians left us and soon after we met a party of citizens coming out from Mount Idaho to our assistance. We, however, continued on to Grangeville and on arrival there found Captain Trimble and some of the men of both companies. I belonged to Captain Trimble's company.

Ques. by Capt. Perry: Was or was not the position on the right occupied by your company ("H") a more advantageous one that that occupied by "F" Company?

A. Yes, very much.

Q. Had Captain Perry any officer with his company beside himself?

A. Lieutenant Theller 21st Infantry, was temporarily attached to his company.

Q. Was this officer with the company on the left, did he remain there?

A. He was on the left I presume when the line was formed. He came up to where I was when they changed their positions. He was dismounted and seemed somewhat confused and excited. I caught a horse and gave it to him.

Q. Did the citizens on the extreme left hold their position?

A. They did not. I think they left that knoll at the first fire when one of their men was wounded. After that knoll was taken the line had to retire. The Indians got completely in rear of the left flank.

Q. Did this position command that taken at first by "F" Company?

A. It certainly did.

Q. At the time you saw Captain Perry apparently trying to gain the bluff, was, or was not the whole command broken up?

A. It was very much broken.

Q. Did you arrive at the top of the cañon or bluff about the same time as Captain Perry?

A. Yes. We joined forces there. We had evidently moved back simultaneously. I moved up the cañon and he along the bluffs. We could see nothing of each other as we moved back.

Q. Did the Indians make a hot pursuit to Johnson's Ranch and after we left there?

A. The[y] did. They kept pushing our line in front and on both flanks. They very much out numbered our party. They came near enough for me to use my revolver on one of them. I would have charged them several times on my way back, but the company was not armed with revolvers.

Q. How many men had you and Captain Perry together upon arriving at Johnson's Ranch and how many upon your arrival at Grangeville?

A. We had about 27 or 28 men, somewhere about that.

Q. Was fighting kept up to within 4 miles of Grangeville or longer?

A. The fighting was kept up until we were about 4 or 5 miles from Grangeville. The Indians then numbered 4 or 5 to one, of the party we had there.

Q. Where was Captain Trimble during the retreat you described?

A. I saw nothing of him after the line commenced to fall back until I arrived at Grangeville. I saw a party of men after I got to the top of the hill after I joined Captain Perry. I saw 6 or 7 men down on the prairie going toward Mount Idaho. It must have been three miles off. I afterwards found out it was Chapman and Captain Trimble and some of the enlisted men of both companies, who were following Chapman back to Mount Idaho.

Q. How long a time elapsed from the beginning of the fight until the retreat began?

A. I think about a quarter of an hour or twenty minutes. I think I was on the knoll there about that time. I would say the fight commenced before our line was formed.

Q. Did you consider Captain Perry in any way responsible for the confusion and rout which occurred on the left of the line? Or to what was this due?

A. I don't think he was responsible for it. I think it was due to the flank movement made by the Indians. They were able to do so as soon as that knoll was abandoned by the citizens.

Q. Did it seem possible to control this panic?

A. I done [sic] all I could and could not succeed. I don't think we could have done it, we three officers. I don't think Lieutenant Theller could do anything. He seemed to have lost all control of himself. We had a great many green recruits in the company. The horses were green and flighty.

Q. Was there or not, much confusion in the ranks of "H" Company at the time they were on the right and before retreat began?

A. There were some of the men huddled up under the cover of some rocks there. Some were mounted and some dismounted. Some of that confusion I attribute to that by band of stock coming in on our right that drove some of the men in on the centre of the company.

Q. In your opinion could a successful stand have been made on the position occupied by "H" Company after the left gave way?

A. Yes. I think we could have made a stand there, but it would not have lasted long. We would have got out of ammunition and been worse off than ever. We would have lost our horses there for it was much exposed. The Indians could have got round on our flanks and killed the horses.

[December 26, 1878]

Ques. by Recorder. Was the position taken up by the command an advantageous one, where the Indians were met?

A. Yes, I think it was, as far as the right of the line was concerned, our position was a good one.

Q. You have mentioned a knoll, occupied by citizens on the left. Was that not the key point to the position?

A. It was the key point to that section of the line. The Indians could have worked up on the bluffs on our right if they had wanted to. The knoll was the most important point. It covered low ground on both sides.

Q. Why was it not more strongly occupied then?

A. We did not have sufficient force to put any more men on it. There were six or seven citizens there and they should have been able to hold it.

Q. Would not prudence suggest that the knoll, being so important a point, a stronger force should have been stationed there?

A. I think there was [sic] enough men to hold it. I think if I had been there with six or seven men I could have held it.

Q. When the intentions of the command's giving way were apparent, did Captain Perry use proper efforts to rally it?

A. I could not see Captain Perry until the line was already broken. "F" Company was out of sight down in a hollow. I could not say what was being done on that flank.

Q. How long after the attack commenced did Captain Perry make his appearance near your company ("H")?

A. It was about 20 minutes I guess.

Q. Was there any order observed in the retreat from the first position?

A. No sir. The command was very much mixed up, when "F" Company came up on our left. Our line was not regular. It was broken up. The men of "F" Company came in straggling order too.

Q. Did Captain Perry make any disposition of the men to get them back on the bluffs?

A. "F" Company moved up, as I supposed to take ground on the right of our company ("H"). I did not hear any orders given. All the orders I heard was [sic] given by Captain Trimble to form into a column and fall back. Our company formed twos or fours moving to the rear.

Q. Do you think a passage could have been forced to the river?

A. No sir. That was suggested. I said that would be murder or words to that effect, and afterwards it was found it could not have been done. I do not think any of the command would have got out at all if it had been undertaken.

Q. Did the men fail to obey the orders of their officers?

A. There was very little attention paid after the line commenced to fall back.

Q. Did the non-commissioned officers do their duty?

A. Some of them did. What few came up the cañon with me behaved very gallantly.

Q. How did you become separated from your own company?

A. I waited to get some men off that knoll. I think some five or six men on a rocky point. I had majority of the company with me when they commenced to fall back.

Q. After joining Captain Perry on the bluffs, how was the retreat conducted, and what was his conduct?

A. He fell back in the same order in which I met him. I took the left of the line. I don't think he could get the men to stand. There was [sic] two citizens with him who did more harm than good. I could see nothing wrong in it, except on one instance for which I blamed him somewhat, but which he explained afterwards. He asked me to hold a ridge while he crossed a cañon and got on the other side. I told him I would try to, and did. I watched for him climbing the bluffs on the other side expecting to see the men make a stand there until I crossed. They did not do that. After we got to Johnson's Ranch I asked what was the matter. He said the citizens that were with him would not remain and the men seemed to be governed by the examples of the citizens. When I met him he was working hard to contest the approach of the Indians. He was working as hard as I was.

Ques. by Court: Who were the two citizens with Captain Perry, referred to, who prevented Captain Perry's covering you?

A. I did not know their names, they were part of the men on the knoll. I did not know any of them except Chapman and he had already gone.

Q. Did you see Captain Perry when he first commenced to retreat? Do you know anything of the circumstances about his being mounted behind a trooper?

A. I saw nothing of his getting up behind a trooper. I saw him when he came up from the left of the line. That was soon after "F" Company came up to the position we were in. He was then mounted on his horse. Several of the men came out of the fight two men on one horse.

Q. What time did the command leave Fort Lapwai, what time reach Grangeville, and what is the distance between those points?

A. We left Lapwai about 8 o'clock on Friday evening, arrived at Cottonwood about 9 o'clock on Saturday morning, halted three hours to make coffee and feed our horses, and reached Grangeville about 6 o'clock p.m. Saturday. The distance between Lapwai and Grangeville is about 55 or 60 miles. We went slow on account of the roads. They were muddy and swampy in the timber. I had charge of a skirmish line and flankers from the top of Craig Mountain to Cottonwood house. We advanced cautiously. The ground was very broken and we progressed slowly.

Q. What was the order of March?

A. I do not remember which company was in advance. We halted several times after we left Lapwai waiting for "H" company pack train of 5 mules. When we had marched about 18 or 20 miles I took charge of a platoon as skirmishers and some flankers on both flanks. The advance was unavoidably slow on account of the ground we had to go over. The skirmish line was from 150 to 200 yards in front, then came a small reserve, a hundred yards in the rear of that a column and pack mule. The flankers were ordered to keep as near as practicable, about 150 yards, from the flank of the column. We made occasional halts to let the flankers get around thick brush and across ravines. We anticipated striking the Indians at any point after adopting these precautions. This order was maintained until we halted for breakfast at Cottonwood when pickets were thrown out in several directions and after leaving Cottonwood we marched in the same order as we arrived at Cottonwood.

Ques. by Court. Was the presence of the Indians first made known by their firing into the command?

A. I do not know. My company was in the rear.

Q. How far from the knoll occupied by the citizens was the left of "F" Company when the citizens abandoned it?

A. I don't know sir. I could see but very few of "F" Company the ground was so low.

Q. How far from the same point were the Indians?

A. I don't know. They were 75 to 100 yards from where we were.

Q. Was there any other attempt made to reinforce and hold this important point?

A. That I do not know either. I don't know what happened at all down on the left.

Q. At what point in the line was stock driven with reference to the right point occupied by a Sergeant and several men?

A. The stock was driven in on the right of it and several men were forced to the right by the stock striking the right of the company. I thought there was [sic] 600 or 700 head of them.

Q. How far did the Indians pursue the command?

A. They pursued us until we got very near Grangeville. It was fifteen miles in my opinion from where the fight first commenced to Grangeville.

Q. If the horses of the Command had been left to the horse holders and the men required to carefully use their ammunition, could not the Indians have been beaten at the first point of attack?

A. It was very probable. It is very hard to say, they were pretty tough customers as we found out afterwards.

Q. What time in the day did the command reach Grangeville in the retreat?

A. Captain Perry and myself got in about 10 o'clock in the morning. I think about 10 o'clock a.m.

Q. How far from point of attack to Johnson's Ranch?

A. About seven miles I guess. I think about seven miles.

Q. Were any wounded men brought off the field? Citizens or soldiers?

A. One soldier found his way back to Mount Idaho and one citizen that was wounded on the knoll in the morning came back.

Q. What were the losses of the command?

A. One officer and 33 men killed, besides the two that were wounded.

Q. Was the confusion and rout of the command attributed to the bad handling or disposition of the troops in the beginning of the fight or to the want of courage of the men?

A. I do not think it attributable to either. Many of them were green hands. Many of our company were undisciplined. A great many recruits that had very little drill. There was no lack of courage. The men that came up with me through the cañon showed that.

Q. Did or did not the men of "F" Company break, some of them to the rear and in confusion before any soldier had been wounded?

A. I don't know whether any of them had been wounded or not. Two of them got into Lapwai between 2 and 3 o'clock that afternoon. Two Indians that came out as guides also got back there about the same time.

Q. On arriving at Cottonwood, did you have a general view of the "Camas prairie"?

A. From one or two points we had a very good view. We saw a burning haystack towards Johnson's Ranch which we thought was a house.

Q. Did you, or not, then receive reports of the burning of ranches towards Salmon river and were the Indians seen in that direction?

A. I heard nothing about reports myself. That I can recollect. I couldn't see anything else burning except this straw stack. I had a good pair of glasses. I lent my glasses to an Indian scout but when he gave them back he said nothing about seeing anything burning.

Q. You say that very probably the Indians could have been beaten, had the horses been left to the horseholders. Should not this then, in your opinion have been done, and would not the retreat be attributable in part, if not whole, to the fact of its not having been done?

A. No. Upon reflection and subsequent events I think we would have been in a very bad fix. Our ammunition would have given out. We had no provisions and our ammunition would not have lasted until night. I attribute the whole confusion to the lack of discipline. We could do nothing with the men.

Q. Would it not have been better if the horses had been ridden harder and made more manageable, than to have been in the condition they were?

A. I don't know. I am not sure how that would be. We didn't anticipate fighting when we started from Lapwai. I think the command was sent up there more as a safeguard for the citizens about Mount Idaho. I would say in connection with the fight that when my company formed line, I expected the command to be given to dismount. The men could have sought shelter. The men could not control their horses nor use their arms.

Q. You state in your evidence 5 or 6 men were in behind some rocks, some on foot and some on horseback. Were these men engaged in fighting or hiding?

A. Those were dismounted and sent up there to hold that point. They were fighting the Indians. There were other men at another point of rocks where Captain Trimble and myself were. Some of these men were ordered to dismount in order to take more accurate aim from cover. They dismounted regardless of numbers, the line was then in confusion, there was no line and no regularity. It was from that point we commenced to fall back in column.

Ques. by Capt. Perry. Did the ridge you were occupying at first at White Bird Cañon *connect* with the bluffs on your right or was there any low ground between?

A. They connected with the bluffs if I remember correctly. It sloped up gradually to the bluffs as it appeared from my position. The bluffs were then very steep. A person could climb them.

Q. How far from Johnson's Ranch was the point at which you expected Captain Perry to await you, after he crossed the ravine?

A. I think it was from three quarters to a mile.

Q. Who should have given the order to dismount your company after taking position on the right?

A. Captain Trimble I suppose. He was in command of the company. Captain Perry was down on the left. I did not see him at all. That would depend upon what orders he (Captain Trimble) had received. If I had been in command of the company I should have ordered the men to dismount. I think it was the proper thing to do under the circumstances.

. . . Quarter Master Sergeant Michael McCarthy, 1st Cavalry, witness, was called before the Court and having been duly sworn testified as follows:

Ques. by Recorder. Please state your name, rank and regiment.

A. Michael McCarthy, Quarter Master Sergeant, 1st Cavalry.

Q. Were you present at the fight at White Bird Cañon in June, 1877? If so in what capacity?

A. I was. I was First Sergeant of Company "H" 1st Cavalry.

Q. What time did you see the Indian[s] after the fight commenced?

A. I saw them while the line was being formed. I saw one or two retreat towards their camp.

Q. Did they make a strong attack upon the troops?

A. No sir. They did not.

Q. Did the troops repulse them easily?

A. If there was any attack at first, it was the troops that made the attack when the first Indian was seen. As the first shot was fired Company "F" formed right front into line on the advance guard and Company "H" formed on the prolongation and deployed as skirmishers on "F" Company right, and the citizens placed themselves on the line as it was formed. I could then see but this one Indian running towards the camp, but I could see several other Indians following a large band of horses that had stampeded up the ravine and side hill to our right. The line after it was formed advanced and inclined a little to the left and halted overlooking the Indian Camp and commenced opening fire upon the Indians in the camp, quite a distance from them though too far to do any execution. There was a bluff near where the right of our line rested, and I was detached by Captain Trimble with 5 or 6 men to occupy the right front of the bluff. I dismounted and secured the horses and commenced firing upon some Indians that were in my front taking up a position on a round knoll in front. For a few minutes I lost track of the movements of the rest of the command. I was firing whilst there several minutes. We fired quite a number of shots me and my party. The line approached me again very close and then surged back to the right. A few of "F" Company men were detached and took position on the left of where I was posted. It got back at least 400 yards, as well as my memory serves me, and somebody called to my party on the rocks to get back, we were going to charge. I mounted my party and started them back, and somebody called out to go back again Sergeant and hold that bluff. I only succeeded in bringing back three men with me; the rest had gone out of my control. When I got back a second time I dismounted and sheltered the horses behind some boulders. It was then that the Indians commenced to advance. Previous to that time they seemed to be acting on the defensive. They then commenced to ride in small parties by my position up towards the right in the direction the herd had gone before. A small party coming under the shelter of this bluff got between me and the rest of the line. I could see the men through the smoke. Their position also sheltered them from the fire of the line. We had then fired about ten rounds apiece, the men firing singly. Then there were signals for me to get back again. Soon as we stood up and showed ourselves, shots came obliquely from the right as they had been coming from the left. I mounted my party as before and started back with a rush. Two of the party must have been killed as I never saw them anymore.

Q. How long before the company was formed in lines were you ordered to the bluff?

A. Almost as soon as they commenced firing, some were firing with pistols some with carbines.

Q. Could you from your position on the bluffs, see the left of the line where the citizens were stationed?

A. No I could not. I saw only one citizen who took post near me.

Q. What was the nature of the point where you were, was it large enough to shelter a large body of men?

A. Fronting the Indian camp it was a natural breastwork and from the rear it was open except a few boulders on the slope.

Q. What was the position of "F" Company and the citizen[s] with reference to the position you occupied?

A. "F" Company and the citizens were on the left of me on the road that passed the bluff by the left going down, and commanded the road.

Q. Do you know why the line gave way on the left?

A. I do not.

Q. Do you know how the men of your company behaved in the fight?

A. While they were under control and were given the proper commands they behaved splendidly. Those that were with me did very well. When they first came into line they seemed eager to advance.

Q. Do you think that an advance could have been made at that time with success?

A. In the first formation I think we could have advanced down the cañon with complete success in five minutes. It was a complete [?] as near as I can understand and from my observation.

Q. Could you see the Indian camp?

A. Yes, sir. I saw the camp, I saw the bushes where the Indians were coming out. I did not see the lodges.

Q. What was the nature of the ground in front of you?

A. From where we were the ground sloped down towards the Indian camp, towards the creek; it was broken through. We were higher than they were. We could have charged over that ground.

Q. Was there a large body of Indians below you?

A. No. They were in small squads. They were just coming out of the bushes in ones and two[s] occupying the points in front of me. They were very slow in occupying the points. Altogether I think there were about 60 more or less.

Q. Why was the command not dismounted when the men commenced firing?

A. I do not know. The first fire was open mounted. After that I was detached. I do not know whether any command was given to open fire or not.

Q. Did you see Captain Perry at any time during the fight?

A. I saw him when the line was first formed, he was with his company on the left I think. I saw him again when the word was passed to charge. He was on the right rear of the line. The line was then intact.

Q. Who gave the command to your company?

A. Captain Trimble gave me all the commands I got.

Q. How long after the firing commenced did you see the line retreating?

A. It was after I had been on the rocks and fired several shots. I saw it pushed back to the right. I did not know it was retreating. It afterwards fell back. I should think it was at least 400 yards. The road at this time I thought was uncovered.

Q. Did you see the citizens at any time during the fight?

A. I saw only one. He was by the side of me. He fired two shots, got on his horse, and rode off.

Q. Who withdrew you from the advance point?

A. No one sir. I was isolated there the last time, completely cut off. Some of the men made signs to me.

Q. Where was your Company Commander then?

A. I did not see my Company Commander again after he came near me on the rocks. I pointed out a squad of Indians that were getting around our right flank. When I saw those Indians on my right rear I called out and directed his attention to them. I did not see him after until I got in on the 19th.

Q. Where did you go when you started for the rear?

A. I went towards where the line had been when I last saw it. I laid flat on my horses [sic] back. When I got to where the line had been, I found only Lieut. Parnell with only a platoon deployed and he was about ten yards in advance of them towards the enemy and he was urging the men to advance and get out some wounded and dismounted men in his front. Nearly all the dismounted men got in the rear of my party, but I could do nothing for the wounded. They seemed to be wandering about. We were under a very heavy fire at the time on the face of the slope. In a few minutes some of my party were dismounted and some ran away galloping up the ridge on the right. I started back myself then and tried to get them to make a rally. They made no effort to stop. They kept running on, some with their carbines over their shoulders as if they were going to mount. My own horse was shot then, and I had to dismount and tried to urge my horse along. I ran down to-

wards the road and overtook one of my own company and an Indian. This
man took me on behind and the Indian caught a loose horse, and they both
helped me to mount. I continued on with these men and I was soon joined
by two others coming down the ridge. I moved to the next rise. We halted a
few moments and dismounted and fired, a few shots at the Indians following and a little further on I overtook Lieut. Parnell on the road. He had a
few men with him, and they were marching in columns of files up the road.
The men occasionally wheeling out and firing as they retreated. I continued
on with him until we reached where the road is graded. Here I was riding as
the last file of the column of the files. The Indians were riding on our right
and on our left and some were coming up the road. My second horse was
disabled. The column was then moving at a trot and I dismounted and tried
to keep up by running. The column was disappearing around a curve in the
road. I fell down two or three times from fatigue. I halted and fired my
pistol at the Indians who were not more than 50 yards from me at the time.

[*December 27, 1878*]

Q. Did you see any more of the column or army of the command that
day?

A. No sir. That was the last I saw of them.

Q. During the retreat did the men seem to be panic stricken?

A. Those I were [*sic*] with were not.

Q. Did the men obey the orders given them up to the time the retreat
commenced?

A. I do not know exactly when the retreat did commence. Those men in
my detached party obeyed my orders. A few from the party that Lieutenant
Parnell turned over to me broke away and rode up the ridge.

Cross Examination

Ques. by Capt. Perry. Could you see the ground to the left of the position occupied by the citizens?

A. I could see all to the left at the first glance as we were forming. I
could see it.

Q. Had you heard any firing on the extreme left previous to your going
to the point of rocks the second time?

A. The line was back about 400 yards the second time and the troops
were firing. There was firing while I was there the first time.

Q. Do you know whether or not the men of your company, besides those
immediately with you, behaved well after fighting commenced?

A. No sir, I do not.

Q. Had the men of your company pistols?

A. No sir, except the two trumpeters and myself and I think one or two
sergeants.

Ques. by Court. State if you know — how many men of your company
had been engaged with Indians previous to this campaign?

A. I don't know. I should judge perhaps ten that had been engaged with
Indians, not more than that. I think about the same proportion of "F" Company.

Q. Were any of the men armed with sabres?

A. No, sir.

Q. At what point of the line did the Indian's herd pass?

A. It passed by the right up the ravine beyond the right of the line. A half mile I should judge from the line.

Q. Were you posted at first in front of the centre or right of "H" Company?

A. I was detached from the right and gained ground to the right front.

Q. Did Lieutenant Parnell return to you with help or not?

A. No sir. I overtook him as I said on the road. There was one man come back to my help, Private Shay of "H" Company. That was the only attempt at rescue that was made.

Q. What was the nature of the ground generally in the cañon?

A. There was a ridge run [sic] through the cañon and it became a hill to the right hand as you rode down. There was a ravine on each side of the ridge. The ridge ended in a bluff looking down the cañon and near the bluff as I remember the ground flattened out. That is my recollection of it from the hurried glance during the retreat.

Q. Give the names and companies of the soldiers who reached Fort Lapwai on the afternoon of the fight?

A. They were Corporal Fuller "F" Company and Private White "F" Company.

Ques. by Recorder. What portion of the men of your company were recruits?

A. In the proper sense of the word there were but few recruits, but there was [sic] a good many young soldiers.

Q. Were they well instructed in horsemanship and the use of arms?

A. I think their horsemanship was good. Of "H" Company with a few exceptions they could stick a horse bareback and lead another at a gallop. We had target practice during the preceding winter. We had mounted drill at Lapwai during May and "F" Company had target practice while we were there. The horses were not accustomed to firing.

Ques. By Capt. Perry. Did this herd you have mentioned, or any part of it, pass *through* the line of troops?

A. No sir. I couldn't see any of it pass through the troops. It passed away to the right. I should judge half a mile. Some of the men were trying long range shots for that distance.

Sergeant Richard Powers Company H 1st Cavalry, a witness, was then called before the Court and having been duly sworn testified as follows:

Ques. by Recorder. Please state your name, rank, company and regiment.

A. Richard Powers, Sergeant "H" Company, 1st Cavalry.

Q. Were you at the fight at White Bird Cañon in June, 1877?

A. Yes, sir. A private of "H" Company.

Q. Were you in a position to see the Indians on their first appearance?

A. Yes, I was.

Q. When you first saw them, where were they?

A. The first Indians I saw were with the Indian herd. It was after "H" Company had come into line. We hadn't advanced yet. Captain Perry's company advanced to the front and inclined to the left. Captain Trimble's company formed right front into line. The herd got out of sight shortly after that.

Q. Did any portion of the herd pass through the line of troops?

A. None that I had seen sir.

Q. Could you see the citizens on the knoll on the left of the line?

A. I could not say they were citizens on the knoll at the Indian graveyard. I saw some citizens riding down from there.

Q. Could you see all the line from that point to where you were?

A. No sir. Not all the line. There was a small depression in the ground between the graveyard and where we were stationed. Captain Perry's company was stationed there.

Q. How long did the citizens, or party, stay on the knoll at the graveyard after the firing commenced?

A. I could not state the time, as my attention was drawn to my front at the time.

Q. Was "H" Company formed in line in good order?

A. Yes, sir.

Q. How long after the line was formed, before the shots of the Indians began to tell?

A. I should judge it was about three or four minutes.

Q. Did the men remain steady under fire?

A. Yes, sir. They did at this time. I couldn't state the time. We had a position on a bare knoll of rocks with a very deep cañon in our front. Shortly after Captain Perry rode down to "H" Company's line and gave an order to Captain Trimble. I did not thoroughly understand the order, but think it was to take his horses out of range of fire. We had some wounded horses there then, from there they commenced falling back in disorder. At about 50 yards I should judge, as near as I can recollect I saw Mr. Chapman on the right on a high ridge — at this time I was riding close by Captain Perry — I heard Mr. Chapman cry from the ridge, "Colonel Perry here is a chance for a charge." Captain Perry rallied the party that was with him at this time, advanced to the top of the ridge and formed in line; 'twas at this time I saw the largest body of Indians coming up the ravine to the front and left. The troops seemed to break from this position at this time. I heard no order to retreat. I don't know by whose order it was made. We had fallen back some distance I should say some 30 or 40 yards. I there again saw Captain Perry try to rally these men on the ridge. They would only stand for a very short time and still keep retreating. Keeping up a fire at short intervals as they went along.

Q. What do you think caused the confusion among the men so soon after the firing commenced?

A. I could form no idea, after the retreat once commenced. There seemed no stopping it.

Q. Do you think that the command could have beaten the Indians at the time the retreat commenced?

A. Yes, I think they could had they ma[d]e a stand.

Q. Did the men disregard the orders of their officers?

A. It appeared in that way. The officers were doing their endeavors to rally them.

Q. Could you see the position of the Indians['] camp from where you were?

A. Yes, sir. From the first ridge we formed on I could see the Indian camp.

Q. How many Indians made their appearance during the fight do you think?

A. Fifty or sixty as near as I can judge.

Ques. by Capt. Perry. What was your position with reference to the line formed by your company?

A. I was in the right center.

Q. When you saw the Indian herd was it moving *in the direction* of the line of troops, or away from it?

A. It was in our front and was running to the right flank.

Q. You say there were 50 or 60 Indians. Could you from where you were see any Indians who may have been on the extreme left beyond the graveyard knoll?

A. Yes, sir. I could see some Indians on the road in the cañon from our first position.

Q. Could you have seen the Indians had they been close to the knoll and on the left?

A. Yes, sir. I could some portion of them.

Q. Was this knoll higher or lower than the point where you were?

A. Our position was higher.

Ques. by Court. At what time in the day did the command reach Grangeville?

A. I could not state the exact hour. It was in the forenoon.

. . . Mr. George M. Shearer, a witness, was called before [the Court] and having been duly sworn testified as follows:

Ques. by Recorder. Please state your name and residence.

A. George M. Shearer, Mount Idaho, Idaho Territory.

Ques. by Capt. Perry. Were you at the White Bird fight on the 17th of June 1877?

A. Yes.

Q. Did you see the line give way at that fight?

A. No sir. I did not see the line of troops give way, only the volunteers who were under me at the time.

Q. Please state the circumstances connected with the first giving way of any portion of the line?

A. Mr. Chapman was in command of the volunteers. I was second under him. He had gone away with Captain Perry and I was in command of them. That was just before the action commenced. I saw Captain Perry forming his line. I went down on the extreme left that carried me under some hills that hid his line completely from my view. On arriving on the flat to the left of those hills, I saw some Indians running on low ground, toward us and we opened fire on them. Those Indians then immediately took to the brush on the bank of the creek which was about 75 yards to my left. From there they opened fire upon us. I ordered the men to dismount. Some of them obeyed this order. Others turned round and put out. In the meantime firing had been going on to our right beyond the line of hills. I could hear the firing but could not see the troops. I then called upon my men to follow me to the top of the hill between me and Captain Perry's men. I immediately went to the top of the hill and found myself in the presence of Indians who were within about 50 yards of me, and flanking Captain Perry's left. At this time I saw his line was broken and on the retreat and I followed as quick as possible.

Q. Did you retreat with the troops?

A. Yes.

Q. Did you observe Captain Perry most of the time on the retreat and did he do all that was possible to rally the men?

A. In my opinion he did all a man could to rally the men.

Q. Did Captain Perry receive any assistance from Captain Trimble in attempting to rally the men?

A. I never noticed Captain Trimble during the action until we reached the first ridge that was susceptible of being held after the retreat commenced. It was there I said to Captain Perry we had a good strong position, thinking he was not acquainted with the country. He remarked we would hold that ridge and immediately took steps to organize a line, and about the time I thought he had a very fine line organized the Indians made their appearance following pretty closely, and the line immediately gave way. I think first the left of the line. When I again saw Captain Perry and Captain Trimble, Captain Trimble was some 50 or 60 yards ahead of Captain Perry up the mountain, and Captain Perry called upon Captain Trimble to rally some men and hold a position at the top of the hill until the balance of the men could get up. Captain Trimble replied that Mr. Chapman had said the best place to hold was the summit, which I should judge was someplace in the vicinity of half a mile above us. Captain Perry called to him again to take some position and hold it. Captain Trimble moved on up the hill, and I saw nothing more of him during the fight.

Q. Did you with Captain Perry proceed on to the summit which had been referred to by Captain Trimble?

A. Yes, sir.

Q. Was an attempt made to make a stand there?

A. There was by Captain Perry. By calling on his men to stop there and wait until every man got up the mountain, and I suggested to Captain Perry there was a stronger position to hold on our left, that would command the road that the Indians were going up and could not be seen from where he was. He asked me if I would go with some of his men and show them the position. I told him that I would and he called upon a Sergeant or a Corporal, I do not remember distinctly which, to take some men and go with me. On getting there I discovered that the Indians had already passed up to our left and getting in our rear following the men that ran from the first line Captain Perry formed after the retreat commenced.

Q. Had the men ahead of you under, or with, Captain Trimble made a stand there — on the summit?

A. I didn't see any of them when we came on the hill. I did not see Captain Trimble.

Q. Was it possible for Captain Perry to rally the men other than in small squads and when so rallied would they remain where stationed?

A. No it was not, and I noticed that he never was able to hold more than 10 or 15 men around him; while some would stand, others would get away. In this connection I would say I heard Captain Perry repeatly threaten to shoot men running by him, and requested me to do the same thing.

Q. [Were] you in company with Captain Perry all the way up the bluffs, and did he have a horse or not?

A. Yes sir. He was on foot.

Q. When you arrived at Johnson's Ranch could you see the country beyond and towards Grangeville, and if so did you see any men in advance on the road to that place?

A. From Johnson's Ranch you can see all over that country for four miles. The only person we could see at all was one lone Indian.

Q. Did you remain with Captain Perry during the entire retreat to Grangeville? If so please state whether or not Captain Perry did all that an officer could do to check the Indian[s] and save his men.

A. After leaving the summit of the mountain mentioned a few moments ago, we proceeded to Johnson's Ranch where Captain Perry succeeded in rallying what men was [sic] left. I should judge he held his position at Johnson's Ranch for about 15 minutes; in the meantime impressing upon the minds of his men the necessity of keeping cool and stopping that stampede. He then called his men off this rocky butte we were occupying and formed them in the road in columns of fours. A portion of them under Lieutenant Parnell to be used as skirmishers. We took up our march to Grangeville. I believe never after that breaking our walk at all. I remained with Captain Perry during the entire retreat to Grangeville.

Cross Examination

Ques. by Recorder. Was the knoll you occupied with your command in the cañon a strong defensible position?

A. No it was not, but we had but a short distance to climb to get a good position.

Q. Why did you not take it then?

A. I did attempt to take it, but when I called my men up on the hill they would not come. They ran.

Q. Did the giving way of your men seriously endanger the left of Captain Perry's line?

A. Yes. It uncovered his left entirely.

Q. Did you see the first giving way of the company ("F") next to you?

A. I did not.

Q. How soon after your men gave way did you see Captain Perry?

A. I think I did not see Captain Perry until we had retreated half a mile.

Q. Was the organization of the troops entirely broken up when you encountered him?

A. Yes.

Q. Had the officer lost control of the men?

A. Apparently so.

Q. What do you estimate the number of Indians at?

A. I have never been able to make up my mind that I saw more than 60 Indians engaged at one time.

Q. Did they push the troops hard during the fight and after the retreat commenced?

A. Yes, sir.

Q. Would it have been practicable to have pushed on towards the river after the Indians were first seen?

A. No, sir. From my knowledge of the ground along the creek there, I think it would have been a very imprudent movement, because when we first saw the Indians they were preparing to receive us. The road was bordered by a very heavy growth of thorn brush and the Indians could have occupied and cut the column all to pieces, and the troops could not have maneuvered or penetrated it.

[*December 28, 1878*]

1st Sergeant Charles Leeman Company "F" a witness, was then called before the Court and having been duly sworn testified as follows:

Ques. by Recorder. Please state your name, rank, company, and regiment.

A. Charles Leeman, 1st Sergeant, Company "F" 1st Cavalry.

Ques. By Capt. Perry. Were you in the fight at White Bird cañon on the 17th of June 1877?

A. Yes, sir.

Q. What orders were given by Captain Perry when the Indians were first discovered and subsequently?

A. Orders were, "Left front into line," dismount and form skirmishers. Number fours were holding the horses and the other men were deployed as skirmishers.

Q. Were the orders promptly obeyed?

A. They were.

Q. What officer was in immediate command of the line?

A. Captain Perry was in immediate command. His order was through Lieutenant Theller.

Q. Did you see the position taken by the citizens at that time, and did it or not, protect the left flank of "F" Company?

A. Yes, I saw the position of the citizens on a knoll on the left flank of the company. It protected that flank.

Q. Did they hold that position?

A. A short time only.

Q. Did the line of troops begin to break before their left was exposed by the retreat of the citizens[?]

A. No, sir.

Q. How many men of the company were killed before the line broke?

A. I should judge six to eight possibly ten. Not less than six.

Q. How long a time elapsed from the time the Indians were first discovered until the line broke?

A. I should judge it was not less than half an hour, possibly three quarters. I am certain it was not less than half an hour.

Q. Were the led horses under cover, or protected from fire after the line was formed?

A. Yes, sir. They were in a ravine in rear of the company. They were perfectly protected until the left flank was uncovered by the citizens giving way.

Q. To what do you attribute the breaking of the line of the company?

A. I attribute it to the citizens giving way and the Indians getting a cross fire on us. Of course the Indians getting in rear of the company and several men being killed there, had a demoralizing effect upon the men.

Cross Examination

Ques. by Recorder. Were the men protected by anything in their front?

A. Yes, sir. Occasionally by a rock or something of that kind. The ground was generally open there, not much cover on the line we were then on.

Q. Did you see a herd of stock in your front? If so what direction did it take?

A. Yes I did as we came down the cañon. It was not what you would call a herd; it was a small number of animals. It was going down the cañon towards the river.

Q. Did any stock pass the line of troops before or during the fight?

A. Not to my knowledge.

Q. What part of the line were you on?

A. On the right and on the centre. Part of the time on the right and part of the time on the left centre.

Q. Could you see the whole line to your left?

A. I could.

Q. What portion of the line of your company gave way first?

A. The left.

Q. Where was Captain Perry at that time?

A. In the rear of the company about 15 or 20 yards where he could superintend the movements.

Q. Was the fire of the Indians very hot?

A. Very.

Q. Could not the Indians on the left have been met by drawing back the left of your line?

A. No sir. Not after the citizens had given way.

Q. How far from the left of your line was the knoll where the citizens were posted?

A. It connected with the left of the line as near as I can recollect. The extreme left.

Q. When the men began to give way was any effort made to [?] them there?

A. Yes, by Captain Perry and Lieutenant Theller and the non-commissioned officers of the company.

Q. Where was the first stand made after the line broke?

A. On a knoll. I suppose about 75 or 100 yards in rear of the original line.

Q. What portion of the company stopped there?

A. I should suppose about two thirds stopped there.

Q. How long a stand was made there?

A. Well, it is almost impossible for me to say now. I recollect well we made a stand there.

Q. Did the men show signs of a panic?

A. Well, they did, yes, sir. I saw Captain Perry there doing all a man could do and Lieutenant Theller. I did all I could, and the other non-commissioned officers but it seemed to be impossible to get them to stand.

Q. Was the pursuit of the Indians very close?

A. Very.

Q. After the first effort to make a stand, after the line was first broken, how did the men act?

A. They acted as if they were frightened. There were most of them young men. After they were once routed it was hard to restore order among them again.

Q. Was there any attempt made to reinforce and hold the point on the left when the citizens were driven off?

A. Yes, sir. Well, sir, after the citizens fell back and the Indians got a cross fire on our flank it had a very demoralizing effect, but we endeavored to rally then and regain the ground again.

Q. Were the six men killed at the first attack known to you?

A. Four of them were. I afterwards heard more were but I did not give it credence for I did not see them.

Q. At what time in the day did the command reach Grangeville and were you where you could see Captain ·Perry all or most of the time? If so, what was his conduct?

A. I should judge it was between 12 and 1 o'clock in the day. I was where I could see Captain Perry most of the time. I did not see anything extraordinary in his conduct more than usual. He seemed to be perfectly calm.

Q. From what distance were the shots fired that killed these men?

A. I should suppose they were not more than 20 or 30 yards away.

Ques. by Capt. Perry. From where you were in line covered could you see the entire line occupied by "H" Company on your right?

A. Not the entire line. No, sir.

Q. Do you mean to say you were on the right on the *entire* line or that part only occupied by your own company.

A. My own company.

Q. How far was it from the right of "F" Company to the left of "H" Company at the first formation?

A. Not far, sir. I do not remember the exact distance. Those minor points I have almost forgotten. I can't say with accuracy.

Ques. by Court: How far off were the Indians when you first saw them?

A. I did not see them myself until we were formed in line. I should judge they were a hundred yards off, perhaps two hundred. I could see a few of them after we formed line.

Q. Were they in camp when you first saw them, or were they advancing to attack?

A. I should judge they were advancing to attack. I could not see their camp.

Q. What became of the small herd you saw when going down the cañon, and was it supposed to belong to the Indians?

A. It was supposed to belong to the Indians. It was driven to the rear I suppose by the Indians towards the mouth of the river.

Q. How far was it from where you saw the herd to [the] point at which the line was first formed?

A. Well, I should think it was probably a thousand yards. A long distance.

Q. How far from the left of "H" Company was the point on which the citizens were posted?

A. Well, sir, it was more than the length of the skirmish line of "F" Company, probably a hundred yards, probably more than it. I was quite a distance anyway. The distance between the skirmishers was about three yards in some places, more or less according to the nature of the ground.

Sergeant Bartholomew Coughlin, Sergeant Company "F" 1st Cavalry, a witness, was called before the Court and having been sworn testified as follows:

Ques. by Recorder. Please state your name, rank, company and regiment.

A. Bartholomew Coughlin, Sergeant Company "F" 1st Cavalry.

Ques. by Capt. Perry. Were you in the fight at White Bird Cañon on the 17th of June 1877?

A. Yes, sir.

Q. What orders were given by Captain Perry when the Indians were discovered?

A. The order to form line of skirmishers to the front. We advanced until we got on to the line mounted and then dismounted.

Q. Did the men hold the position? If not, to what was their breaking due?

A. The men held the position on the center and on the right; and on the left until the Indians got in a heavy cross fire and six of the boys fell that I know of and I think one of the citizens named Swartz was shot. Then I remember that the citizens started and we gave way further towards the right of the command.

Q. Were efforts made to rally the men?

A. Yes, sir. Captain Perry called to the men loudly and the First Sergeant Baird. The men were very much demoralized on the left. The right being the strongest and "H" Company being in reserve came upon the right. We made several stands for a short space of time until we got up on the ridge.

Cross Examination

Ques. by Recorder. Did you see any herd of stock pass the line of skirmishers?

A. I saw the stock, but that was all. They did not pass through the line. I do not know which way they went.

Q. Did the men remain steady until the left flank was turned?

A. Yes.

Q. Were any efforts made to make a stand after the line first broke, before going up on the bluffs?

A. Yes. Captain Perry repeatedly called on the men to rally and they did stop several times and turned and fired as many as two or three rounds.

Q. Where was "H" Company at this time?

A. They were scattered in different places, several of which were in the party with myself and Captain Perry.

Ques. by Captain Perry. Could the herd have passed through the line of "H" Company on the right without you seeing it?

A. Yes.

Ques. by Court. What was done with the horses, after you had formed the line?

A. They were given to number fours to hold down the ravine, in rear of where we were on the hill.

Q. Were the men you speak of being killed or wounded, on the skirmish line, or among the horse holders?

A. On the skirmish line. The horse holders could not be reached. They were down lower, and the hill was between them and the Indians.

Q. Was there any attempt at any time to rescue the wounded?

A. There was a wounded man came out with myself and party. He was given a horse and an overcoat put on the horse for him to ride on by one of the men of the Company. That was the only man that I saw that could be lifted. Sergeant Gunn was given a horse but he could not get on him.

Q. Did you remain with Captain Perry most of the time from the commencement of the fight until it was over?

A. At the commencement of the fight I was on the skirmish line very near the left and Captain Perry was near the centre and when the left gave way towards the command on the right. The command was given to remount, and from that time I was with him until we got to Grangeville.

Q. Was Captain Perry most of the time on his own horse or that of one of the troopers?

A. He was on a trooper horse from the top of the hill to Grangeville after we got up out of the cañon.

Q. Was it on the horse of a man wounded or killed?

A. He was on Bugler Jones' horse. He was killed almost at the first fire.

[January 30, 1879]

Captain Perry then through his counsel requested to be examined in his own behalf, and having been duly sworn testified as follows:

Ques. by Capt. Perry. Please state to the Court all the facts and circumstances governing your official conduct while in command of the Cavalry of the column under General Howard operating against hostile Nez Perce in 1877?

A. On the evening of June 14, 1877, a letter was received at Fort Lapwai from L. P. Brown of Mount Idaho, saying that some of the settlers had moved into town on account of the threatening attitude of the nontreaty Indians, but that he (Brown) did not feel any alarm as the 15th was the day appointed for them to move on the Reservation. I thought it well enough to have them watched, so I accordingly dispatched my interpreter and two men at daylight on the 15th with instruction to proceed to Cottonwood and from that point to observe the movements of the Indians. About 9 a.m. on that day the detachment returned in great haste, having met an Indian on Craig Mountain who told them that the Indians had murdered three or four men on Salmon River. I immediately prepared my command ("F" and "H" Company, 1st Cavalry) to march at once, but did not move as the news needed information. In the afternoon a letter was received from L. P. Brown confirming the reported murders on Salmon River and giving particulars of additional murders on Camas Prairie.

I have neglected to state that General Howard commanding the Department was at the Post from the first. Upon receipt of the last letter from Mr. Brown, Lieutenant Bomus was sent to Lewiston to procure pack animals to enable me to move with sufficient supplies. Not returning at Retreat, I proposed to General Howard to move at once to the relief of the citizens of Mount Idaho carrying three days rations in my saddle bags.

The General acceded to my proposition and at 8 o'clock p.m. on the 15th of June I left Fort Lapwai with the following command: Company "F", 1st Cavalry, Captain D. Perry, 1st Lieutenant, E. R. Theller 21st Infantry, attached 50 enlisted men, three days rations cooked; Company "H", 1st

Cavalry, Captain Trimble, 1st Lieutenant W. R. Parnell and 41 enlisted men,
5 pack mules, and 5 days rations. I reached Cottonwood at 9 o'clock a.m. on
the 16th, distance 40 miles. I was obliged to halt frequently and wait for the
pack train as the roads were very muddy in places. I halted at Cottonwood
three hours, when from the high ground in the vicinity, three large smokes
could be seen, supposed to be burning houses or straw stacks (proved to
have been the latter) evidently fired by the Indians as signals.

From Cottonwood to Mount Idaho the road passes over an open rolling
prairie a distance of 18 miles. I reached Grangeville, 2½ miles from Mount
Idaho, at 6 o'clock p.m. When within about 3 or 4 miles of Grangeville I was
met by a party of armed citizens led by Captain Chapman.

Chapman informed me that the Indians had crossed the prairie about 11
a.m. that day, traveling in the direction of White Bird crossing of Salmon
River. He further represented that unless they were pursued and attacked
early the following morning, they would have everything across the Salmon,
and be comparatively safe from pursuit, and the Buffalo trail, via Little Salmon, open before them; thus escaping without any attempt being made to
punish them. I saw at once that if I allowed these Indians to get away with
all their plunder without making an effort to overtake and capture them, it
would reflect discredit upon the Army and all concerned, so I replied to
Captain Chapman that I would give him an answer on my arrival at
Grangeville. Upon arriving at the latter place, I laid the matter before my
officers, and it was unanimously decided that it was best, in fact the only
thing to do, viz: — make the attempt to overtake the Indians before they
could effect a crossing on the Salmon. It was also urged by Chapman that
the Indians would in all probability commence crossing at once, and I
should thus strike them while divided. I informed Chapman that I would
make the attempt, and should be in readiness to start as soon as the horses
had been fed, and the men cooked their coffee, at the same time requesting
him to bring as many volunteers as possible, also a guide.

About 9 o'clock that night I started for White Bird crossing of Salmon
River and at midnight reached the summit of the dividing ridge between
Camas Prairie and Salmon River.

My command consisted of eighty eight (88) enlisted men and eight (8)
volunteers. At this point I called a halt and waited for daylight. Soon as
dawn appeared I saw that the road led down a long narrow gorge, but was
assured by the guide, that it opened out into a comparatively open country,
but this I afterwards ascertained to be a mistake, as the country was all
rough. At dawn I commenced the march down. When part way down the
ravine in which the road ran, a woman and two children (Mrs. Benedict)
came out of the bushes and implored our protection. I at once offered to
send her to the rear by one of my friendly Indians, of whom I had two or
three along for messengers, but this she declined, saying she preferred waiting my return. As there was no other alternative, not having any men to
spare guarding her back, I directed one of my men to give her a blanket,
and my trumpeter gave her his lunch. Promising to return for her, I then
proceeded down the canyon. At this time I gave the command to load also
detailed Lieutenant E. R. Theller with eight (8) men if he saw any number
of Indians to halt, deploy men, and send me word.

About four miles from the top of the ridge, before mentioned, and at a
point where two (2) high ridges run diagonally across the low ground which

we were traversing and flanked on the left by two round knolls of considerable heights, and on the right by a long high ridge running parallel with our road. Between this ridge, however, and two ridges above referred to was a long deep valley of considerable width, and beyond the two knolls on the left ran White Bird Creek. On the more distant of the ridges Lieut. Theller halted and deployed his advance guard, at the same time sending word that the Indians were in sight. I immediately formed my company *"left front into line"* at a trot, gave the order to drop carbine and draw pistol, intending to charge the Indians. I turned to my trumpeter to give the order when I found out that he had lost his trumpet. In the meantime I had, with my company, reached the position occupied by Lieut. Theller and could see the Indians coming out of the brush on the river bank, also rushing up to get on my flanks. Taking a hasty look I saw that if I charged, it would only be to drive the Indians into the brush, where they would be under cover and my command in the open and exposed to their fire. I also saw that the ridge I was on was the most defensible position in that vicinity. I gave the order for my company to *"dismount to fight on foot,"* at the same time sending word to Captain Trimble to look out for my right. I gave Lieut. Theller instructions to deploy the men and take command of the line. While this order was being executed I reconnoitered and found the citizens had taken possession of the round knoll on the left, and which completely covered my position lead horses and all.

All that I have above stated took place under a heavy fire.

I now started for the right of my line for the double purpose of ascertaining my situation on that flank and if possible procuring a trumpet, as a Cavalry command on a battlefield without a trumpet is like a ship at sea without a helm perfectly unmanageable. I had proceeded two thirds the way to Captain Trimble's position, when I was made aware of a commotion among the lead horses (they having been sent to my rear in the low ground between the two ridges alluded to), and saw that the citizens had been driven from the knoll, and it was now in possession of the Indians, and they had my whole position in flank, and were pouring a deadly fire into my line. As I was too far away to order a charge and retake the hill, I concluded the only thing to do now, was to take a new position on the ridge in the rear, and which did not seem to be commanded by the knoll occupied by the Indians. I accordingly gave the command for the line to retreat to the ridge in the rear, and not having any trumpet, ordered the word passed along the line. I then went to Captain Trimble's position for the purpose of getting a trumpet, intending to superintend the reforming of my line as it moved back. Captain Trimble informed me that *his* trumpet had been lost. I found Captain Trimble's company on a high point, the extreme right of the ridge, or two ridges before described, as they seemed to be branch[ed] out from this one point. His company was not deployed, but most of the men huddled together and some dismounted. I had only time to observe this, when I galloped down towards my line. My order had evidently been misunderstood, and the men understood it an order to retreat. They were getting on their horses and everybody in a perfect panic. With no trumpet and only my voice, I tried in vain to reform the line. I then went to Trimble and told him we must retreat, to some point up the cañon, that we could hold. At this time a good many of "H" Company had gone and the rest very much demoralized. The Indians were all this time pressing us in front and flank and from this time, getting around in our rear. I could only make a show of resistance by galloping in front of the men, and facing them about to defend such positions as I could for a short time, or until I was flanked out of them. Once when near the trail leading up the bluff, I saw a position which I thought might be successfully defended. I called to Trimble who was quite a distance to my rear, about to go up the trail, and asked him to halt a squad of men near him and place them on the point indicated by me, to which he replied, "Chapman says there is a good place further up to defend." I repeated my order, when he (Trimble) placed the men as directed. I then turned to Sergeant De Haven [sic] "H" Co., who had a little squad of men on another point, and asked him if he couldn't control those men, and he said he could. I then told him to hold that position, until I could place some men on a point commanding a portion of the trail, also the position occupied by him and the men placed by Trimble. After giving these instructions I turned and saw that Trimble himself had continued to the rear, and was now part way up the trail. This was the nearest that I ever was to him during the retreat. But to go back a little. Just before giving the orders above recorded, my horse which I had been riding very hard was nearly exhausted. Seeing the men on the point above referred to, and recognizing the importance of defending them as long as possible, and fearful that these men would leave before I could reach them, I asked one of my men who was riding a comparatively fresh horse to carry me quickly behind him to this point (the one occupied by Sergeant De Haven). Soon as I reached the point, I dismounted and after making the dispositions as stated and finding they could not be held, I took up the trail on foot. The men placed by Trimble, seeing that officer going to the rear, followed his example. Sergeant De Haven and party also following. As I was on foot at this time, it was impossible for me to exercise any control over the men near me as they did not pay the slightest attention. On my way up the cañon, probably half way, I succeeded in catching a loose horse and rode him the rest of the day. When I reached the top of the ridge I saw Trimble some distance to the rear, too far away to make myself heard. I motioned him to the left, as Parnell, I knew, and also Theller with a squad of men were coming up the road which we went down. But Trimble did not stop, and that was the last I saw of him until I reached Grangeville. With the few men I had, I worked my way over to the right and reached the head of the cañon, just as Parnell emerged with about a dozen men. He as well as myself had been obliged to contest every step of the way. Our two squads united made all told about 28. We scarcely had time to acknowledge each others [sic] presence when the Indians were upon us, and we had to continue our retreat fighting all the way and in the same order, until we reached a rocky knoll at Johnson's Ranch from 3 to 4 miles from where we joined squads. At this point I thought we ought to be able to defend ourselves, so I halted the detachment and dismounted the men, but finding that the Indians were crawling down to kill our horses, I gave the order to mount, and as we now had to pass over a level prairie I thought we could keep the Indians off. This little halt had done much to calm the men, and as we moved on I cautioned them to close up in columns of four. As soon as that was completed I wheeled them into line and Parnell taking the "H" Co. men deployed them as skirmishers, while I marched mine in column, and in this way we crossed the prairie about a mile wide. Once the Indians charged us with a large party, but finding they could not break or scatter our little squad, they, as soon as we reached the fence on the opposite side of the prairie, abandoned their pursuit. When we reached Grangeville, we found Trimble already there.

[Perry then testified about later events.]

Cross Examination

Ques. by Court. Did all the officers in your command obey your instructions as given them and behave properly or were they panic stricken as well as the men?

A. I saw Lieutenant Theller, he seemed much excited and did not seem to know what he was doing. Captain Trimble failed to obey my order on the retreat and seemed to be in a hurry to get away.

Q. Did you take official action in regard to Captain Trimble's conduct, by preferring charges or arresting him?

A. No, I merely stated it verbally to the General when I saw him.

Q. Was the disaster at White Bird due to the misconduct of either of the officers named in your evidence?

A. No, I do not think it was. A panic was caused by the Indians getting in on my left flank, by the citizens abandoning the knoll, thus exposing my whole line and lead horses.

OPINION

That up to the time of the fight at White Bird Cañon (except that no evidence appears that a suitable quantity of ammunition had been provided in case of an emergency), every precaution that good judgment dictated was taken by Captain PERRY; that at White Bird Cañon the disposition of the troops was judicious and proper, with the exception of leaving his left to be protected by some citizens, — possibly unavoidable. That soon after the fight began, this point was abandoned by the citizens in a panic extending to nearly all the troops, who became so disorganized and dispersed as to be unmanageable.

That Captain PERRY, after the panic took place, did all in his power to collect and organize the men for a defense, without success, owing partly to the troops not being well drilled in firing mounted; and the Court does not deem his conduct deserving of censure.

*   *   *

It further appears to the Court, from the written statements of some of the officers of the First Cavalry, submitted to the Court, a coloring by insinuations has been given, prejudicial to the conduct of Captain PERRY, unwarranted by the evidence.

The Reviewing Officer approves the proceedings, findings, and opinion of the Court, excepting this shade of difference: that it does not appear to him, from the evidence, that Captain PERRY is at all answerable for the limited quantity of ammunition on hand at the engagement of White Bird Cañon; neither is it clear that the citizens (volunteers) were misplaced upon his left. Their subsequent conduct could not have been foreseen.[2]

2. The Court's opinion was handed down February 1, 1879, and published as General Orders No. 1, Department of the Columbia, on February 4. Appended to it is Howard's revision as Reviewing Officer. That portion of the opinion which deals with the Battle of White Bird Canyon, together with Howard's comments, is printed here as reproduced in Brady, *Northwestern Fights*, pp. 121–122.

Appendix 2

FULL CITATIONS FOR "WHAT THEY SAID"

Chapter 1

1. "Lawrence Ott, *"North Idaho*, p. 513.
2. Old Timer's Statement, item 29, packet 150, McWhorter Collection.
3. Babcock, "Joseph, The Nez Perce."
4. McCarthy, Diary, June 27, 1877.
5. "The American Indians," *The Times* (London), July 3, 1877, p. 10.
6. Trimble, "Soldier," pp. 47–48.

Chapter 2

1. Popham, "Hostilities."
2. Robie, November 9, 1889, Claim of Isabella Robie.
3. Isabella Benedict in Kirkwood, *Indian War*, p. 51.
4. Walsh, "Incidents."
5. A[lonzo] Leland, "Letter from Slate Creek," *Lewiston Teller*, June 30, 1877, p. 4.
6. Helen Walsh to her husband, June 16, 1877, Slate Creek, *Idaho Tri-Weekly Statesman*, June 30, 1877, p. 3.

Chapter 3

1. Wilmot, "Norton Massacre," p. 24.
2. Kirkwood, *Indian War*, p. 55.
3. Norton, "Norton Speaks," p. 39.
4. Greenburg, "Victim."
5. Adkison, "Norton Rescue," p. 37.
6. McWhorter, *Yellow Wolf*, p. 49.

Chapter 4

1. "Mount Idaho."
2. Chapman, November 23, 1886, Chapman 1102.
3. Adkison, "Inside Mount Idaho Fort," p. 44.
4. Wilmot, "Norton Massacre," p. 25.

Chapter 5

1. McCarthy, Diary, June 14, 1877.
2. Fitzgerald, Report for June 1877.
3. McCarthy, Diary, June 15, 1877.

4. Trimble to Wood, January 29, 1878.

5. "An Attempt to Make False History," *Lewiston Teller,* December 15, 1877, p. 6.

6. Howard, *Nez Perce Joseph,* p. 93.

Chapter 6

1. Crook to Assistant Adjutant General, Department of the Columbia, March 27, 1868, Letters Received, DC.

2. McCarthy, Journal, p. 102.

3. Statement of Surgeon C. H. Alden and Asst. Surgeon G. E. Bushnell, April 1, 1855, Retirement Board Proceedings, File of Parnell, ACP.

4. First endorsement, Jones to Howard, May 14, 1877.

5. "Jim Shay" in McCarthy, Journal.

Chapter 7

1. Perry, CI, p. 116.

2. McCarthy, Diary, June 16, 1877.

3. McCarthy, Journal.

Chapter 8

1. Trimble, CI, p. 51.

2. Shearer, CI, p. 93.

3. Perry, CI, p. 120.

4. Leeman, CI, p. 100.

5. Parnell, CI, p. 61.

6. Coughlin, CI, p. 105.

7. Trimble to Adjutant General, USA, April 14, 1897, McCarthy, Medal of Honor File.

8. Perry to Forsyth, *c.* October 22, 1878.

Chapter 9

1. Account of About Asleep.

2. Account of John Miles in McWhorter, *Hear Me,* p. 249.

3. McCarthy, Journal.

4. W. A. Birch, "In Memory of Lieutenant Theller," in Kirkwood, *Indian War,* p. 7.

5. Brice, November 23, 1897, Brice 7427.

Chapter 10

1. "Keep Cool Gentlemen," *Lewiston Teller,* July 7, 1877, p. 2.

2. "White Feather," *Lewiston Teller,* July 14, 1877, p. 3.

3. Account of E. J. Bunker in Kirkwood, *Indian War,* p. 6.

4. SCOUT, "Letter from Lewiston," *Lewiston Teller,* June 30, 1877, p. 4.

5. McWhorter, *Hear Me,* p. 498.

Chapter 11

1. JUSTICE, "Reason Why," *Lewiston Teller,* September 29, 1877, p. 2.

2. "White Feather."

3. Howard to Assistant Adjutant General, Division of the Pacific, December 13, 1877, Letters Sent, DC.

4. Forsyth to Assistant Adjutant General, Department of the Columbia, November 14, 1878, Letters Received, DC.

5. Trimble, CI, p. 51.

6. Shearer, CI, p. 90.

Chapter 12

1. JUSTICE, "Reason Why."

2. Whittaker, "The American Army," p. 398.

3. G. W. Baird, "The Capture of Chief Joseph of the Nez Perce," *International Review* (1879), 7:214.

4. Stranahan, "Taciturn Chief Joseph."

5. Greenburg, "Victim."

Chapter 13

1. "Non-Commissioned Officers in the U.S. Army," *Idaho Tri-Weekly Statesman*, August 18, 1877, p. 2.

2. Trimble to McCarthy, October 29, 1894. Pasted to p. 85 of McCarthy, Journal.

3. Howard to Maj. Gen. John M. Schofield, December 28, 1894, Parnell, Medal of Honor File.

4. "Theodore Swarts," *North Idaho*, p. 474.

5. Kirkwood, *Indian War*, p. 57.

6. Birch, "Lieutenant Theller."

Bibliography

1. Parnell, "Recollections," p. 264.

What They Said

Without some aid, in the shape of memoranda, personal or official documents, diaries, or the suggestions and assistance of comrades, one is certain to commit blunders, or, to say the least, be guilty of errors on both flanks, front and rear.

WILLIAM PARNELL

Bibliography

MANUSCRIPT MATERIAL

National Archives

Records of the Assistant Attorney General for Claims Cases, Record Group 205. The Claim of Isabella Robie, no. 10557.

Records of the United States Army Commands, Record Group 98.
1. Records of the Department of the Columbia.
   a. Letters Received, 1877–1878. See especially Joel G. Trimble, Report of the Nez Perce Campaign, *c.* December, 1877, Fort Walla Walla, letter no. 131; and David Perry, Detailed Account of the Affair in White Bird Cañon, June 17, 1877, October 22, 1878, Fort Walla Walla, letter no. 1024.
   b. Letters Sent, 1877–1878.
2. Records of Fort Lapwai, Letters Received, 1877.

Records of the United States Court of Claims, Record Group 123.
   See claims filed by Arthur Chapman (1102), L. P. Brown (2714), Benjamin F. Morris (2718), Catherine Cleary (2723), John J. Manuel (3496), Henry C. Johnson (3501), Hiram Titman (4945), Patrick Brice (7427), Henry Croasdaile (7439), James Chamberlin (8632), and Jennie Bunker (9816).

Records of the Office of the Adjutant General, Record Group 94.
1. ACP File. Personnel files of Perry, Trimble, Parnell, and Theller.
2. Medal of Honor File. See folders on William Parnell and Michael McCarthy.
3. Registry of Enlistments in the United States Army, 1798–1914, vols. 72–73 (1871–1877), microfilm copy no. 233. The records contain basic statistics on enlisted men, including place of birth, age, previous occupation, height, and place of discharge, arranged alphabetically within each year.
4. Regular Army Muster Rolls. Companies F and H of the First Cavalry, 1875–1879.
5. Records of the Office of the Surgeon General. Medical History of Fort Lapwai.

Records of the Office of the Judge Advocate General, Record Group 123.
   Transcript of a Court of Inquiry Concerning the Conduct of Captain David Perry During the Nez Perce Campaign of 1877, file no. QQ1738. Contains testimony by Trimble, Parnell, McCarthy, Powers, Shearer, Leeman, Coughlin, and Perry on the Battle of White Bird Canyon.

Records of the Office of the Quartermaster General, Record Group 92.
  List of Remains of Soldiers and Others Disinterred in Post Cemetery at
  Fort Lapwai by Second Lieutenant N. F. McClure, *c.* November 14,
  1890, General Correspondence, Military Cemeteries File.

Other Manuscript Material

Buck, Henry. "The Nez Perce Indian War of 1877." Montana Historical
  Society, Helena, Montana.

Cone, H. W. "White Bird Battle." Idaho State Historical Society, Boise,
  Idaho. Typewritten copy.

McCarthy, Michael. The Journals and Papers of Michael McCarthy. Library
  of Congress, Washington, D.C. Found in the material are his Diary for
  the period May 6 to August 6, 1877; his typewritten Army Sketches,
  which is a reminiscence based on his diary; and his Journal, which he
  kept in later years.

McWhorter, Lucullus Virgil. The Papers of Lucullus Virgil McWhorter.
  Washington State University Library Archives, Pullman, Washington.
  This is the finest collection of Nez Perce Indian material in the United
  States. Although Lucullus McWhorter published many of the Indian ac-
  counts he recorded in his two books, *Yellow Wolf: His Own Story* and *Hear
  Me My Chiefs!: Nez Perce History and Legend*, there are also unpublished
  fragmentary accounts of interest. Among them are the accounts of
  About Asleep, First Red Feather on the Wing, and Arthur Simon, which
  deal with the Battle of White Bird Canyon. Most of the material is described in Nelson Ault, *The Papers of Lucullus Virgil McWhorter* (Pullman:
  Friends of the Library of the State College of Washington, 1959).

Peo-Peo Tah-likt. "Stories about Indians as told by Chief Peo-Peo Tah-likt to
  Sam Lott (Many Wounds), February 25, 1935." Washington State University Library Archives, Pullman, Washington.

Walsh, Helen J. "Personal Experiences of the Nez Perce War." University of
  Washington Library, Seattle, Washington. Copy in Idaho State Historical
  Society, Boise.

SIGNIFICANT NEWSPAPER ARTICLES

The Daily Oregonian (Portland)

Brown, L. P. Letter from L. P. Brown to Commanding Officer of Fort Lapwai, June 17, 1877, Mount Idaho. June 21, 1877, p. 3.

Chase, H. M. Letter to the Editor, June 22, 1877, Lewiston. June 26, 1877,
  p. 3.

Frank Leslie's Illustrated Newspaper (New York)

"Statistics of the Army." February 8, 1879, p. 415.

The Idaho Statesman (Boise)

Fenn, Frank. Letter to A. F. Parker, September 4, 1927, section 3, p. 2.

"Idaho County Marks Sites of Nez Perce Battleground." September 4, 1927, section 3, p. 2.

Schorr, John. "Participant in Whitebird Massacre Recalls Fatal March into Ambush." September 13, 1931, section 2, p. 2.

Stranahan, C. P. "Taciturn Chief Joseph Refuses to Discuss War." June 8, 1933, section 2, p. 4.

Willey, Norman B. "Letter to Editor." December 8, 1877, p. 2.

Idaho Tri-Weekly Statesman (Boise)
Goulder, W. A. "Northern Idaho." March 4, 1876, p. 2, and February 24, 1877, p. 2.

"Non-Commissioned Officers in the U.S. Army." August 18, 1877, p. 2.

"Shocking Details." July 21, 1877, p. 2.

Walsh, Helen. Letter to her husband, June 16, 1877, Slate Creek. June 30, 1877, p. 3.

Idaho World (Idaho City)
Benedict, Isabella. Letter to Mrs. Orchard and Mrs. Dougherty, June 19, 1877, Mount Idaho. July 13, 1877, p. 1.

Brice, Patrick. "The Nez Perce Outbreak." September 14, 1877, p. 2.

Kooskia Mountaineer
Fenn, Frank. September 3, 1925.

Lewiston Morning Tribune
Greenburg, D. W. "Old Luna Clock Rich in History." May 3, 1936.

Lewiston Teller
"An Attempt to Make False History." December 15, 1877, p. 6.

Benedict, Isabella. Letter to Alonzo Leland, April 17, 1878. April 26, 1878, p. 1.

Brown, L. P. "From the Scene of Hostilities." June 30, 1877, p. 1.

Chapman, A. I. "More of the Murderers." February 23, 1878, p. 2.

"Indian Status Since Our Last Issue." July 7, 1877, p. 4.

JUSTICE. "Reason Why." September 29, 1877, p. 2.

"Keep Cool Gentlemen." July 7, 1877, p. 2.

"Killing of Norton." June 30, 1877, p. 2.

Leland, A. "Letter from Slate Creek." June 30, 1877, p. 4.

"Mount Idaho." June 2, 1877, p. 1.

Poe, J. W. "Beginning of Nez Perce Hostilities." April 13, 1878, p. 2.

————. "Letter from Mount Idaho." July 28, 1877, p. 1.

Popham, George. "From the Scene of Hostilities." June 30, 1877, p. 4.

SCOUT. "Letter from Lewiston." June 30, 1877, p. 4.

Swarts, Theodore. Letter to Alonzo Leland, July 21, Mount Idaho. July 28, 1877, p. 4.

"Theller's Remains." December 15, 1877, p. 2.

Walsh, Helen J. "Incidents of an Indian Murder." September 9, 1877, p. 2.

"White Feather." July 14, 1877, p. 3.

The New North-West (Deer Lodge, Montana)
MacDonald, Duncan. "Goaded to the War-Path." June 21, 1878.

New York Times
"Soldier Life and Death." July 12, 1877, p. 2.

The Times (London)
"The American Indians." July 3, 1877, p. 10.

ARTICLES IN MAGAZINE AND BOOKS

Adkison, Harriet Brown. "Inside Mount Idaho Fort." In Norman B. Adkison. *Nez Perce Indian War and Original Stories*. Grangeville, Idaho: Idaho Country Free Press, 1966. Pp. 42–45.

Adkison, John R. "The Norton Rescue." In Adkison. *Original Stories*. Pp. 36–37.

Babcock, W. H. "Joseph, The Nez Perce." *Harpers New Monthly Magazine* (1878), 58:109.

Baird, G. W. "The Capture of Chief Joseph and the Nez Perce." *The International Review* (1879), 7:209–215.

"Blackeagle, Chief Joseph's Nephew, Has Passed Away." *The Nez Perce Indian* (Lapwai Agency) (1918), 14:1.

Brimlow, George Francis, editor. "Nez Perce War Diary — 1877 of Private Frederick Mayer of Troop L, 1st United States Cavalry." *Seventh Biennial Report of Trustees of the Idaho Historical Society, 1939–1940*. Boise: The Society, 1940. Pp. 27–31.

Carpenter, John A. "General Howard and the Nez Perce War of 1877." *Pacific Northwest Quarterly* (October, 1958), 49:129–145.

Chaffee, Eugene B., editor. "Nez Perce War Letters to Governor Mason Brayman." *Fifteenth Biennial Report of the Board of Trustees of the State Historical Society for the Year 1935–1936*. Boise: The Society, 1936. Pp. 37–128.

Chief Joseph. "Chief Joseph's Own Story." In Cyrus Townsend Brady. *Northwestern Fights and Fighters*. Garden City, N.Y.: Doubleday, Page & Co., 1913. Pp. 48–75.

"Chief Joseph Was a Great Indian." *The Indian School Journal* (1904), 5:37–39.

"Death Comes to Josiah Red Wolf, Last Nez Perce Flight Survivor." *Montana Post* (May-June, 1971), 9:6.

Faxon, H. A. "Survivor of Nez Perce War." *Winners of the West* (February, 1937), 14:7.

Forse, Albert Gallatin. "Chief Joseph as a Commander." *Winners of the West* (November, 1936), 13:1, 3–6.

Greenburg, D. W. "Victim of the Nez Perce Tells Story of Indian Atrocities." *Winners of the West* (February 15, 1926), 3:8. Account by Jennie Norton Bunker.

Haines, Francis. "Chief Joseph and the Nez Perce Warriors." *Pacific Northwest Quarterly* (January, 1954), 45:1–7.

————, editor. "The Skirmish at Cottonwood: A Previously Unpublished Eyewitness Account of an Engagement of the Nez Perce War by George Shearer." *Idaho Yesterdays* (Spring, 1958), 2:2–7.

Howard, O. O. "The True Story of the Wallowa Campaign." *The North American Review* (1879), 129:1–7.

Hutchins, James S. "Mounted Riflemen: The Real Role of Cavalry in the Indian Wars." In *Probing the American West*, edited by K. Ross Toole, *et al.* Santa Fe: Museum of New Mexico Press, 1962. Pp. 79–85.

Laird, Floyd, editor. "Reminiscences of Francis M. Redfield, Chief Joseph's War." *Pacific Northwest Quarterly* (January, 1936), 27:66–77.

Moody, Charles Stuart. "The Bravest Deed I Ever Knew." *Century Magazine* (1911), 55:783–784.

Norton, Hill Beachy. "Hill Beachy Norton Speaks Out of The Past." In Adkison. *Original Stories*. Pp. 38–39.

Parnell, William R. "The Battle of White Bird Cañon." In Brady. *Northwestern Fights*. Pp. 90–111.

————. "The Nez Perce Indian War — 1877: Battle of White-Bird Cañon." *The United Service*, n.s. (1889), 2:364–374.

————. "Recollections of 1861." *The United Service* (1885), 13:264–270.

Perry, David. "The Battle of White Bird Cañon." In Brady. *Northwestern Fights*. Pp. 112–118.

————. "The First and Second Battles in the Lava Beds, and the Capture of Captain Jack." In Brady. *Northwestern Fights*. Pp. 291–304.

Redington, J. W. "Battle of White Bird Canyon, Idaho, June 17, 1877." *Winners of the West* (April 30, 1929), 4:2.

Rowton, J. G. "A Tribute to Mrs. Bunker." *Winners of the West* (March 30, 1926), 3:2.

Ruby, Robert H. "First Account of Nez Perce War by Man Who Went: Josiah Red Wolf." *Inland Empire Magazine*, November 17, 1963, p. 3.

Schorr, John. "The White Bird Fight." *Winners of the West* (February 28, 1929), 4:7.

Trimble, Joel G. "Carrying a Stretcher Through the Lava-Beds." In Brady. *Northwestern Fights*. Pp. 314–319.

———. "The Country They Marched and Fought Over." In Brady. *Northwestern Fights*. Pp. 281–285.

———. "The Killing of the Commissioners." In Brady. *Northwestern Fights*. Pp. 286–290.

Trimble, Will J. "A Soldier of the Oregon Frontier." *The Quarterly of the Oregon Historical Society* (March, 1907), 8:42–50.

Whittaker, F. "The American Army." *The Galaxy* (1877), 24:390–398.

Wilmot, Luther P. "The Norton Massacre." In Adkison. *Original Stories*. Pp. 21–25.

Wood, C. E. S. "Chief Joseph, The Nez Perce." *Century Magazine* (1884), 28:135–142. Reprinted in *The Red Man* (1915), 7:189–204.

Woodruff, C. A. "Battle of the Big Hole." In *Contributions to the Historical Society of Montana*. Vol. 7. Helena: Montana Historical Society, 1910. Pp. 97–116.

BOOKS AND GOVERNMENT PUBLICATIONS

Adkison, Norman. *Nez Perce Indian War and Original Stories*. Grangeville, Idaho: Idaho County Free Press, 1966. See Articles.

An Illustrated History of North Idaho. [Spokane?]: Western Historical Publishing Company, 1903. A great deal of useful information included on the settlers and settlements involved in the beginning of the Nez Perce Indian War.

Bailey, Robert G. *River of No Return*. Lewiston, Idaho: Bailey Publishing Company, 1943. Contains accounts by H. W. Cone and Grant Benedict.

Bancroft, Hubert Howe. *History of Washington, Idaho and Montana*. San Francisco: The History Co., 1890.

Beal, Merrill D. *"I Will Fight No More Forever": Chief Joseph and the Nez Perce War*. Seattle: University of Washington Press, 1963. Good summary. Best on later phases of the war.

Beyer, W. F., and O. F. Keydel, editors. *Deeds of Valor*. 2 vols. Detroit: Perrin-Keydel Co., 1903. Contains highly romanticized account of Sergeant McCarthy's part in the Battle of White Bird Canyon.

Brady, Cyrus Townsend. *Northwestern Fights and Fighters*. Garden City, N.Y.: Doubleday, Page & Co., 1913. See Articles.

Brown, Mark H. *The Flight of the Nez Perce.* New York: G. P. Putnam's Sons, 1967. Contains much new material. Good account of military operations.

Contributions to the Historical Society of Montana. Vol. 7. Helena: Montana Historical Society, 1910. See Articles.

Curtis, Edward S. *The North American Indian.* 20 vols. Seattle: E. S. Curtis, 1911. Volume 8 contains accounts by Yellow Bull and Three Eagles.

Defenbach, Byron. *Idaho: The Place and Its People: A History of the Gem State from Prehistoric to Present Days.* 3 vols. Chicago: American Historical Society, 1933. Volume 1 contains account by Maggie Manuel.

Drury, Clifford M. *Marcus Whitman, M.D.* Caldwell, Idaho: Caxton Printers, 1937.

Elsensohn, M. Alfreda. *Pioneer Days in Idaho County.* 2 vols. Caldwell, Idaho: Caxton Printers, 1947, 1951. Second volume edited by Eugene F. Hoy. Rambling but valuable local history.

Fee, Chester Anders. *Chief Joseph: The Biography of a Great Indian.* New York: Wilson–Erickson, 1936. Part fact and part fiction. Undocumented, but does have bibliography.

Gaston, Joseph. *Portland, Oregon: Its History and Builders.* Chicago: S. J. Clarke Publishing Co., 1911. Volume 3 contains biography of Col. William Chapman.

Haines, Francis. *The Nez Perces: Tribesmen of the Columbia Plateau.* Norman: University of Oklahoma Press, 1955. One of the best studies available. Critical bibliography.

Hawley, James H., editor. *History of Idaho.* Chicago: S. J. Clarke Publishing Co., 1920. Volume 4 contains biography of Dr. John Morris.

Heitman, Francis B. *Historical Register of the United States Army, 1789–1903.* 2 vols. Washington, D.C.: Government Printing Office, 1903.

Howard, Helen Addison. *Saga of Chief Joseph.* Caldwell, Idaho: Caxton Printers, 1965. Latest revised edition of the author's history of the Nez Perce Indian War, which, unlike earlier editions, plays down the role of Joseph as a military strategist. Good bibliography.

Howard, O. O. *Nez Perce Joseph: An Account of His Ancestors, His Lands, His Confederates, His Enemies, His Murders, His War, His Pursuit and Capture.* Boston: Lee and Shepard, 1881. Excellent for understanding the workings of the military, but Howard is highly imaginative in discussing Indian motives and tactics.

Hunter, George. *Reminiscences of a Old Timer.* San Francisco: H. S. Crocker and Co., 1887.

[Idaho] State Historical Society. *Eleventh Biennial Report of the Board of Trustees of the State Historical Society of Idaho.* Boise: The Society, 1928. Contains a biographical sketch of Frank Fenn.

―――. *Fifteenth Biennial Report of the Board of Trustees of the State Historical Society for the Years 1935–1936.* Boise: The Society, 1936. See Articles.

————. *Tenth Biennial Report of the Board of Trustees of the State Historical Society of Idaho for the Years 1925–1926*. Boise: The Society, 1926. Contains a biographical sketch of Dr. John Morris.

Jocelyn, Stephen Perry. *Mostly Alkali*. Caldwell, Idaho: Caxton Printers, 1953.

Josephy, Alvin M., Jr. *The Patriot Chiefs: A Chronicle of Indian Leadership*. New York: Viking Press, 1961. Chapter 9 is devoted to Joseph.

Josephy, Alvin M., Jr. *The Nez Perce Indians and the Opening of the Northwest*. New Haven, Conn.: Yale University Press, 1965. Perhaps the best book yet written on the Nez Perce. Certainly the best account of the tribe prior to the outbreak.

Kirkwood, Charlotte M. *The Nez Perce Indian War Under Chiefs Joseph and Whitebird*. Grangeville, Idaho: Idaho County Free Press, 1928. Contains accounts by E. J. Bunker, Helen Walsh, and Isabella Benedict in the first person, and accounts of Catherine Elfers, Jennie Norton, Lynn Bowers, and H. C. Brown based on interviews.

Knight, Oliver. *Following the Indian Wars*. Norman: University of Oklahoma Press, 1960.

List of Field Officers, Regiments, and Battalions in the Confederate States Army, 1861–1865. n.p., n.d.

Malone, Dumas, editor. *Dictionary of American Biography*. 22 vols., New York, 1928–1944. Volumes 9 and 10.

McWhorter, Lucullus Virgil. *Hear Me My Chiefs!: Nez Perce History and Legend*, edited by Ruth Bordin. Caldwell, Idaho: Caxton Printers, 1952. In many cases the author lets the Indians speak for themselves. Of particular value for this study are the accounts of Two Moons, Camille Williams, Wetatonmi, Nat Webb, Wounded Head, Black Feather, Bow and Arrow Case, and Roaring Eagle.

————. *Yellow Wolf: His Own Story*. Revised edition. Caldwell, Idaho: Caxton Printers, 1948. The best account of the war by a Nez Perce.

Murray, Keith A. *The Modocs and Their War*. Norman: University of Oklahoma Press, 1959.

Pollock, Robert W. *Grandfather, Cheif Joseph and Pyschodynamics*. Caldwell, Idaho: Caxton Printers, 1964.

Report of the Secretary of War, 1878. Washington, D.C.: Government Printing Office, 1878.

Spinden, Herbert Joseph. *The Nez Perce Indians*. Memoirs of the American Anthropological Association, vol. 2, part 3. Lancaster, Pa.: New Era Print Co., 1908.

Secretary of the State of Idaho, *Twenty-Seventh Report of the Secretary of the State of Idaho, 1943–1944*, Boise, 1944. Contains biographical information on L. P. Brown, Frank Fenn, B. B. Norton, and George Shearer.

Toole, K. Ross, *et al. Probing the American West.* Santa Fe: Museum of New Mexico Press, 1962. See Articles.

U.S., Congress, Senate. *Claims of the Nez Perce Indians.* Senate Executive Document 257, 56th Congress, 1st session, 1899. Testimony of many of the Nez Perce who acted as scouts for Perry.

Webb, George W. *Chronological List of Engagements Between the Regular Army of the United States and Various Tribes of Hostile Indians, Which Occurred During the Years, 1790 to 1898, Inclusive.* St. Joseph, Mo.: Wing Printing and Publishing Co., 1939.

Index

219

A Note on the Author

John D. McDermott is Director of Special Studies for the Advisory Council on Historic Preservation, a federal agency established to encourage the protection and preservation of historic properties. Born and raised in Redfield, South Dakota, and holding degrees in history from the University of South Dakota (B.A.) and the University of Wisconsin (M.A.), McDermott began his government career in 1960 as historian for Fort Laramie National Historic Site, Wyoming. In 1964 he moved to the Washington office of the National Park Service, where he worked as a research historian and later as historian for the National Historic Landmarks program. He began his service with the Advisory Council in 1970. He is co-author of *Fort Laramie: Visions of a Grand Old Post*, which appeared in 1974, and a frequent contributor to historical journals. McDermott, his wife, and their three children reside in Arlington, Virginia.